RUNNING FREE

Richard Askwith is Associate Editor of the *Independent*. His first book, *Feet in the Clouds*, won Best New Writer at the British Sports Book Awards and the Bill Rollinson Prize for Landscape and Tradition. It was shortlisted for the William Hill and Boardman-Tasker prizes and was named by *Runner's World* as one of the three best running books of all time.

Also by Richard Askwith

Feet in the Clouds:
A tale of fell-running and obsession

The Lost Village:
In search of a forgotten rural England

Running Free

A runner's journey back to nature

Richard Askwith

YELLOW JERSEY PRESS
LONDON

Published by Yellow Jersey Press 2015

1 3 5 7 9 10 8 6 4 2

Copyright © Richard Askwith 2014

Richard Askwith has asserted his right under the Copyright, Designs
and Patents Act 1988 to be identified as the author of this work

First published in Great Britain in 2014 by
Yellow Jersey Press

Vintage
20 Vauxhall Bridge Road,
London SW1V 2SA

www.vintage-books.co.uk

A Penguin Random House Company

global.penguinrandomhouse.com

A CIP catalogue record for this book is available from the British Library

ISBN 9780224091978

Penguin Random House supports the Forest Stewardship
Council (FSC®), the leading international forest certification organisation.
Our books carrying the FSC® label are printed on FSC®-certified paper.
FSC® is the only forest certification scheme endorsed by the
leading environmental organisations, including Greenpeace.
Our paper procurement policy can be found at:
www.randomhouse.co.uk/environment

Printed and bound by CPI Group (UK) Ltd, Croydon, CR0 4YY

Contents

I

The race against time

Sometimes I wonder what non-runners daydream about. For me, most reveries lead to running. I may not start there; I may not finish there. But there's usually a stage when I realise that, in my mind's eye, I've been running.

Even when the window through which I'm gazing belongs to an urban office, my notional self will skip unthinkingly over jostling traffic jams and pavements, escaping to unexplored parks, rivers and open spaces – irrespective of the fact that I'm principally thinking about something else. But I notice it most when I'm looking at the passing countryside from a car or train. No matter what else is in my head, something will grab my eye: an empty field; an inviting path; a soft green roll of rural landscape glimpsed through trees. And my drifting mind begins to sense the familiar rhythm, the patient reeling in of each slope and turn, the thrill of discovery as each new corner is turned or summit crested; the bright release of the downhill dash...

Then I remember that there is no actual runner doing this. And I wonder why not.

This happened recently when I spent an October night in Edale, en route to an engagement in Buxton. Edale is a tiny Derbyshire village at the southern end of the Pennine Way, in the aptly named Hope Valley, shielded on all sides by the great green hills of the southern Peak District. Paths flow out from it in all directions: low routes and high routes, flat and steep; long, short, muddy, firm. There are deserted lanes, riverside footpaths, the wide, well-marked beginnings of the Pennine Way, and faint sheep-trods leading up to the open fells.

I'd been noticing them in the final miles of the journey up, and had had to make a conscious effort to focus on the road instead. No one with the slightest taste for running could come here and not feel their legs grow restless. If the sport leaves you cold, go to Edale and you'll understand.

Yet there weren't, as far as I could see, any runners. Where had they gone?

It was still light when I finished checking in at the bed and breakfast, so I decided that I, at least, would make the most of a place that seemed to have been created with runners' pleasure in mind. A path through a farmyard led me quickly to the Pennine Way.

It seemed as good a route as any: rich with the texture of an English autumn. I jogged gently, enjoying the feel of the ground as much as the surrounding views. The tensions of the long drive from Northamptonshire slipped away within minutes.

Detail after detail of the land around me snatched at my attention. One moment my eyes were feasting on the mes-merising complexity of the damp leaves, jagged and brilliant in the contrasts of their golden yellows and darkest browns, like smashed Marmite jars. Then I was on a sunken section of path – an ancient holloway, I thought, pressed into a trench by centuries of hooves – that filled my nostrils with the scent of mud and leaf mould and my mind with long-lost memories of childhood conker gathering.

The bubbling of an adjoining stream dispelled these thoughts. How, I wondered, might that noise be replicated on a printed page? Shwshwshwshw? Gaaaaaaaaaaah? Blwblwblw? Each time I tried to spell it out, it sounded different.

Then – barely noticing that I was running – I was out in the gently sloping pastures beyond, where wide-eyed sheep gawped like bonneted extras in a costume drama, dumbstruck and woolly-headed. 'What are you looking at?' I snarled at one; then felt ashamed. There was really very little to be grumpy about.

I breathed in the delicious air, sweet with agricultural smells and touched with the moisture of the deepening evening. Its flavour could barely have changed in centuries. My mind wandered further, taking my feet with it. At one point I think I was running and daydreaming about running at the same time.

On the skyline to my right the higher slopes were lit up, golden from the shining sunset. One bare fell-top in particular – the nearest – seemed to have turned to molten metal: it glowed in the darkening sky like the flattened tip of a red-hot poker.

I left the Way and climbed towards it, following a thin half-path of flattened grass straight up the slope until I was breathless, drenched in sweat and striding out across the windy summit. I roamed where the land took me, haphazardly, relishing the feel of the soft, dry turf. I followed sheep-trods when I found them and my nose when I didn't, listening as the skylarks' songs came and went in the gusting wind and glancing only occasionally at the distinctive promontory to the north that I was using as a navigational reference point.

3

Worries about work, money and family were blown from my mind; for the first time in hours I wasn't subconsciously keeping track of what needed to be done next. Instead, I let myself be mesmerised by the lengthening shadows of the wind-swept grass and, increasingly, the lichen-coated stones strewn all around. What, I wondered, was each one's story? Some were clearly the remnants of walls, piled up by farmers within living memory. Others might well have been untouched since being thrown up by nature tens of thousands of years ago. And the rest? I had no idea, but did not let that stop me speculating about hill forts and battles, ancient Britons, Romans, Mercians and Danes, and any number of long-forgotten lives lived out against a backdrop scarcely distinguishable from what I saw around me. Did their ghosts ever wander on this hilltop? Were they mingling with these shadows now?

That's one of the things I love about running. It's the part of my life where I regularly jump on to trains of thought with no idea of where they're going – thinking, while running, about not running – and then find myself at unexpected destinations. By the time I remembered myself the sun had almost slipped below the opposite skyline. I hurried down the fellside, enjoying the perfect texture of the turf – dry enough to grip, soft enough to be painless – and feeling, for no earthly reason, rather pleased with myself.

Then, as I neared the bottom, I saw what looked like a ghost running towards me.

He was tall and haggard, dressed in a clumsy combination of singlet, long-sleeved top and baggy shorts, each in a slightly different shade of pale, washed-out yellow-gold. He may have been as young as thirty; if so, something about his expression or complexion seemed to reveal the future old man within. His sallow face seemed etched with shadows, like those on a playing-card king. I suppose he was exhausted, but his grimace suggested horror rather than pain. Never, not even at a marathon finishing line, have I seen a runner whose gait was so overwhelmingly suggestive of suffering. He wasn't moving particularly fast and seemed to wince with each step. Yet he looked like a serious runner, not least because of the hydration pack he wore on his back, and because he kept looking anxiously at his watch.

By the time I had rejoined the Way he had gone, but I headed off in what I presumed were his footsteps, vaguely curious that someone could be running here, on an evening such as this, with so little apparent enjoyment. When I caught sight of him again, the setting sun had turned his flesh the same pale yellow-gold as his clothes – making me think, for some reason, of the little yellow man that Google uses as the guiding icon for its Street View service.

The path led quickly down into a quaint old stone farm, with a shaggy-hooved horse grazing in one field and black-legged chickens clucking to one another on the path. Did Street View's reach extend this far, I wondered? I hoped not, and resolved not to find out.

When I caught sight of him again he was leaning against a wooden signpost by the main farm gate, bent almost double. Was he being sick? Was he dying? Had he reached the end of his run? Or was he just having a rest?

I never found out. By the time I got there he was gone. I carried on up the next stage of the Pennine Way for a while, looking; but there was no sign of him. Then I ran back to the signpost. There was no corpse, and no vomit, so I assumed that he had gone in a different direction – unless he really was a ghost. But it was the signpost itself, by this stage, that fascinated me.

I had noticed it the first time I passed. Now I paused to study it properly: a white metal box fixed to the post at chest height, bright and hard against the soft, lichen-stained wood and the moss-carpeted drystone wall behind it. It was a bit bigger than a pack of cigarettes, with a hole in its front for inserting some kind of electronic device, together with a big red flame logo, a small Natural England acorn logo, and the word 'Trailblaze' in large type. There was also a short explanatory blurb ('A hand-picked portfolio of demanding endurance challenges, which runs through the world's most inspiring landscapes') and a web address at which to 'find out how you can take part'. Had this been what the ghostly runner had stopped here for? And, if so, what did it mean?

It was a small thing, and I resumed my run with no intention of giving it further thought. Yet somehow it preyed, intermittently, on my mind: then, later on, and for days afterwards – even after I had checked out the Trailblaze website and discovered what the little box really meant.

It wasn't the only thing that prompted this book. But it may have been the final catalyst that prompted me to begin it.

2

Big Running

In the dusty wastes of east London, a few hundred metres from the stadium where Mo Farah, Jessica Ennis and the rest performed their Olympic miracles at London 2012, Westfield shopping centre was a hive of activity. Eager shoppers buzzed in their thousands through the three floors of Europe's biggest shopping mall, visibly animated with anticipation, like fans arriving at a football match.

It would have been easy to miss Britain's biggest specialist running store among the brilliant shopfronts of more than 250 other retailers (including major Nike and Adidas outlets). But I knew that Sweatshop was there somewhere, and I needed – on strict instructions from my wife – to buy myself a birthday present. I hadn't spent a penny on my running habit for years, and I reckoned it couldn't take long to find something I needed.

I hadn't bargained for the Aladdin's Cave I eventually found, on the middle floor, tucked between Crocs and Lush. It seemed at first glance a modest place – compared with, say, the giant Ann Summers store opposite – but the understated shelves and rails within were loaded with small items of great value. It was a bit like entering a jeweller's shop.

Hundreds upon hundreds of pieces of shiny kit gleamed like Christmas tree baubles, each crying out to be touched and tested. I counted more than a hundred different kinds of running shoe on display, forty models of sports watch, nearly fifty different ways of getting hydration or nutrition on the move, thirty different types of headwear, fifty kinds of sock, and more shorts, singlets, jackets, tights, gilets, tops, T-shirts and thermals than I could even categorise, let alone count.

I didn't need any of them.

I wanted to buy them all.

A quick look at the price tags dispelled that notion. In fact, a sense that I was in danger of succumbing to ruinously expensive kit-lust made me feel suddenly uneasy about the whole idea of shopping here. Maybe I'd get myself a book instead. But, in the meantime, another idea had entered my head. What if I were a new runner: a young couch potato, inspired by the Olympics to try out running for the first time? What would it cost me to get myself kitted out, from scratch, assuming that all these products were as vital as the blurbs on their packaging suggested?

I began to fill an imaginary shopping basket with running basics: some trainers (Mizuno Wave Prophecy 2, £170); some shorts (Gore Men's X-Running 2.0, £60); a top (X-Bionic Powershirt, £70); some socks (X-Socks Effektor XBS Accumulator Competition Socks, £50); some gloves (Gore Mythos SO Running Gloves, £35); a windproof jacket (Nike Vapor Windrunner Men's Running Jacket, £150); some leggings (Nike Stretch Woven Men's Running Trousers, £40); a headband – don't ask me why, but there were thirty different kinds available (Nathan LED Headband, £30); a high-visibility bib (Sweatshop Hi Viz Run Bib, £6) and snapband (Ronhill Vizion, £5); some running sunglasses (Sunwise Waterloo GS,

£77.99); an armband for iPod or iPhone (iFitness Neoprene Armband, £20); some runners' headphones (Yurbuds Ironman Inspire, £60); some Brooks Race Day Arm Warmers – again, don't ask me why (£15); a combined sport watch, heart-rate monitor and GPS route-recorder (Garmin Forerunner 610, £279.99); a Mizuno Bottle Waist Pouch (£23); and a small selection from getting on for fifty different nutrition and hydration products: 500 grams of GO Electrolyte Sports Fuel (lemon and lime, £10.20), 1.6 kilograms of SIS Rego Rapid Recovery (strawberry, £31.80), three pouches of SIS Go Plus Carnitine Gel (lemon, £2 each) and three Lucozade Sport Carbohydrate Energy Gels (orange, £1.40 each).

My imaginary bill came to £1,144.18, and I hadn't even started on the various products relating to the treatment or management of injuries (including some seriously state-of-the-art 'compression pants' with built-in icepacks, from £80 to £100). I felt sick at the thought of it.

I was being profligate about price, of course. That's the joy of imaginary shopping. But even when I repeated the exercise selecting the very cheapest product in each category rather than the top of the range, I couldn't get the total below £494.16. Nor did I have any reason to suppose that Sweatshop charged more than its rivals. Later, I performed a similar experiment at upandrunning.co.uk and spent – notionally – £1,348.45 (although that did include an extra £29.99 for a Power Balance silicone wristband and £6 for a jar of Halo Proactive Sports Wash – 'the World's first Non Bio Laundry Detergent designed specifically for Sports wear clothing').

The worrying thing was that it took a real effort to walk out of Sweatshop without buying anything. Never mind the price tags; never mind the fact that I'd been running happily for decades without this stuff; never mind the fact that the credit card in my pocket was throbbing from imaginary overuse. I felt incomplete without these tantalisingly pristine products, whose blurbs made them sound so indispensable ('to improve your performance like nothing before...'; 'you'll notice improved core body control and power, as well as less post-exercise muscle soreness...'; 'power-mesh contrast panels for breathability and ventilation...'; 'the world's most complete training watch ever...enabling you to re-live, track and learn from every session to constantly improve your performance'). I was still feeling pangs of desire – a physical ache deep inside me – when I drove away afterwards.

I glanced back wistfully and caught a glimpse of the mall and the stadium facing one another: two vast and windowless structures – a Large Hadron Collider and a giant brown box – towering above Stratford's wide concrete spaces, like secular cathedrals: twin monuments to the dreams of twenty-first-century Britain. Winning and shopping: what more does one need?

A bit later, I thought: this is insane. Times are hard. All but a handful of us are tightening our belts. We've less in our take-home pay (if we're lucky enough still to have any), less in the bank and less reason to feel secure about the future. Yet we're spending more than ever before on running.

The details are breathtaking. Running, as an industry, is barely less significant in British life than farming. Look around you, anywhere, and you'll see its products: running shoes, running clothes, running books, running DVDs, special running equipment (from heart-rate monitors to treadmills), special running drinks and foods, running shops, glossy running magazines, advertisements in the glossy magazines for every conceivable running-related product. Estimates and definitions vary, but a low-end estimate, from the consultants

NPD Inc., puts the 2012 value of the UK running market at retail alone at £425 million. That's just the stuff you see in shops. There's also a vast running economy beyond the high street. Think of the bright young things, hundreds of them, who work for bodies such as Sport England, or who spent years working for the London Organising Committee for the Olympic Games (LOCOG). Think of the gym workers and personal trainers; the go-getters who organise for-profit races; the people who sell race T-shirts and race goodie bags; the people who put on running festivals and running holidays; the therapists who treat running-related injuries; the sponsorship brokers; the corporate ladder-climbers at the running shoe multinationals.

It's hard to put precise figures on it: how many of the 26,000 people who work in the British gym industry, for instance, should be counted as part of the running economy? But it's clear that, even without the competitive elite (and their coaches, managers, sponsors and agents), it all adds up to a big, big business. Globally, according to a 2013 report by Bloomberg, the running industry is worth nearly twice as much as the football industry: NPD Inc. values the retail part of it at £16.5 billion a year, including £5.5 billion spent on 'running shoes used for running' (just over half of the overall running shoe market). In England alone, 441,000 people work in sport-related jobs – twice as many as work in agriculture, forestry and fishing combined. Even if only 33,000 of these jobs are categorised as running-related (a back-of-an-envelope extrapolation based on running's 7.5 per cent share of the UK's £5.7 billion sports retail market), that's significantly more people than, say, the Church of England employs. And the numbers are getting bigger. In the past twenty years the running market has grown by 500 per cent.

And the insanity? It comes down to one question: how can running be an industry at all? Can you think of any other human activity, apart from eating, drinking, sex and defecating, that is so utterly natural as running? It's as simple, spontaneous and life-enhancing as singing. We've been doing it for tens of thousands of years: for necessity (hunting, fleeing, etc.) and, over countless generations, for pleasure. A child doesn't need special training or equipment to discover the joy of running for fun, any more than a dog or a horse does. There's no more need for a running industry than there is for a tree-climbing industry or a hide-and-seek industry.

Except, of course, that that's not how the modern world works. The opposing forces of capitalist consumerism and the socialist-inspired nanny state have between them squeezed all but a few drops of spontaneity from our lives. (Come to think of it, they turned eating, drinking and sex into industries long ago. Watch out for Big Defecation.) It may seem perverse, in these economically stagnant times, to moan about the fact that one of our industries, based on popular enthusiasm for a life-enhancing activity, is booming. But every boom comes at a price, and in this case – I'd argue – the price is paid by ordinary consumers, impoverished by the relentless pressure to buy more or better kit or, alternatively, marginalised, excluded or deterred because they can't afford it.

This isn't just a running issue; it's true of many of life's basic pleasures. It's still theoretically possible to enjoy them without spending a fortune on equipment, ingredients, packaging and extras, but the twenty-first century's agencies of persuasion encourage us to consider it weird to do so. Indeed, that may, sadly, turn out to have been the most enduring legacy of London 2012. Long after the athletes and volunteers and others who created the magic had gone home, the sponsors were still booming out the same deafening message from the billboards: if you want to amount to anything in your chosen sport – or, by implication, in life generally – then, obviously, you'll need to buy the same state-of-the-art clothing, equipment, nutritional aid, shampoo or even junk food that your particular Olympic hero or heroine has been paid to endorse. One year on from the Games, grassroots participation in sport had fallen, by 100,000 a week. But television viewing figures were at an all-time high, while a sponsor such as Procter & Gamble (makers of the Olay products endorsed by Jessica Ennis and Victoria Pendleton) was on target to record £325 million of extra sales. So no one can say that a generation wasn't inspired.

And while the Olympic fortunes of our elite athletes are as likely to go down as up at future Games, you can be pretty certain that, for expenditure on grassroots running, the trend can only be upward. Renaud Vaschalde, sales and sport industry analyst at the aforementioned NPD Inc., forecasts that the market will continue to grow by 6 per cent or more per year until at least 2016. 'Running is definitely the fastest growing sport at global level,' he adds.

Within a year or two, those products in my imaginary Sweatshop shopping basket will have been superseded by new ones: more sophisticated, more expensive, more achingly essential. Never mind if we can afford them or not. Running is now a market, not a recreation: buying products is what ordinary runners are supposed to do. If you're not a consumer, you're at best ridiculous, at worst weird.

A similar kind of twisted logic has persuaded any number of modern children that, for example, a packaged sandwich is more desirable than a homemade one; or that clothing with logos is better than clothing without. It is, I suppose, a rational response to a lifetime of being carpet-bombed by advertising. The bought things in life are better – more desirable, more trustworthy, perhaps even more real – than those that you simply improvise for yourself.

So it is that – to return to the point where the previous chapter left off – by 2013 there were two very different ways for a runner to enjoy a rural trail such as the Pennine Way. You could go to the trail and start running. Or you could go to the Trailblaze website, set up an account there (£20 a year at the time of my visit), get a digital toggle, insert it into every Trailblaze box you passed on any one of a dozen of England's best-known scenic trails (as my 'ghost' was presumably doing) and, in return, have your trail-running achievements recorded and published online and, if you ran far enough, rewarded with various coloured wristbands.

Does either of these approaches strike you as ridiculous? And, if so, which one?

In fact, by the time you read this, the Trailblaze 'project' will have been discontinued. Concerted opposition by an alliance of rural traditionalists has caused a drying-up of the enterprise's public funding – of which there was at one point a surprising amount (from, among others, the EU, Defra, the South West Regional Development Agency and the South Devon AONB Sustainable Development Fund). A knock-on effect on profits was unavoidable, and the people behind it, a Devon-based outfit called Endurancelife, pulled the plug on it. None the less, it's striking that, between 2011 and 2013, hundreds of people found the Trailblaze concept sufficiently convincing to buy into it. Many went further and shelled out extra cash for bronze membership: £61 a year, including membership card, stickers, visor and branded arm warmers. Presumably they felt that they got enough out of the transaction for it to be worthwhile; and it is not for me to question their judgement.

Yet I can't help feeling a lingering distaste for the enterprise: not because of its alleged desecration of the countryside (in fact, you could barely notice it), but because the core idea was so perverse. Why pay to run when you can run for free? Why brand something when it is part of our common heritage?

Rightly or wrongly, the short-lived concept of Trailblaze has come to symbolise, for me, a wider and more fundamental surrender to consumerism in twenty-first-century Britain. More people than ever before are struggling to make ends meet and yet we seem to have lost the will to question or resist the propaganda of big business. Advertisers target us virtually every minute of our waking lives, online and off, and sometimes it seems as though just being a person is no longer enough. Instead, for your life to be worth anything, you have to be a consumer, defined by the objects you covet or spend your money on. It is, similarly, no longer enough simply to do something. For an activity to count, money and products must change hands; ideally, the transaction must be 'shared' online.

As a runner, I notice this trend particularly in running. A pleasure that ought to be gloriously simple has been made prohibitively complicated and expensive: not by law but by a kind of unthinking consensus. 'Go outside, put one foot in front of the other, continue until you've had enough' has become 'Spend several weeks' wages on state-of-the-art shoes and purpose-made clothing; consume large quantities of specialist high-energy food and drink from brightly coloured pouches; buy hi-tech equipment to measure time, speed, distance, strides, heart rate, weight loss and more; subscribe to every possible running magazine and website; buy any new products you see advertised there; perform complex warm-up routines, preferably tailor-made for you by a professional "expert"; use a specialist app to determine optimum route; measure performance against norms for your age, gender, weight, etc.; calculate your body mass index, body fat percentage, power-to-weight ratio, etc., to several decimal points; download as many as you can afford from a choice of several hundred running and fitness apps; keep a digital log, preferably online, of every run you do (if not via Trailblaze then via Garmin – makers of the £279.99 training watch mentioned earlier and, it seems, a market leader in this fast-expanding field); monitor (and share) your calorie expenditure, steps taken, achievement levels and much else with a £129 Nike+ FuelBand or similar; seek specialist medical treatment for repetitive strain injuries that your state-of-the-art running shoes have mysteriously failed to prevent; buy even more expensive, more state-of-the-art running shoes to reduce (supposedly) the risk of injury recurrence . . . and so on until you can no longer afford to continue.'

The strange thing is, the more we spend on running, as a nation, the less fit and more fat we collectively become. In the past twenty years (when, remember, expenditure on running has increased fivefold), the incidence of obesity in the UK has doubled.

Or perhaps it isn't so strange. If even the simplest kind of outdoor exercise has been converted into a form of consumption, is it really surprising if those without money to burn opt to remain on the sofa? On the contrary: being a couch potato is the logical response.

'They took all the trees,' sang Joni Mitchell, 'and put 'em in a tree museum,/ And charged the people a dollar-and-a-half just to see 'em.' It's much the same with running, except that it will cost you a lot more than a dollar-and-a-half to get yourself kitted out as a proper modern runner; and more still to start running in the way that politicians and health professionals generally recommend – that is, on a treadmill in a members-only gym.

Runners are born free, and everywhere they run in chains. Or, if you prefer, in chain stores. This book is written in the hope of helping at least some of those runners to liberate themselves.

It is, among other things, a manifesto for a different kind of running: a de-commercialised, lo-tech kind of running, accessible to all. I hesitate to call it a new kind of running, because most previous generations will have run in the ways and settings that I describe. But it is 'new' in the sense that many of us may need to relearn it, in the same way that a calculator user might need to relearn mental arithmetic or a satnav user might need to relearn to read a map – and in the same way that millions of us might one day need to learn the basic cooking and making-and-mending skills that our grandparents took for granted. You could even think of this book as a manual: a 'how to' guide for those for whom the tried and tested ways of the past represent scarily unfamiliar territory.

It is about the kind of running that involves getting wet, and muddy, and lost; the kind of running where you'll be more concerned with the rhythms of the agricultural year and the ways of wild and domesticated animals than you will be with split times and recovery rates. You won't need a stopwatch for it, or a heart-rate monitor, or any other special equipment (or, for that matter, skills): just a sense of wonder and a resolution to live in the moment.

I've no more claim to proper expertise in athletic matters than I have to be a doctor or an accountant. Yet there is one subject in which I consider myself reasonably knowledgeable: namely, the art of incorporating a running habit into a normal modern lifestyle – busy, stressed, time-poor – in such a way that it never becomes an unsustainable chore.

In more than thirty years of amateur running I've approached the sport from many angles: competitive, recreational, hi-tech, lo-tech, consumerist and natural. I've run on roads, pavements, parks, treadmills, footpaths, fields, moors, mountains, beaches, stairwells, escalators – even, occasionally, running tracks. I have no special talents as a runner but might at different times have reasonably been described as keen, half-hearted, obsessive, a kit junkie, a nutter, quite good, pretty pathetic, middle-of-the-pack and plain useless.

But I've never stopped enjoying it, or doing it.

'Gosh, you must have a lot of willpower,' people often say when they hear that I still go running every day at the age of fifty-three. To which I reply: bollocks. I exercise no more willpower in going running than I would in eating a bar of chocolate. I don't do it for self-improvement, or to keep me slim or healthy. I do it for pleasure. It's my little treat. Or, rather, my big treat: a seemingly inexhaustible stream of free, life-affirming brightness from which I constantly refresh myself, spiritually and physically.

The aim of this book is to share this indulgence with other people; to help any runner whose running habit has become a dutiful, expensive routine to convert it into a sustainable, affordable pleasure. It's partly a manual, partly a description of a typical year in the life of a rural runner, and partly an account of a journey: my own long, unexpectedly liberating journey through a succession of different approaches to running.

If I sometimes come across as being critical of other, non-rural forms of running, remember: the person I'm criticising is me. Road-running, gyms, obsessively competitive running – I have devoted years of my life to each and have no wish to attack such approaches. We all run in the ways that seem most appropriate to us, at different stages of our lives. I'm merely suggesting – and celebrating – an additional, neglected kind of running: not an 'instead' but an 'as well'.

And if I sometimes get carried away with enthusiasm as I try to share an aspect of my life that has brought me huge amounts of joy, please don't mistake my enthusiasm for self-congratulation. In many cases, I'm only just discovering those joys myself.

3

Clock-watching

Is it only me who sees his life melting away behind him: thousands of packed, unique, exuberant days merging into pale decades that dissolve in turn into a tired, misremembered fog? Or is that just what middle age feels like?

I can't be the only modern fifty-three-year-old to look back on the prime of his life and think: did I really need to spend quite so much time at work? Did I really need to meet all those targets? To earn so much? To spend so much? To waste so little time?

I can't be the only one to think: is that it?

But I may be the only one to blame it on running.

It's a long story. Let's begin it, more than three decades ago, with a feckless young man in south London, drifting through life and work in a post-teenage daydream, who decided, belatedly, that it was time to get a grip. The dissolute lifestyle of a would-be journalist has much to be said for it, unless you try to combine it with the pitiful income and career prospects of a permanently hungover office junior. By the time I realised that my way of living was unsustainable, I could barely see my way out of it.

Then, one summer evening, hungry, hungover,

frustrated, down to my last cigarette, too penniless to go out but too bored to stay in, I remembered an article I'd been proof-reading about the psychological benefits of exercise and, in desperation, decided to go for a run.

I dug out my old gym shoes, borrowed a pair of shorts, slipped out of the overcrowded house I was sharing and, for a strange half-hour, puffed, spluttered and shuffled my way to the local common and back again.

Millions of other runners will have had comparable experiences. We all come to it in different ways, but there is still usually an 'it': the equivalent of a smoker's first cigarette. It's not necessarily the very first: it's the first that leads to another, and then to another.

The thing itself is usually forgettable. All I remember of mine – the run, not the cigarette – is the coughing, and the sense that my chest was about to split open, and the shocking redness of my face when I noticed my reflection in a window. Actually, my first cigarette was much the same. But with that first run – a decade later, on a busy Clapham Common rather than in the woods behind the school gym – there was also the unaccustomed peace and depth of the night's sleep that followed, and the disorienting sense of self-worth the next day.

It takes more than one fix to establish a habit; sometimes, a degree of willpower is required. But once it's part of your life you can look back to that very first time as a landmark: the watershed between (in this example) life as a non-runner and life as a runner. Years later, we can look back and say: that was the night (or day) when I started to become who I am.

It took a few months to catch on, for me. But it did, and within a year I had recognised it as a life-changing liberation. I had stumbled upon a way of letting off steam that got me into neither trouble nor debt.

Within three or four years I had grown used to it – and was acquiring a more or less lasting sense that I was not quite as helpless in the face of life's turbulence as I had imagined. I can't pretend that my life was never again a mess: one burst of super-intense strength training, a year or so into this phase, was inspired by a threatened visit by some angry sounding debt collectors. But it was never again an entirely helpless mess. As I discovered myself as a runner – and learnt to ignore the inner voice that continued for years to whinge about not really feeling like it today and couldn't we do it tomorrow instead? – so I acquired an increasingly firm faith that I had it within me, through self-discipline and perseverance, to make more of a difference – to my own life and to others' – than my old, hopeless, apathetic self had ever believed possible.

Some people tag their memories with pop music. Call up the right song, and great handfuls of the past – friends, places, holidays, jobs, parties, kisses, homes, dreams – will surface with it. Runners, if they choose, can do much the same with runs. If I want to retrieve the texture of a period in my life, I think back to where and how I would have been doing most of my running at the time. Then I focus on the details of the route and wait for the past to resurface.

If it is slow to do so, I try to think my way through the relevant route in more detail, step by step: where I would have started; what time of day it would have been; who, if anyone, would have run with me; what sights, sounds and smells I would have encountered at different stages on the route; what my likely frame of mind would have been.

With sufficient focus and persistence, every stride of the route returns, vividly, in real time, each step leading logically to the next. By the time my mental run is over I will some-times feel so in touch with the person I was then that I have almost become him: as if I were about to wake up from a strange dream about the future and re-enter the world that I lived in then.

Here I am, for example, on one of those Friday evenings when, having seen off the almost irresistible temptation to blow my week's wages on beer and bad behaviour, I would work off the resulting frustration with a long, slow run, just keeping on going, sometimes for hours, until I felt happy again. On a good night I could make it from south London to the Thames and beyond, into the royal parks, as I worked my way through my various resentments and worries.

Sometimes I would meander through the almost-empty parks until late at night, marvelling at my good fortune at having all this expensively landscaped space more or less to myself. And once, at least, a dark summer evening grew suddenly sweet with the scent of a rose garden, presumably from behind some palace walls, and I laughed out loud at the thought that I was getting more pleasure from those flowers than the people for whom they were planted.

Naturally, as I meandered, my troubles would drift away, one by one, and my mind would fill instead with thoughts from books and films, with jokes and sports highlights and dreamy plans for love, work and adventure – with, in short, all the nonsense with which youths everywhere have always filled their heads.

If I'd passed you, you'd probably have avoided my glance. I was shabby, crop-haired, muscular, with none of the shiny kit that might have denoted a respectable, competitive athlete; you might even have scrutinised me to check that I wasn't running away with someone's handbag. Inside, however, I was just an ordinary young man: clumsy, well-meaning, vulnerable; searching for certainty and confidence; flitting from pose to pose; an insecure blunderer whose hard-boned head was full of poetry and yearning. Like many runners, this tortured-looking individual was striving for something that could be encapsulated by the phrase 'personal best'. In his case, however, the words had nothing to do with time, speed or distance. Rather, he was trying — with a certain feeble heroism — to realise, for once in his life, something of his personal potential.

It frightens me that I could have forgotten someone who was once so real. Yet retracing my regular running routes brings it all back, so vividly that I feel that I could stretch out and touch myself. (And, indeed, I long to do so. I want to reach back through time and tell him: 'Don't worry. It will be all right. Every step you take is a step in the right direction.')

Such memories present themselves as single episodes: individual runs with a beginning, a middle and an end. They're kidding me. They feel authentic but these visions are in reality misleading tapestries, woven from countless different occasions into a self-serving whole. Examine their internal logic and they fall apart like dreams. Yet they're no less intoxicating — to me — for that.

Here I am again, for example, in another retracing of the same block of memory, running north from the Oval, up the long plane-lined avenue of Kennington Road, up through Lambeth, working up a rhythm and a sweat. By the time I have reached the parks of central London I have shaken off the day's rage and frustration at my boring, ill-paid job as (by now) a junior magazine sub-editor. Yet the chronology doesn't add up. In between those two moments, as I cross Westminster Bridge on that same nostalgically retrieved run, it is early morning, with the air fresh and the Thames sparkling peacefully beneath me in the dawn's first warmth and the streets barely awake and (as William Wordsworth observed two centuries earlier) all London's mighty heart lying still.

In my remembered run, I am always alone at that point – although in reality I don't think I ever ran in the early morning in those days unless I was dragged out by one or more housemates. Conversely, there are usually two or three of us by the time I recross southwards at Lambeth Bridge. The warm breeze that drifts up to us from the broad river is less bitter than the air we have been breathing on the city streets, and a few gulps of it are usually the perfect incentive to kick on for the final couple of miles. It is still light at that point – it feels like a late Sunday afternoon – with a rose-tinted sun sinking into the ripples to the west; yet by the time we emerge from the railway arches on Lambeth Road – a few hundred metres later – the remembered scene is as dark and deserted as midnight, with the scent of the next morning's bread wafting from the Lambeth Walk baker's.

And then there's the mile-long dash for home, and once again I'm alone, watching for Sunday afternoon traffic out of the corners of my eyes as I cross half a dozen side roads without breaking my stride, insulating myself from the pain of the final sprint by reciting poetry to myself. (I had taken to heart the teachings of Percy Cerutty, the great Australian coach-philosopher of the 1950s whose training methods placed almost as much emphasis on spiritual conditioning as on physical.)

You get the picture. If you've done any kind of running you can probably conjure up an equivalent of your own that is as poignantly evocative for you as mine is for me.

The point is not the details of the scenery but the person running through it. The former are just a means of evoking the latter. And the purpose of evoking the latter is not (in this context) the alarming thrill of remembering the people we once were but, more modestly, the insight that comes from remembering the kind of runners we once were.

Suppose – and I'm only guessing here – that there are Seven Ages of Running. What might they be? The First is presumably the total novice: hesitant, embarrassed, still only provisionally committed, and pleasantly surprised on first completing a distance that can be measured in miles rather than metres. (As with the first of Shakespeare's Seven Ages of Man, a certain amount of 'mewling and puking' is sometimes involved, too.) That would be me on Clapham Common.

The runner of the Second Age is more of a zealot. Going for a run no longer feels like a mad experiment. You know you can do it. You know you feel better when you do it. You know that, the more you do it, the better you get at it. So the challenge and the excitement relate mainly to the simple life discipline of doing it more.

Somehow you have to carve out spaces from your life for running where no such spaces existed before. Other routines have to give. Pubs? Television watching? Work? Meals? The friends who bring out the worst in you? Different lives have different default modes, good and bad. In the Second Age of Running, the thing that absorbs and excites you is changing the default: resetting your life to accommodate your new habit. Many of us find ourselves feeling dramatically better about life as we do so – which explains why so many of us, in this phase, are inclined to bore our friends with our excitement, like new parents who prattle as though no one had ever had a baby before. Those scenes in the parks and bridges of central London were from my Second Age of Running.

Let's rejoin my younger self, a year or two later. I'm living in a different part of south London now, in Camberwell, cohabiting with Clare, my future wife. The daily run has become as instinctive as brushing my teeth. It still makes me happy – or, at least, it makes me unhappy if I don't do it. But it no longer fills me with wonder.

I normally go in the evening, first thing after getting back from work. That way there's still some evening left afterwards. There's less romance to the running by now. Get changed, jog up and down the street a couple of times, stretch a bit, then off, fast, pushing myself from the first stride. If there's a friend around who wants to come with me, well and good; if not, I'm not going to waste time trying to rustle someone up.

I'm usually able to sustain the fierce rhythm for the whole run – typically five or six miles – but I have to concentrate. So there's less room in my head for idle dreams. If my mind does wander, it does so across a range of concerns that are increasingly grown-up: work, wedding plans, the pros and cons of house-buying – that sort of thing.

The various routes I used to take in this period are oddly lacking in detail when I try to re-run them in my head. Narrow pavements. Busy roads. Some ups and downs along Herne Hill Road and Red Post Hill. A vague sense of relief on reaching Dulwich and, eventually, Dulwich Park. And then, with a few variations, the whole thing in reverse.

The thing that comes back with most clarity is the sense of how much faster I was getting – and of how absorbing I found this. Each evening, as I started, I would check my watch. It was a pre-digital model, one with hands, so I could time myself only by memorising the exact time that I started. Oddly, I never once forgot it. I knew the records for all my principal routes; and I was more likely to break a record than to be significantly outside it.

When I visualise myself pounding through Dulwich Park, the main sense impressions that return are of the pounding rather than the park. The latter comes back to me as a vague blur of grass and trees; but I can remember vividly the feeling of pressing, relentlessly, against my limitations, always pushing myself forwards, straining against some invisible force of resistance at the front of my chest. The fitter I got, the further I could push it back. But it was always there; and I never eased off from pushing.

If there was any poetry in my soul as I ran, it, too, was running-specific. Where once I had merely daydreamed as I ran, I now enriched my routine with visualisations of track heroes: of the perfect symmetry of Coe, the implacable rhythm of Cram, the weightless elasticity of Aouita. Where once I had fantasised about being a better person, I was now concerned mainly with being a better athlete. Focus was the key. Exclude all other thoughts, concentrate only on that perfect rhythm, that perfect balance, with every stride; let rhythm and balance and suppleness fill every corner of your soul – and before you know it they will fill your running, too.

Such living in the moment has much in common with some forms of meditation, and I suspect has similar psychological benefits. Yet I don't look back to these runs with as much affection as I do to earlier or later phases in my running evolution. All that focus could too easily turn into a form of joylessness. Road crossings, for example – jogging on the spot waiting for a gap in the traffic – were no longer a welcome break but an irritation. I found myself choosing routes less for their interest than for the amount of uninterrupted full-speed running they offered. Increasingly, I preferred half a dozen quality circuits of Ruskin Park to a more discursive journey through south London on which I might have to slow down or stop from time to time.

There weren't any iPods then, but if someone had offered

me an easy way of delivering rhythmic music to my ears while I ran I would certainly have taken it. Anything that helped me to eliminate distractions and focus on the job in hand was welcome.

I suspect it's no coincidence that I was, by now, finally starting to get somewhere in my career. Nothing spectacular, sadly, but employers were beginning to recognise and value my ability to focus, to set and meet targets, to make adequate preparations, to be honest about progress, to stay the course, to push myself – all qualities that flowed from my running.

At some point in this period I moved to a job where there was an office gym – offering the even more focused option of doing all my runs at a constant, measurable pace on an indoor treadmill. The only thing that stopped me from doing so was the fact that (in those days) the treadmill didn't go fast enough for someone with aspirations to being a proper middle-distance runner.

I also trained regularly on a public running track – with friends, on Sunday afternoons – where, again, the act of running could be distilled to its purest form, without distractions. Occasionally, I raced: not on tracks but on roads, at distances from 2.5 miles to half-marathon. I didn't win anything, but I was often near the front; and the harder I trained, the better I performed.

Seasoned runners will recognise the gist, if not my specific combination of details. This is the Third Age of Running, when a general desire for self-improvement gives way to a yearning for 'peak performance'. You're already relatively near your natural peak, and your times no longer improve in huge leaps and bounds as you shed the accumulated unfitness of the years; instead, you forage through the collective know-how of the running world in search of tips, tricks, techniques and technology that might help you achieve what Team GB coaches call 'marginal gains'. You might be well below Team GB standard – I certainly was – but the principles are the same: half a per cent here, a tenth of a per cent there, and it all adds up.

The other thing that distinguishes this Third Age runner from the previous two is the kit. In my case, the frayed Green Flash gym shoes had by now been replaced by an expensive pair of Asics, identified for me by a biomechanics expert at a specialist running shop as the model most appropriate for my (pronating) running style. My heavy, sweat-drenched T-shirts had given way to bright, lightweight, synthetic vests; my stiff cotton rugby shorts to purpose-made Lycra running shorts; and so on.

Actually, it's hard to think of much else that a runner in London could need, except possibly socks. None the less, I found ways to fill up our home with lots of it: windproof and waterproof outerwear, gloves, sweatbands, water bottles, spare clothes, spare shoes, and, yes, special runners' socks. There were also running magazines, fitness magazines, even a sports science book or two. Anything that could conceivably narrow the gap between me and my Olympic heroes was irresistible to me. And, for that brief window of affluence when Clare and I had two good incomes and no children, the cost seemed tolerable. If I didn't buy a heart-rate monitor or a back-mounted hydration pack, that was only because they weren't yet available. The running industry must have loved me. Big Running loves Third Age runners.

And the Fourth, Fifth, Sixth and Seventh Ages of Running? The sad truth is, most of us never get that far.

4

Running wild

Somewhere in the years that followed I got lucky. Clare married me. We had two lovely children. We, and they, stayed healthy. We stayed employed. And our working lives developed in such ways that we were able, gradually, to leave London.

My running habits changed. Parenthood meant snatching runs when I could. Living in rural Northamptonshire meant finding new routes. There were no parks or pavements but plenty of deserted lanes, and it didn't take long to work out suitable circuits: the four-and-a-half-mile run, the seven-mile run, the ten-mile run, the two-mile mini-run.

In terms of physical demands, this kind of running was barely different from being in London: just a little hillier, with less traffic, fresher air, greener views – and the notable advantage of no busy junctions or crossings requiring me to break my rhythm.

I'd grown up, as had Clare, in a small rural village; but my life as an adult runner had been entirely urban until then. I just thought of the lanes as an imperfect rural substitute for pavement.

The nearest running club and track were ten miles away,

as was the nearest gym; the time spent getting there and back would have taken longer than the actual training. As for what lay on either side of the tarmac – a vast, undulating, thickly hedged patchwork of rough pastures and ploughed fields – the idea of venturing into it barely occurred to me.

When it finally did, I explored the unfamiliar wilderness of fields and woods with apprehension. I recall going out one damp autumn evening, a half-remembered map in my head, cursing each time the footpaths I had been expecting failed to show up on the heavy ground. Before I knew it the sun was sinking, the bare ash trees on the skyline had turned black, an icy mist was rising from the sea of furrows around me, and I realised that the solitary pigeon that flapped urgently past me towards the woods, starkly audible in the deserted sky, was hurrying to reach its roost before nightfall. I felt suddenly small and lost. The fact that the setting sun told me plainly which direction was west was of little comfort. I hardly knew where our house was, let alone where I was in relation to it.

Of course I was bound to get home eventually, simply by trial and error. But with my legs already heavy from five or six miles of hard running, my appetite for trial and error was limited. Should I head for that apparent gap in the hedge on the far side of the ploughed field I was in? Should I fight my way through the impenetrable thicket directly in front of me? Should I retrace my steps half a mile to the point where I was last on an unambiguous footpath? When you've no idea where or how you went wrong, you can never be sure that your attempted corrections won't make things worse. And with each extra fruitless mile, your legs grow heavier and the night grows darker …

Such mishaps confirmed me in my prejudice that, if I was

to extract the maximum training benefit from the limited time available to me, I would be better off sticking to the roads.

I was – I'm pretty certain – the only runner in our village. Nor was I aware of runners in any neighbouring villages. This was the early 1990s, and recreational running was a pastime still largely confined to town- and city-dwellers. My Day-Glo kit, my fancy trainers, my glazed expression and my fast, rhythmic gait all screamed 'incomer', and I grew used to faintly disapproving stares from passing motorists.

Then, one spring morning, running on a back lane so deserted and cratered with pot-holes that it almost qualified as 'off-road', I sensed an inexplicable panting sound swelling behind me. By the time I was fully aware of it, it was surging everywhere. I was waist-deep in a warm, tempestuous, smelly, black and brown sea of dogs, leaping and squirming like a school of excited porpoises. There were about twenty of them, each the size of a small calf and each slobberingly thrilled to see me. By the time they had all put their paws on my shoulders and licked my face I had worked out that they were bloodhounds: huge, gentle beasts with melancholy eyes, worried, jowly faces, dangling ears and exuberantly optimistic body language.

I was still wiping saliva from my face when the pack was joined by its leader: a young, weather-beaten, serious-browed man on a quad bike, with a tatty khaki coat, a big sheath-knife on his belt and what looked like a miniature bugle hanging from a cord around his neck.

'What do this lot hunt?' I asked him.

'People like you,' he said.

A brief chat revealed that these were the Farmers Bloodhounds, central England's premier pack of people-chasers. Based in kennels on a remote farm outside a village a few miles from mine, they belonged to a consortium of enthusiasts who used them for fox-free hunting on farmland right across Northamptonshire, Warwickshire, Oxfordshire, Worcestershire and Gloucestershire. Graham Tutton, the young man on the quad bike, was the kennel huntsman – a hard, lonely, ill-paid role that involved, in effect, acting *in loco parentis* for the entire pack. Every detail of the life of each hound – food, drink, shelter, health, hygiene, breeding, training – was his responsibility, from dawn until dusk, every day of the year; although it was the hunt committee that came up with the cash for the £500's worth of raw meat the hounds wolfed down every week.

It was not, Graham said, what he had set out to do in life, but it was employment, and he was pleased to be working outdoors, and with animals. The hounds, which looked up to him as a god-like figure, were entertaining and enthusiastic companions. The biggest headache of his job, he added, was finding runners who were able and willing to act as quarry at the right place and the right time. What did I reckon?

I couldn't think of a plausible reason to refuse, and so began an unexpected episode in my running life that would gradually transform my ideas about what constituted 'normal' running.

Graham tried me out the next day on a small circuit he'd devised nearby. 'Go across that field there, though the gap in the hedge, across the next field diagonally, then down the slope on to the disused railway...' All I had to do was remember his instructions, avoid falling over on the rough ground, stop in the place where he had told me to stop, and remember to distribute the chopped liver he had just given me when the hounds caught up with me a minute or two later.

I passed the test and was soon being tried out on proper

hunts. This was a strange experience for someone who, despite a rural upbringing, had never felt the remotest urge to participate in any form of hunting. But 'hunting the clean boot', as hunting a runner with bloodhounds is known, is quite different from other country sports. Not only does it not involve killing anything; it doesn't even use the unmissable chemical 'drag' that foxhounds follow in drag-hunting. Much of the interest, for those who follow it on horseback or on foot, lies in seeing how the hounds respond to the challenge of following a relatively mild, unenhanced human scent; the horseback followers also tend to experience a much more exhilarating ride than foxhunters, because the human quarry can be relied on – if they follow the kennel huntsman's instructions – to take the hunt on a route with lots of fast riding and feasible jumping.

For a formal hunt there were usually two of us, picked from a pool of three or four regular runners across central England. We would set off fifteen or twenty minutes before the hounds and horses, run for about five miles, rest for a few minutes while everyone else caught up, then set off again on another 'line' of around five miles. A full afternoon's hunting could involve anything from ten to twenty miles' running, which wasn't always as hard as it sounds: partly because of the rests but also because we often weren't going particularly fast.

The instinctive human response to being hunted is to run as quickly as possible: the faster the hunters, the greater the speed required. In practice, for the runner being hunted by bloodhounds, this instinct is barely relevant. The hounds are quick, certainly: three or four times the speed of a human over rough ground, once they're certain of your scent. And it's considered highly undesirable for them to catch you up

– not for your sake, but because that would mean that the
'line' was cut short; and because they might be tempted to
hunt by sight rather than scent. But that's all in the hands of
the huntsman, not the quarry. No runner can outrun the
hounds, but the huntsman can ensure that they never quite
catch up, simply by giving the runners enough start.

Graham was uncannily good at this, generally calculating
timings on a formal hunt so that, no matter how wild and
unpredictable the terrain, the runners finished with exactly
two minutes to spare. For our training runs – which became
an increasingly important part of our relationship – he liked
to cut it a bit finer, arranging things with sadistic precision
so that I could avoid being overtaken only if I ran the final
mile more or less flat out. Either way, it was interesting that
I never quite shook off my lingering irrational fear that I was
likely to be ripped apart and eaten if I allowed the pack to
catch me.

One moment I'd be plodding through the fields, drinking
in the scenery or chatting (if applicable) with my fellow quarry.
Then, from nowhere, I'd hear Graham's horn – shocking as
the last trumpet – and the half-forgotten sound of the pack
would explode all around: a crescendo of discordant yelps,
like metal scraping on metal, that swelled into the howling
music of hounds in full cry, echoing from the sky. Involuntarily,
my gaze would snap towards them, in the knowledge that, if
I couldn't see them at first, they would materialise at any
moment: black shapes, shooting from hedgerow or undergrowth one by one, like lethal, malevolent insects from under
a slab, swarming over the landscape until they had resolved
themselves into a more or less coherent shoal of rippling,
clamouring black and tan. At the same time, instantly, my
heartbeat would change up a gear, and I would find that,

without conscious thought, I had sprung into a sprint.

This would be sustained for however long it took to reach the end, give or take the odd backward glance, which would invariably yield the dispiriting sight of the hounds gliding with no apparent effort over slopes, furrows, bogs and ridges that had taxed me to the limit when I was labouring through them a few minutes earlier.

Any worries I might have had about a loss of quality in my training when I ran for the hounds rather than on the road was dispelled by such moments. Those final kicks for home – spurred by the distant thunder of Graham's horse's hooves as well as the pack's ever-closer baying; straining to rise above the mud and knotted turf; fuelled by primeval fear – were among the most demanding sessions I have ever done.

There was, of course, no real need for fear. When I greeted the bloodhounds at the finish, they would merely take it in turns to lick me, slobber over me and (paws on shoulders) gaze soulfully into my eyes – pausing only to snarf up the biscuits or chopped liver that I would distribute for them as they arrived.

I grew quite fond of them, eventually learning to recognise most of them by name. They seemed to think of me as a genuine friend: not as a member of their pack (as Graham, the pack leader, was), but as some kind of much-loved old acquaintance whom it was always a pleasure to see again – not least because of the biscuits and chopped liver.

'I've never known them hunt anyone as well as they hunt you,' said Graham one day. 'You must give off a really distinctive scent.' Some people might have taken umbrage at such a remark, but I was only too delighted to have finally discovered, in my early thirties, a sport at which I was naturally talented.

For much of one season (October to April, roughly), I used to act as the hunt's quarry on most Sundays, as they plied their trade in assorted parts of central England.

It was a fantastic chance to see some beautiful tracts of countryside close up, often on land that wasn't usually accessible to the public. But Clare and the children, who loyally tagged along as hunt followers for a while, soon began to pine for other ways of spending Sunday afternoons, and I could see their point. So I settled for a less ambitious routine, whereby other people would have the glory of running for the proper hunts, while I would turn out two or three times a week for early morning training runs with just Graham, Graham's horse, the bloodhounds and me.

For several years, on weekdays during the hunting season, we'd meet up at various prearranged dawn rendezvous in the local fields; I'd do my morning run, on a route chosen by Graham; and the hounds, their memories of me periodically refreshed by the loan of one of my smelly old running socks, would set out after me a bit later, with nothing to guide them but whatever traces of scent I had left.

This worked well for all concerned. Graham was able to train the hounds far more thoroughly than would otherwise have been the case. And I was able to incorporate my hound-based runs into my normal training routine, rather than giving up family weekends for them.

There were drawbacks. The fact that I needed to earn a living meant that we had to do all these training runs very early in the morning. The fact that the season fell mostly in winter meant that, when we did, it was often very dark. And wet. And cold.

I grew used to finding my way by starlight, feeling my way through black tree-shadowed paths with my hands held

out in front of me as I jogged, eyes screwed up against dangling branches, until I gradually realised that (although
someone who had just left the house would have insisted that
it was pitch dark) I could see enough of the landscape's key
features to be able to run fairly freely and then, a little later,
to be able to run flat out. The more familiar I grew with the
contours of our favourite hunting ground – the south-facing
slopes of a barely inhabited ridge about a mile south of my
village – the easier it became.

I grew used, too, to falling over and getting up again, and
to slithering down waterlogged slopes, or squelching through
fields churned into knee-deep bogs by livestock. The bloodhounds had to have their exercise come rain or shine, and
Graham, who was exposed to the elements all day long, was
gloriously unsympathetic – although he did once check, on
a particularly flooded morning, that I could swim.

The cold took more getting used to. Rural temperatures
are usually about two degrees colder than urban ones, and
the further you go from human habitation the more you
notice it. On a dark winter morning, on rough, frost-hardened
Northamptonshire grassland, your feet inevitably succumb to
freezing sooner or later, no matter how vigorously you try
to keep the blood circulating. This is tolerable at the time:
you simply lose all feeling in your feet. It's bringing them
back to life indoors that's so agonising it makes you want to
howl – especially if, as often happened to me, your post-run
morale has already been battered by ten or fifteen minutes
spent trying to remove tightly laced shoes whose laces have
been frozen too solid to be untied by normal fingers, let alone
numb ones.

But the bonuses outweighed the discomforts. Most rural
dawns are beautiful. Few are so soul-warmingly lovely as

those that creep up on you when you are outdoors, cold and inwardly praying for the darkness to pass – until suddenly you're aware that the empty fields, woods and hills around you are flooding with light and colour, miraculously reinfused with life. It's hard to begin a working day with that kind of thrill and not feel a little better for it.

My daily duel with the hounds also introduced me to a new kind of intimacy with nature. Where previously I had merely glanced at these fields and thought 'That's nice', I now learnt to note and remember minute variations in gradient and texture – and to sense what was within the ground as well as on its surface – because all of these factors affected my experience as a runner. If I read the ground accurately, I could escape all sorts of unpleasantness, from boggy patches to thorny ones, avoidable steep bits to dangerously rutted ones; and, conversely, I could pick out more forgiving lines, where the running would be pleasant and free.

It seemed extraordinary that I could have missed so much before.

Better still, I began to get a sense of how such details might appear to the mind of a hound. Looking back at my pursuers, I could see easily where my scent was obvious to them and where it was confusing or elusive. Eventually, I began to understand why, as I realised how variations in temperature, moisture and wind – and the activities of nearby wildlife – can influence the perceptions of creatures that interpret the world primarily through scent.

On a warm, wet day my trail would be indistinct. On a windy one, it would be blown away from where I had left it, and the hounds would be lured off course. (I found it helpful to visualise the scent as a long, slowly fading cloud, like an aircraft's vapour trail, hovering about a foot above the ground.) Across a yielding, slippery ploughed field, or a path that was much crossed by wildlife, they could quickly become confused – especially early in the season, when half the pack were little more than puppies. But on dry, frosty mornings the scent would be so clear and resonant that I could almost see it myself, as the hounds, baying with delight, hurled themselves after me unhesitatingly.

The training had a seasonal shape to it. Younger hounds would be initiated into the pack in late summer; hunting would begin in October; and the season would end around Easter – at which point we'd go our separate ways for a few months. The late summer runs would be relatively short, as the young hounds built up stamina, discipline and know-how. By the time the clocks went back, we'd be doing longer distances, on trickier terrain; and by January Graham would be picking out extra-demanding routes with a view to pushing man and dog closer to their physical limits.

My fitness fluctuated with this cycle. On balance I welcomed this. A regime of unrelenting intensity might have proved too wearing, on my enthusiasm as well as my joints. I was already starting to notice that several of my London running friends, discouraged by injury and family demands or simply stale from lack of variety, were losing their appetite for the sport, and I felt grateful that I, by contrast, was at least still doing it, with regularity, pleasure and a strong incentive never to slip too far away from peak condition.

In any case I had by now another kind of running to keep me on my toes. A chance chain of friendships and conversations had led me to discover – within about a year of my first bloodhound encounter – the obscure northern pastime of fell-running. I have written about this at length elsewhere, in a book called *Feet in the Clouds*, and will therefore pass over it here with a cursoriness that underplays the sport's impact on my life. In brief: having discovered that a sport existed that involved running up and down trackless mountains, on all terrains and in all weathers, several of my old running friends and I devoted a ludicrously large proportion of our free time, over a period of about five years, to visiting suitable parts of Britain (notably Cumbria) and trying to master some of the sport's key challenges. These are considerable and various, from short, straight-up-and-down dashes lasting barely fifteen minutes to multi-peak long-distance challenges that can go on all day or, in some cases, longer. What unite them are three key facts. First: the surfaces involved (grass, mud, rock, scree, heather, bracken, bog, etc.) are generally so rough, steep and uneven that you can run on them only in defiance of common sense. Secondly, the mountain environment means that weather plays a huge (and often unpleasant) role in everything you do. And, thirdly, to be any good at any kind of fell-running, it is not enough simply to possess such conventional athletic qualities as fitness, stamina and speed: you also need to be brave, agile, resourceful and mentally and physically resilient, with enough mountaincraft to find your way safely even when conditions are severe, and enough general hardiness to endure a much wider range of discomforts (e.g. cold, fear, disorientation, minor injury, etc.) than conventional running normally produces.

Without going into detail, I think I can say that my fell-running phase constituted my version of the Fourth Age of Running. By this I mean the stage when you finally pit yourself against the very biggest, craziest, most daunting challenge you can possible imagine. For some this might mean going for Olympic gold; for others it might mean running a marathon, or perhaps some kind of adventure race or triathlon.

What matters is that, in your terms, it is extreme, improbable and perhaps on the borders of lunacy – but still, just about, theoretically, within your grasp.

Some never get round to trying their 'impossible' dream before it's too late, and then spend their post-running years wondering what would have happened if they had. For the rest, it barely matters, ultimately, whether you succeed or not. The point is that you give it your very best shot, and, in doing so, discover the absolute limits of your talent, strength and determination.

For a moderately talented runner like me, fell-running offered just the right combination of daunting difficulty and tantalising achievability: especially one particular ultra-distance challenge that I describe in *Feet in the Clouds*. I'll resist the temptation to retell that story here, beyond saying that the Bob Graham Round is a notorious circuit of forty-two of the Lake District's highest peaks, and that the challenge, which defeated some of the twentieth century's toughest athletes and mountain adventurers, is to complete the seventy-odd mile course within twenty-four hours. How I could ever have imagined that I would possibly be able to complete it is anyone's guess. But I did imagine it and, as often happens for runners who are lucky enough to reach that Fourth Age, the romance of the impossible dream temporarily took over my life.

It wasn't the only thing in my life during that five-year period in my mid-thirties. Family, work, friends and assorted other interests (including the bloodhounds) all occupied me as well. But I doubt there was a single day when I didn't (a) give it considerable thought and (b) put time and effort into trying to make myself better at it.

Big Running must have loved me more than ever. Every

spare penny I could find – apart from the small fortune I spent on trips to the Lake District – went on running kit and outdoor kit or, failing that, on maps, navigational aids, sports nutrition, training manuals and magazines and anything else I could think of that might make me a slightly better fell-runner.

It wasn't just about buying things, or even mainly about buying things. Most of it was simply about incessant training, in every relevant way I could think of. (Remember those tower blocks and escalators I mentioned earlier?) But the real clue to this being my Fourth Age of Running was simply that, had you visited our house, you'd have noticed the Stuff: the muddy leggings hanging out to drip outside the front door; the battered, muddy shoes (best, second-best, too-damaged-to-use-but-it-seems-a-shame-to-throw-them-away, etc.) propped up to dry in various locations; the heap of stinking clothing by the washing machine; the giant map in the bathroom (which I used to memorise each time I brushed my teeth); and so on.

If you've ever experienced the Fourth Age of Running yourself, or know anyone who has, or, for that matter, have experience of similar phases relating to other sports, you'll recognise the symptoms. The nature of the Stuff varies according to the challenge – anything from track-racing to triathlon, adventure-racing to marathon-bagging. What doesn't vary is the way the challenge (and the Stuff relating to it) seeps out to infuse the entire texture of your life. Perhaps that's why so many running books refer to this phase.

Normally, the obsessed runner grows out of it, the impossible challenge either achieved or abandoned. But he or she is usually left with, at least, a rich stock of memories, some of which may seem barely credible when reviewed a decade or two later, or, later still, evoked for sceptical grandchildren.

Some of my fell-running memories seemed barely credible even at the time. There were moments – usually when lost, bruised, exhausted, frightened and miles from the reassuring comforts of civilisation – when I asked myself why I did it. There were several answers, one of which has grown clearer with hindsight. Fell-running is rewarding partly because it requires you, as few other activities do, to be utterly absorbed in your environment. You have to pay constant attention to the small details of the ground beneath you: which stones are stable and which are not, which rocks are slippery, what lies beneath the heather or bracken, how firm or soggy the turf is, and so on. Otherwise, a painful accident is likely. At the same time, you can't afford to lose sight of the broader terrain: the directions of the various slopes, the upcoming hazards and obstructions and, thus, the optimum route to take you to the peak or valley you are heading for. Otherwise, you might put in far more effort and distance than you need to. And, not least, you can never afford to lose sight of where you are in the overall landscape – even if most of it is obscured in cloud or darkness – or you may become dangerously lost.

You must, in other words, be immersed in it all: which is a great way of forgetting your worries, but also a reliable way of magnifying the intensity of the miseries of the mountains at their worst. A dark, precipitous mountain half hidden in storm clouds is an only mildly bone-chilling sight if you glance at it from the window of a car or train. When you're right in the middle of it, with every fibre of your being straining for more awareness of exactly what is going on around you, it can reduce you to a level of physical despair that all but extinguishes the will to live.

Yet those miseries have an opposite. That same immersion adds indescribable depth and brilliance to the joys of the mountains at their best. All mountain lovers know this, but fell-runners, I think, know it more than most. When the clouds break, when that endless slope finally levels out, when the blizzard stops and you feel the sun on your back and half a mountain range is suddenly visible below you, shining like the Promised Land – at moments like that, the fact that you can barely tell any more where your rain- and sweat-drenched body stops and the storm-soaked mountain begins means that the happiness and wonder saturate your entire being. All the pains of fell-running are justified by such joys.

This formula is equally applicable whether you are approaching the sport with the obsessive drive of a Fourth Age runner or enjoying it in a more relaxed, recreational way. It applies, too (though less dramatically), to being hunted by bloodhounds over the rough countryside of central England; and, I'm sure, to other forms of rural exertion as well. The wilder the environment, the greater the demands it places on you – and, as a result, the more you get back from it.

The drawback is that, for most of us, wild environments – and packs of bloodhounds – are far away and hard to get to. By the time my Fourth Age of Running was coming to an end, I had begun to suspect that the toughest thing of all about fell-running was getting to the fells in the first place. Inevitably, as families expanded and time and spare cash grew scarcer, my friends and I found the sport playing a diminishing part in our lives.

These days I barely participate at all in formal fell races, although I still love running in mountains when the chance arises. Nor, if it comes to that, do I run with bloodhounds any more – or, at least, it has become so vanishingly rare that it barely counts any more as a part of my life. The pack moved to kennels in a different part of the county. Graham moved to a different job. We acquired a dog of our own. The net effect was that it all became a bit impractical.

But I've never formally said goodbye to either sport. And although those parallel chapters of my life are to all intents and purposes closed, I look back on both not just with affection but with gratitude – not least because, between them, they gave me a lasting education in the art of running confidently over rough ground.

There is, to be honest, no secret technique to this, but it still has to be learnt, from many hours of clumsy and sometimes painful trial and error, through which your brain, eyes and feet eventually get the message that it is perfectly possible to run fast and well – or, for that matter, slowly and comfortably – on surfaces that are neither flat nor smooth. It's best if your footwear isn't too thick-soled, and studs sometimes help, but it isn't primarily a question of kit. You just have to be more alert about what's under your feet, and less precious about the hazards of getting muddy, bruised or grazed.

The second half of that sentence is perhaps the most crucial lesson of all. I remember being slightly shocked, in my early days as bloodhound quarry, by Graham's total indifference to the incidental discomforts that those running for him (human or canine) might suffer when required to run through thistles, nettles, barbed wire, brambles, icy bogs or fields sharp with hidden flint. 'He's a bit of an old woman,' he said scornfully of another occasional runner, who had become rather tentative when clambering through thorny hedges. But that lack of sympathy was, essentially, the only lesson that mattered; its implied message brutal but effective. Running over rough ground is often a bit rough. It won't kill you. Get over it.

Eventually, like the hounds, I did.

I don't expect many readers to resolve on reading this to try fell-running for themselves, or even to volunteer to be hunted by a pack of hounds (although in theory there should be plenty of conventional hunts in need of runners to lay artificial trails for their allegedly non-fox-hunting foxhounds). Most will have good reasons not to – mainly geographical ones. But to anyone who raises the common objection that it 'all sounds a bit dangerous', I would offer a counter-argument. There is indeed a dangerous element to fell-running; and, to a lesser extent, to other forms of rough-terrain running. But you could say the same about driving a car. Is that an argument for not learning to drive?

Both activities can kill, done without due care and attention. But if you do learn, and learn properly, and learn, among other skills, to drive with a constant awareness that there is a potentially lethal side to what you are doing, then passing your driving test can confer on you a great freedom that you would never otherwise have tasted.

So it is, too, I think, with 'wild' running. The danger, which is limited but undeniable, isn't a conclusive argument for not learning to do it. It's just an argument for having the patience and responsibility to develop the relevant skills (including navigation and survival skills) before you try it.

And if you do so, and then build up your confidence and experience, you will find that you have conferred on yourself another great freedom: the freedom to cover large distances in Britain's wild places with relative safety at relatively high speeds – and, as a result, to enjoy remote areas of natural beauty that normal people rarely have time to reach.

5

Lost

I said earlier that I have no special running talents. In
fact, I have one: getting lost.

No one gets lost like I do. It's not just a running thing.
It's a getting lost thing.

I've been lost when running, walking, driving, cycling,
sailing, using public transport, even (once) taking a taxi,
on at least three continents, since I first ventured out into
the world as an unaccompanied teenager. I've temporarily
abandoned a car in despair on a roadside in Milton Keynes,
and once phoned Clare from the outskirts of Northampton
to warn her that I might not find my way home for days.
I've never been lost on a running track (yet), but I have
been lost indoors – not just temporarily disoriented, but
properly, sit-down-and-cry-and-wait-to-die lost – on a dis-
astrous visit to the Birmingham branch of Ikea.

But it is, I think, a running thing as well. When you
run, you tend to focus on distance and speed – the two
main objects of the exercise – rather than direction. So it's
easy to find yourself going further than you'd expected,
sooner than you'd expected, without necessarily knowing
where. There's also the need to watch where your feet are

going as well as where they are taking you, and the fact that, if you do find yourself not quite where you'd hoped you'd be, issues of exhaustion limit your options for working out what to do about it. But the main issue, I think, is simply the way that running encourages your mind to wander. You promise yourself that you're going to focus on memorising your route, but before you know it you're in a different world, lured there irresistibly by thoughts banal or profound, and the next time you pause to consider your location, or how you reached it, you realise that you haven't the slightest clue, beyond the fact that you must be many miles from where you started.

Whether you're running on roads or in a wilder environment makes little difference, in my experience. That mishap in my local fields that I mentioned earlier was entirely typical, and no different in kind from a dozen other navigational disasters from my road-running years. It's what goes on in your head that's the problem, not the terrain.

Abroad is worst. My mishaps on foreign holidays and foreign work assignments could fill a chapter of their own. The time in central Spain when I realised that I had not only lost all sense of where the village I was staying at was but couldn't even remember what it was called. The time in Italy when I ended up running twenty miles instead of the planned five, eliminating each different compass point in turn before finally trying the right one. The evening in Brussels when I omitted to memorise the name of either my hotel or the street it was in, and rediscovered it only the following morning, after sleeping on a park bench. The time in a vast, virgin Minnesotan forest when all traces of a campsite – or road, or settlement, or fellow human beings – simply vanished, leaving only me, the endless trees and the bears. And, most frightening of all, the time when I was staying in Bukhara in Uzbekistan and headed off for a late afternoon run beyond the city limits. Gratifyingly soon, I was in semi-desert: dark, flat, barren and criss-crossed with irrigation trenches. To my urban eye there was something irresistibly fascinating about the flat emptiness. I ran, and ran, and eventually realised that there was flat emptiness as far as the eye could see, in all directions. Then the light began to drain from the vast, empty sky, and I realised that I wasn't *absolutely* sure which direction would take me back to the city, and that if I ran in a straight line for several miles in what I thought was the right direction, I could easily be heading deeper and deeper into the desert... (Hours later, exhausted, panicked and dehydrated, I found a road and, better still, a human being – a leather-skinned old man with startlingly pale blue eyes – who I thought might tell me which way to run; at which point I realised that he and I didn't have a single word of language in common...)

It's possible that – like most athletic talents – my propensity for getting lost has faded with age. Perhaps it has finally sunk in that, in unfamiliar places, you need to take special steps to memorise your route. Or perhaps I just travel less these days.

You might expect me to be glad about this (the lack of getting lost, not the lack of exotic trips), but I'm not. On the contrary, from the safety of hindsight I see my talent as a valuable gift, for which I am retrospectively grateful.

It's also something that I associate with one transformative moment in my running history. The incident was so slight and obscure that I can barely pin down what happened or why it mattered. Yet I must try to describe it, because my approach to running has never been quite the same since.

I was in my early forties, in a sleepy corner of south-west

France, on a hot, soundless Sunday morning in September. It was the usual problem: several miles into the run, my pace gradually slowed as it dawned on me that, yet again, I hadn't been paying attention to where I was going – beyond the fact that the dusty track I was following through the vineyards and rough scrub had divided and redivided many times.

Ten minutes earlier I'd been happily dreaming, basking in the scents of wild herbs and the warm Mediterranean light, watching unfamiliar birds of prey coasting on the thermals far above, and journeying mentally through hills that stretched hazily to the distant, beckoning sea.

Now my mental bubble had burst. I had lost all sense of direction or, indeed, of anything much beyond blistering heat and aching thirst. Never mind the sea: the only thing that beckoned now was the usual laborious, spirit-sapping process of trying to unravel my mistake.

You idiot, I said to myself. How difficult can it be, to learn from experience? Even a dog – even a slug – can learn from experience not to keep making the same mistake. Yet every time I went away, for pleasure or work, I'd fall into the same trap, charging off without taking a proper look at where I was going. And every time it came as a surprise when I finally noticed that I was miles from where I wanted to be, but with no idea of how many miles, or in what direction, or what landmarks to look for; and, often, no way of finding out.

What was that thing that Einstein supposedly said, defining insanity as 'doing the same thing over and over again but expecting different results'? What was I, by that definition, if not insane?

Actually, it wasn't the first time this had occurred to me. But it was, oddly, the first time it had really sunk in. (I am,

I should say, a slow absorber of life's lessons. It took me until my mid-thirties to accept the connection between drinking and hangovers.)

Now, as I tried to unravel my latest variation of the mistake, I felt suddenly angry at all those avoidably wasted hours, which began to blend depressingly in my mind with all sorts of other instances of waste and folly in my life.

How many of my other problems, I wondered, came down to the same insanity: the same pig-headed refusal to learn? I didn't dare answer. But it did strike me immediately that, in an awful lot of cases, the same unforgiving logic applies. Go off track – into debt, say, or addiction, or crime, or betrayal or lost reputation or underachievement – and you'll find, just as with running, that it takes you many times longer, and infinitely more effort and courage, to get back to your original state than it took you to go off track in the first place. When you're on track, all alternative directions are the wrong one. When you're lost, only one direction takes you back.

With thoughts like these it was no surprise that energy, morale and time drained away, as I searched feebly for clues to my whereabouts. Arid frustration remained – together with the usual throb of anxiety that I needed to go faster. I was haemorrhaging time. So much for keeping the pace up; so much for getting back while the morning was still young.

Then yet another fork led me up through a clump of tall conifers and I found myself in the unexpected shade of an old garden and, soon, a small, old château.

It seemed solid and well kept, with orderly stacks of varnished barrels by the outbuildings' brown-painted doors, but the windows of the main house were shuttered, and something about the atmosphere – the stillness; the undisturbed coolness – convinced me that the place was deserted. I followed the path round, on to a wider track that looked as though it must lead to a road, hugging the shadows of an avenue of cypresses and feeling a strange sense that I had stumbled into an ancient fable.

Brightly coloured birds flitted and darted at the corners of my vision: blue and gold bee-eaters swooping and red and grey crested hoopoes pecking at the balding lawn. The rest was Sunday morning silence.

Who lived here, I wondered, or worked here? Did any activity ever disturb this soporific air? What charmed lives had run their course in this obscure, privileged seclusion, far from the noise of cities, crowds, revolutions or wars?

A sense of dormant energy, of lost time magically re-encountered, made the hairs on the back of my neck stand up. I even began to feel that an unseen eye was watching me from behind the shutters − at which point I picked up my pace until I emerged from the formal garden on to a wide but entirely empty road.

The sun beat brighter; the silence settled deeper. There was, I realised, not the slightest hint of traffic noise, even in the remotest distance. It was like being in another life.

I returned, in a kind of daze, to my dilemma. Left? Right? I had no idea: no possible reason for preferring one to the other. So I ran for nearly a mile in one direction, then decided that it didn't feel right and doubled back on my tracks. As I passed the château gates again, a peloton of cyclists swooshed past, too fast for me to ask their advice. Then the world fell silent yet again: just me, the sky, the savage sun, the empty road and the pale brown hills, and an ancient pair of huge, spiked metal gates, impregnable to any possible attack from angry peasants (apart from the minor defect of there being no trace of a wall or fence on either side).

I stopped and walked. It was the first time I had yielded to such a temptation for years. Or possibly decades.

Within a few paces I felt an overwhelming sense of liberation. Not only was I lost: I seemed to have lost the world; or, at least, to have lost the world I was used to. Where had life's usual rumble gone: the noise and cars and crowds and buildings? And what about the even deeper accompaniment: the pounding, incessant rhythm of time? Now that I had stopped running, and had given up caring about how fast I was going, or how long it would take me to get back, I could sense the absence of a hitherto unnoticed drumbeat: the relentless urgency of modern living, whirring behind me, measuring and monitoring and driving me forward. It was as if I had stepped off a treadmill.

It felt good: so good that, after a while, I stopped altogether.

I stood by the roadside, savouring the stillness. Without the noise of my own movements, other sounds seeped into my consciousness: insects, birds, the occasional rustle of leaves; and what sounded like a hammer, far away, occasionally striking a stone. How strange that, moments earlier, I had been crashing through this world in my big new Asics trainers, oblivious to the soundscape I was disturbing.

The trainers seemed suddenly incongruous: shiny and absurdly expensive, a totemic product of the then booming global economy, unaffordable to anyone not on the great global growth merry-go-round. There was, I remembered, a world beyond that, and had been all along. And now I was in it.

And whereas not long earlier I had been feeling something close to despair, I was now brightly conscious of being extraordinarily privileged: to have been able, for a few sunlit moments, to enjoy an elusive something that I can only compare to the total freedom from responsibility with which children enjoy the world. I had lost my way many times, but never before had I felt so lucidly aware of the cares of the world having vanished with it.

Eventually, I broke into a happy, unhurried jog, trying to step as lightly as possible so as not to disturb the peace too much. And it occurred to me that the experience of getting lost offers not one but two analogies for life.

The first is the obvious one alluded to above: that it's far, far easier to lose your bearings than to find them. But there's a second lesson, too. Getting lost while running is a vivid symptom of a broader failing, which military types tradition-ally avoid by remembering the Six Ps ('Prior Preparation Prevents Piss-Poor Performance'). My talent for getting lost reflects a mental sloppiness that causes me to go haring off in what seem like promising directions (not just in my running) without having thought through the consequences.

Yet that morning in France, having berated myself, I won-dered: is that sloppiness, that recklessness, really such a bad thing? Thinking back to my previous misadventures, I realised, rather to my surprise, that these were all – now – happy memories. In fact, a startlingly high proportion of my happiest memories of running involved getting lost. That early attempt at off-road running in Northamptonshire; assorted naviga-tional cock-ups from my fell-running years (the warmth of each memory being exactly proportional to the depth of the despair I felt at the time); the shadows of the Uzbek desert (likewise); the time I got lost in Hyde Park late at night and, I think, briefly broke into the grounds of Kensington Palace.

Perhaps it was the same old phenomenon of the remem-bered run acting as a trigger to release happy memories of a former self. But what if I had never had those particular running experiences (which, by definition, must have involved some frustration and despair)? Could I have reached out to my past so effectively via the innumerable runs that had passed without mishap? It seemed hard to imagine it, when so many of them had already dissolved into one undifferentiated blur.

I suppose it's obvious. When you're lost you engage with your surroundings – belatedly, but all the more intensely for that. You focus on details and ask yourself what they signify. Could I really have passed that strangely shaped tree on my outward journey without noticing and remembering it? Could I see that church spire when I set out? Is there anything on that slope over there that suggests a river? The more lost or worried you are, the more deeply you drink in the details.

The other, simpler answer is that the bits of our lives that matter – the bits that stay with us – are the adventures. These don't have to be outdoor adventures: think of getting married, giving birth, starting a new job, trying to master a new skill, or simply standing up for what you believe in. What makes it an adventure is that it's outside your comfort zone. There's an element of risk involved; an element of fear.

This was an encouraging thought because I was, as it happened, just twenty-four hours into a small adventure that had nothing to do with running, but quite a lot to do with that same long-term habit of setting off without giving proper thought to where I was going. Essentially, for reasons that I still hadn't properly understood, we had just emigrated.

It was only a temporary and partial emigration, but it was still a life-changing step, to which we had given surprisingly little thought. A freak chain of problems and opportunities – too convoluted to explain here – had culminated in an abrupt decision to let out our home for a year and move to a friend's house in a little village in south-west France. We'd barely had time to think about the negative implications (for me, a year of incessant £1 Ryanair flights to and from London; for the children, then eight and ten, a new school far from their friends where they wouldn't understand a word anyone said). Just a few weeks after Clare came up with the plan, there we were, in the rural depths of Languedoc-Roussillon, with the final hours ticking away before a new school term.

It could easily have gone horribly wrong, and when the children grew belatedly apprehensive it was hard not to share their fears. But now, on that first sunny Sunday morning, lost on that deserted lane, I began to believe that it would all turn out all right.

Everything seemed clear as the southern sunlight. Yes, we were troubled by the absence of various familiar certainties, but most of those certainties could equally have been described as irritations: the troubled local primary school; a houseful of clutter; a rural existence circumscribed by the tyranny of cars; a comfortable rut of lukewarm routine. Why should we regret having left any of this behind?

Why, if it came to that, should I assume that anything needed to go wrong? What worse example could I give the children than to fret about unseen dangers and difficulties? It was, in any case, too late to do anything about it. Perhaps it was time simply to trust the world.

It was at around this point in my thoughts that an elderly cyclist came wobbling round the corner. He climbed the slope towards me so slowly that it seemed impossible he could keep his balance. He looked grateful to be stopped. Conversation was slow: I found his accent as baffling as he found mine. But we both took irrational pleasure in our attempts at communication, and eventually we managed to understand one another enough to exchange potted life stories and, finally, for him to suggest a route home.

Forty minutes later – footsore, sunburnt, faint with thirst, but curiously elated – I found myself back at our temporary home. I had no rational basis for doing so, but I felt that my morning's experiences presaged well for the year ahead. Never mind that we couldn't be sure how it would turn out. We would have to resolve to make the best of it; and, from that alone, good things might come.

We did, and they did. The children picked up the language painlessly. The tiny school was welcoming. We flung ourselves into village life, and new acquaintances turned quickly into friends. We relished the forgotten sanity of a life where everyone we knew lived within walking distance; where children could wander freely from house to house or play unsupervised in the street; where families and friends lingered for hours over meals and were never too busy for a chat.

I suspect that this rural French approach to life was far too relaxed to be economically sustainable, but the great joy of being a temporary resident is that you don't have to worry about such questions. In fact, most of life's irritations seemed less important that year than before or since. I attribute this partly to the fact that, for a year, we had no more possessions than the four of us could cram into a car for our outward journey; and to the fact that, knowing that our time there was all too short, we lived in the moment and made the most of the good things in life. A wise person would always live thus.

As for running, I found the whole adventure astonishingly liberating. Every time I stepped outside to run, for a whole year, the sense of embracing the unknown returned. The flavour of the air was unfamiliar, the light was unfamiliar, the temperature was unfamiliar, the texture of the earth was unfamiliar. Above all, the context was new. For the first few months my runs were almost entirely about exploration. There was no point in timing them because I had no idea what distances I was covering. But the thrill of discovery – of not knowing what to expect – proved at least as motivating as any stopwatch.

Our village was in the middle of a gently rolling plateau, covered haphazardly with vineyards and a kind of scrubby, rocky moorland known as *garrigue*. Even when I had developed a few regular running circuits, it was never the thought of speed that drove me on. There were more interesting things to fill my mind. In the cold early mornings you could feel the previous day's warmth rising from the undergrowth as you passed, rich with the scents of herbs and wildflowers. Dramatic mountains ringed the horizon, and from certain places you could glimpse the sea to the south.

The ground was rough but soft, the slopes steep but short, the paths confusing but not entirely random. The more I paid attention, the more sense it all made. There were strange birds in the huge skies – kites, falcons, harriers – and exotic creatures – grey hares, red squirrels, wild boars, poisonous snakes – concealed in the vegetation. I found myself running with a new alertness, eyes peeled and ears pricked for clues to the wild world, or trying to creep up undetected on places where I had previously made exciting sightings.

One unexpected side effect was that I stopped getting lost. I suppose that's what happens when you focus more on the landscape and less on yourself. Another was that I got fitter. On a couple of occasions I took part in races back in the UK that I had done before – and noticed significant improvements in my times.

I wasn't sure what to make of this at first, but I suspected it might have something to do with the fact that there was more joy in my daily running than there had been for a long time. That routine reluctance to get started that every runner knows had, for the time being, vanished from my life. No matter how tired or preoccupied I felt when I got out of bed, I invariably emerged from the house for my morning run with a sense of happy anticipation, wondering what adventure the countryside had in store for me that day. Of course I ran with a spring in my step.

It's obvious, on reflection. The more interesting and unpredictable your training regime, the more you will enjoy it, and the more likely you are to stick to it. And I was intrigued, much later, to read of evidence suggesting that, conversely, predictable regimes are associated with unhealthy outcomes, ranging from giving up exercise out of boredom to surrendering to destructive habits. (For example, research for the Medical Research Council's Social & Applied Psychology Unit by Professor Ben C. Fletcher has found a direct correlation between lack of 'behavioural flexibility' and problems such as obesity and addictions.) But that's a digression. The problem with ruts isn't that they can lead to undesirable health outcomes. It's the fact that they are ruts. Life passes quickly. The longer you live, the faster it passes. The moments you spend in ruts vanish as soon as you have lived them; while sometimes it is when we are most lost that we find ourselves.

Of course it's absurd to equate getting lost on a run, or moving temporarily from one prosperous European country to another, or running in the countryside of either, with having a proper adventure. But I can't think of a better word to describe the satisfaction that I have derived from such experiences; and, in any case, it's the broader point that matters. Most of us face daily choices, on a large or a small scale, between sticking with tried and tested routines

or venturing into the unknown. Sometimes the consider-
ations that keep us from trying the adventurous option are
powerful or intractable ones; often the prudent option is
the only sane one. With running, however, the choices
tend to be simple, and the risks of leaving the comfort zone
are usually manageable.

If every day you run or train on the same risk-free route
(or treadmill), taking the same even strides on the same
even surface, you may well be making highly efficient use
of your training time. But aren't you also running in an
utterly forgettable rut – and, as a result, losing out?

Thornton Wilder put it well in his 1955 play, *The
Matchmaker* (better known to millions as the 1969 musical
Hello, Dolly!). 'The test of an adventure,' says the hero, Barnaby
(reflecting on a wild and improbable once-in-a-lifetime night
out in New York), 'is that when you're in the middle of it,
you say to yourself, "Oh, now I've got myself into an awful
mess; I wish I were sitting quietly at home." And the sign
that something's wrong with you is when you sit quietly at
home wishing you were out having lots of adventure.'

The words sum up perfectly the paradoxical appeal of
running in slightly wilder circumstances and environments.
Nearly every time I have gone out running in a strange, wild
or uncomfortable place, there has been a moment, associated
with more than mere exhaustion, when I have thought to
myself: 'Oh dear, I wish this wasn't happening – I wish I was
sitting comfortably at home.'

And nearly every time – especially when I was really rather
surprised to have survived at all – I ended up looking back
on the experience with wonder and warmth, feeling happier
and more alive than I did before I set out.

6

Field days

It's easy to talk about the merits of adventurous living. Most lives don't work out that way.

Mine hasn't. By most standards it's been lived (so far) largely in comfortable ruts.

I'm not complaining. 'Interesting times', as those who have lived in other periods and places have known, are as likely to be tragic as delightful. But there's no point disguising the truth. If I'm sparing with my autobiographical details, it's because they're dull.

I am – if you're curious – middle-class, middle-aged, white, Home Counties-born, university-educated, married with children, employed and healthy, with a car, a motorbike and most of my own teeth. In the rat race of life, as in running races, you'll generally find me towards the middle of the pack: usually much nearer the front than the back, but not by a spectacular distance, and not always, and with only the remotest prospect of winning a significant prize.

I consider myself exceptionally privileged, as anyone who fits such a description should. But not interesting.

In the present context, that's just as well. What matters for the purposes of this book is not what is different about me but what isn't. If I'm telling you at vast length about one particular aspect of my life – running – it's because the details might have relevance to other unremarkable lives.

So, to resume: the years of my prime have (that spell in France apart) been largely spent on much the same banal routines as everyone else: working, driving, shopping, cleaning, feeding, mending and maintaining; keeping the household afloat, caring for dependants young and old; and snatching brief moments of leisure or sociability when events permit. The details are specific to me, the subject headings common to millions.

Sometimes I feel weak at the thought of the tide of things to be done, remembered, resolved or fretted about. Knowing that, on a global scale, I am incredibly lucky does not prevent me from wishing, sometimes, that things could be otherwise; that the ratio of joy to tolerable toil could be adjusted just a little more in my favour.

Perhaps it's a mid-life thing: that fear that, before you know it, your life will have swept past in a flood of haste and drudgery, without your having snatched enough shining memories to brighten your remaining days. Or maybe it's a middle-of-the-pack thing. The poorest have more urgent matters to trouble them; the richest get someone else to do the drudgery. The rest of us have just enough spare capacity to notice and regret the waste, but rarely enough to do anything about it.

In such circumstances – and, indeed, in many worse circumstances – it's worth reminding yourself to take what you can along the way from the range of free gifts that life so generously offers: natural beauty, music, poetry, sex, laughter, friendship – and, if you're a runner, running.

The older I get, the less I see running as a way of developing my self-control and self-respect, and still less as a way of maintaining health, weight or personal attractiveness. Instead, I see it more and more as, simply, a way of escaping from the disciplines of adult life. It's a chance to live in the moment.

Many older runners might claim something similar. I feel particularly privileged, though, because my favourite escape is re-made for me each day by the inexhaustible creativity of nature.

Here I am, for example, on a recent January run, stumbling out of the house at around 7 a.m., barely awake, let alone warmed up, gradually accelerating from shuffle to a slow jog as my feet take me on the easiest of the three or four off-road routes that I most regularly use.

The world is still bleak with the remains of the night as I pad out of the village. Leafless, colourless boughs lean over the sloping back lane from both sides, dark as sleep. A gravestone-grey sky appears slowly beyond them. Within a minute or so we have reached the stile to the first meadow: a small, threadbare, bowl-shaped field with a dozen old trees – ash, beech, oak, hawthorn – scattered randomly across its irregular slopes. The scruffy grass is lumpy with tussocks and strewn with twigs and frozen droppings. A huddle of pale sheep, plump and still, stare grimly from one corner.

There are traces of ancient ridge-and-furrow agriculture in the field's corrugated turf, and the little undulations force me to put more spring into my half-awake step, while the grey and white crust on the crisp grass prompts the vain thought that, if I run quickly and lightly enough, the frost may not penetrate my all but naked feet. (I am, I confess, one of those cranks who run in minimalist 'barefoot' foot gloves rather than conventional running shoes; but let's save that discussion for later.)

Nutmeg, my dog, adores frost, and is soon in a frenzy of delight, swerving crazily from side to side as scent after vivid scent leaps out at her. She is still on her lead — one of those long, heavy-handled extension leads — and her dashing and darting force me to accelerate my plod even more.

My mind is full of ...well, not very much, really. Years of experience tell me that at some stage I will start to enjoy this. Until then, the less thinking the better.

But some things demand to be thought about. Pick my way through the muddy, leafless copse at the end of the field without slipping on the sideways slope. Help Nutmeg over the stile. Check the new field for livestock. (None today.) Release Nutmeg. Consider the texture of the ground: it's been waterlogged for weeks, and before that buried in snow, but this morning it's frozen just hard enough, thankfully, to prevent my feet from sinking through the frozen surface into the icy water that I know lies beneath. On the far side, let Nutmeg through the gate on to the wooden bridge that leads into the next series of fields; make sure the gate is properly closed; then step up my pace a little more so that I don't lose sight of her.

Other things merely ask to be thought about, so gently that I barely notice. I find myself reflecting on, for example, the startling, inch-thick furriness of the frost on the bridge's metal handrail; and the perfect beauty of the bright white spider's web that joins the rail to its far post; and, a bit later, the distant gash of yellow across the bottom of the eastern sky. (How pale and thin the dawn looks — as though it had seen the approach of a terrible storm...)

The path beyond the footbridge follows a wide, grassy field boundary, overhung by a ragged hedgerow. A series of greying snowdrifts blocks the path in the shadows, the last, incongruous remnants of a wintry fortnight that I had thought had finished thawing days ago. The shin-deep snow is soft and, presumably, melting as fast as it can. It still feels like ice on my feet. For Nutmeg (a shaggy, long-bodied, short-legged hound, known as a Fauve, whose ancestors were used by the French to hunt wild boar) the problems are more practical. She sinks in below head height and then, with every stride, leaps slightly more than her own height, before sinking down again. The snow sticks and freezes to her shaggy coat as she does this. When there's lots of snow, this effect can mean that she steadily accumulates it, as a rolled snowball does, until sometimes she is carrying close to her own weight in unwanted frozen baggage. It's not so bad today, but there have been times, in the depths of winter, when after three or four miles of this she has simply sat down and refused to go further.

Generally, though, she shrugs off such inconveniences, and today she carries on cheerfully. Before long we are back on firmer, snow-free ground. There's still plenty of white stuff on it, but I'm pretty certain that that's just thick frost. It's easy enough to tell: frost feels colder to the feet.

After half a mile or so I spot a dark fox, half a field away, tiptoeing across the cold ground, picking up its paws so tentatively that its movements seem almost feline. I've seen it here several times in recent weeks – there's a den down there on the left that foxes sometimes use – and, each time, I've been struck by its blackness. Is it really absence of light that makes it look so dark? Or is it a freak: a black fox? I am starting to detect traces of greenness on the white grass beneath it, and shades of pale brown in the stubble nearby – yet there's still no hint of colour in the fox's fur.

I'm also curious about its gait. Does it feel the frost, I

wonder? Is it making a particular effort to tiptoe noiselessly? Or have I just never noticed before that that is how foxes walk? A dozen such questions suggest themselves each time I run. Most remain unanswered. (This one is an exception. Clare tells me later that foxes do indeed pick their steps with great delicacy: hence the Native American idea of 'fox-footing' to mean something like 'tiptoeing'.)

Nutmeg is oblivious to the fox's presence. It obviously didn't pass along this path, which means that, from her point of view, it's invisible; whereas I had glanced in that direction to see if anything was there. None the less, the next time she's within reach I stoop to reattach her to the lead. Moments later we pass a gap in the hedge where she picks up the fox's scent, and I'm dragged after her at a near sprint. I tolerate this because I can see, as Nutmeg can't, that the fox has now slipped silently through a fence 100 metres away, into an adjoining field where we will not be following.

The wide field verge we're now running on offers two kinds of grass: short and flattened by previous footsteps, but frozen into hard, pointy lumps; or longer and softer, but liable to transfer the softer frost on its upper blades on to and into my feet. Neither is ideal, and I alternate between the two. Running fast reduces the discomfort, forcing me to land right on the fronts of my feet; but I also make a conscious effort to wiggle my toes in mid-stride, to keep the blood circulating in the cold.

By the time we slow down, clambering over a collapsing stile in the shadow of the woods, we're about a mile and a half from the start. I release Nutmeg again, and, as we follow the edge of Grumbler's Holt (as the old wood is known), I'm taken by surprise, as usual, by how comfortable I suddenly feel – as though we had entered a big wooden barn. The sheltered path is carpeted with soft, unfrozen leaves, and, since it also slopes gently downhill, I barely notice the physical efforts I'm making. Instead, I glance repeatedly at the dry, brown, sleeping depths of the wood itself, separated from the path by a half-collapsed wire fence to my right, and speculate about what might be hiding within it. I've seen roe deer, foxes, even a badger here on previous runs, and one sudden rustling is so loud that it seems impossible for it to have been generated by anything smaller than one of those three. But it turns out to be a blackbird, reminding me of the pretty infallible rule that if you can hear it, it's a bird; or, possibly, a squirrel. Earthbound mammals know how to be silent.

On the far side of the wood, we head uphill again, along another ridge-and-furrow field. Ahead, slightly to the right, a huge silver moon still gapes like a hole punched in the metallic blue sky, while daylight streams through that yellow gash on the horizon, which is now to my left, with a molten gobbet of red-gold sun occasionally visible at the centre of it, through the furthest trees. (This positioning doesn't quite conform to what little I know of astronomy. None the less, that was what I saw.)

As generally happens when we take this route, my spirits have begun to rise. Cold? Sleepiness? Heavy legs? Whatever. I'm warm and awake now, and I have more interesting subjects to think about. For example: buzzards. I often disturb a buzzard from its early morning reverie on the branch of a small oak tree near here. It must be used to me by now, and I've concluded that there's less urgency than there used to be in its flight to the safety of the woods. Sometimes it seems as though it can barely be bothered to leave its bough, eventually flapping off so laboriously that it's a wonder it stays airborne.

I may, of course, be quite wrong about this. For all I know it's a different buzzard every day. Perhaps, for that matter, it is fear rather than familiarity that causes a buzzard to fly slowly. Or perhaps there's a different explanation.

It would be easy to find out: that's one of the pleasures of the internet age. Yet I've refrained from researching the subject. I enjoy my ill-informed naturalistic speculation – which in one sense is anything but ill informed. Unbiased by prior knowledge, I see only what I see. To plunder the World Wide Web for the current ornithological consensus on buzzard body language would – I imagine – kill off the wonder and leave my world with one less life-enhancing mystery in it. I'd rather wait for the buzzards to teach me in their own time.

There's no buzzard there today, but there is, at least, the usual sense of being closer to nature than to the internet. I like the fact that, for the duration of this run, I'm in a little corner of modern Britain that isn't wired; a place beyond the reach (for now) of Google Street View's little yellow man. And I like the fact that this is one part of my life that leaves no digital footprint. I am, for a while, below the radar of corporate and official surveillance. You would hardly describe these fields as wild: there's a village within a mile or two in any direction you choose. There's a motorway (sometimes audible) less than ten miles away, and I don't suppose this part of Northamptonshire is any less densely populated than the rest of the county, which has an average of 750 people living within each square mile of it.

Yet I've rarely met a single human being out in these fields at dawn, and those I do meet can usually be assumed to be kindred spirits. And sometimes – as at this particular moment on this particular run – I feel as though I have temporarily escaped the gravitational tug of crowded urban modernity. How many other daily pastimes give you that kind of liberation?

Idle chains of thought like this appear quite regularly in my head when I'm running. They rarely lead far, because there's always something else to think about. On this occasion I have to call back Nutmeg from some particularly compelling scent that is leading her off towards the wrong horizon. There are more gates and stiles to negotiate and then, in the field that leads down towards the tiny village of Plumpton, there is a flock of browsing sheep and lambs that means Nutmeg has to be reattached. For the next few minutes my mind is full of the subtleties of threading a route through the flock that gets us to the next stile without panicking them.

After that, we're starting on the homeward half of the circuit, and the moon is once again directly ahead of me: a shining silver disc whose smooth, bright rim seems unnatural in its perfection, like the peel-off inner seal of a plastic milk carton. I'm struck by the clarity of the man in the moon: you would have had to be wilfully perverse, in the pre-urban age, not to see his face there. I'm struck, too, by how immobile the moon seems, tethered above the same tall trees in Grumbler's Holt no matter which direction our zigzag route takes us in. I suppose that for modern, indoor human beings the idea that the moon moves through the sky each night has nothing remotely intuitive about it.

Then I think: that soundless shape that just glided past me on the very periphery of my vision: did I just fail to notice an owl? Or did I imagine it?

As we come up the hill towards the woods, the ground is softer. It's hard to see how it can have warmed up much in the half-hour since we started, but presumably this particular waterlogged slope of stubble is sheltered from the frost. I slide, squelch and lurch up it, slipping to my knees just once, while

Nutmeg bounds exuberantly ahead, like a long-haired teddy bear on a pogo stick.

By the time we reach the top, we are both caked in mud from our feet to at least halfway up. For the rest of the run I make a point of splashing into every puddle I see. Many are frozen on top, but there's water within, and it helps to get the mud off.

Eventually, we find ourselves back in the big penultimate field – the one that, on our outward journey, was just hard enough for me to remain on its frosty surface. It isn't now, but the icy water doesn't bother me. I'm too busy racing Nutmeg – and, more trickily, her shadow, which stretches twenty feet in front of us.

As we sprint, a flash of pink catches my eye from the puddle-cum-spring in the field's centre. It's the underside of a buzzard, which flaps crossly away as we approach, disappearing behind the broken oak tree far to our right. This is, I realise, one handy thing about the low, late-rising winter sun: it illuminates objects from below.

Nutmeg's shadow wins the race, with me a close second. Nutmeg eases off in the final yards, once she knows she is beaten. As we reach the final gate she looks up at me, and we exchange a look of mutual congratulation. It isn't that we've achieved anything: we've just enjoyed ourselves, taking full advantage of a glorious winter morning. Only when we're back at the house does it strike me that most other adults in Britain are currently peering out of their windows and thinking: 'Bloody hell, it's cold!'

The great thing about such beginnings to my days is that they're never the same. I wouldn't go quite so far as to describe them as adventures: after twenty-three years in the same village, I'm long past the days when there was anything truly unfamiliar about any of the countryside within comfortable running distance. But they are, none the less, consistently unpredictable. Each day is subtly but significantly different. So is each week, each month, as the weather changes, the seasons change, the length of the days changes, the farmers do different things with their livestock and their land, and the wildlife adapts its behaviour to take all these fluctuations into account.

I rarely even bother to try out new routes any more, beyond my fairly extensive repertoire of basic route building blocks. There's no need. I can pass the same tree three hundred times, and each time it will be an unexpected experience. The light will be different, the foliage will be different, the sky behind and the earth beneath will be different; there will be new sounds, new smells, a new wind, and new creatures going about their enigmatic business nearby.

As with any relationship, long acquaintance with the local countryside brings a measure of understanding. I'm no David Attenborough, but I can and do learn from observation. There are always messages that matter to the runner in a given day's landscape 'news'. Is that path waterlogged? Has this field been ploughed? Are there bullocks in the next field but one? Has that patch of thistles grown back? Is there a creature concealed in that hedgerow that will spring out in panic when I pass? The need to take such factors into consideration means that, unavoidably, I run in a more or less permanent state of mild curiosity about my surroundings. And this, I think, is one reason why running makes me happy. Once I ran looking inwards, focusing on the physiological and psychological struggles within. Now I look outwards, and the struggles take care of themselves.

There is (again) evidence to suggest that I'm not the only

one to benefit from this kind of shift in perspective. Studies on both sides of the Atlantic have found a strong link between exercise taken in green and wild places (as opposed to exercise taken indoors or in city centres) and general wellbeing. Benefits include increased energy, feelings of revitalisation and positive engagement, and reduced tension, anger and depression. The most spectacular boosts are psychological: for example, in the 2008 Scottish Health Survey, a team of researchers at Glasgow University, led by Professor Richard Mitchell, found that exercising in 'natural environments' such as parks or woodland was 50 per cent more beneficial for mental health than exercising in a gym; while a 2012 study in Belgium found that people who exercise in city centres perform significantly worse in cognitive tests than those who exercise in the countryside; and a study by scientists at Edinburgh and Heriot-Watt universities, published in the *British Journal of Sports Medicine* in 2013, found that going for a walk in a natural environment produced more 'meditative' brainwaves than performing the same activity in a man-made environment (where levels of anxiety and frustration rose). The mental health charity, Mind, promotes 'green exercise' as a healthier and more affordable alternative to antidepressants, following studies at the University of Essex in 2007 in which users of Mind services took part in such exercise – and 94 per cent reported mental health benefits. There are even hospitals where victims of severe burns are given pain relief in the form of virtual recreations of walks in the countryside. 'People enter a highly relaxed state,' Birmingham University's Professor Bob Stone, a pioneer of the therapy, told the *Independent on Sunday* in 2013. 'When that happens, as well as regulating such processes as respiration, digestion, circulation and so on, the body experiences a restorative effect.'

This may be brain science but it's hardly news. Many of our greatest thinkers and writers – Wordsworth, Rousseau, Kierkegaard, Dickens, Emily Brontë, Nietzsche, Kant and Einstein, to name just a few – have relied on walking to aid their thought processes, and most (although not Kant) have preferred to do so in as rural a setting as possible. 'A man walks that he may be impregnated by Nature,' wrote the philosopher C.E.M. Joad. 'There is, it seems to me, a something in Nature which enters into and mixes with the spirit of man.'

There are also physical benefits to outdoor exertion: for example, burning extra calories from the effort needed to maintain stability on rough surfaces; or simply keeping at it for longer. A 2012 study by Dr Jacqueline Kerr, at the University of California in San Diego, found that older adults who exercise outdoors do so for longer, and more frequently, than those who work out indoors. And there is evidence (still inconclusive, but cited in the 2011 review of evidence commissioned by the National Institute for Health Research in collaboration with the European Centre for Environment and Human Health) that those who exercise in natural environments are 'more likely to repeat the activity at a later date'.

For me, most of those points, especially the last one, are so overwhelmingly obvious that I struggle to believe that anyone could believe the opposite. Countless runners lose their appetite for their sport in middle age. Of course, boredom will have been a factor for many. Of course, a more stimulating environment reduces the likelihood of boredom and increases the likelihood of continued enthusiasm. If science doesn't bear that out, science is an ass.

My interest is also maintained by the fact that the experience of running in rough countryside can vary intriguingly over longer cycles. For example: twenty-three years ago,

that 'big, penultimate' field that I've mentioned was barely
ever dry. There was a large, permanent puddle near the
middle of it that was marked on old Ordnance Survey maps
as a 'spring' and a mass of more or less permanently waterlogged ground around it. Then it dried up, along with several
other local springs. We assumed that the water table was
falling, as it was said to be doing in much of Britain, thanks
to a combination of climate change and increased human
consumption. Then, recently, after a decade and a half of
dryness, the springs seem to have been rising again.
Presumably, successive waterlogged winters in the years since
2010 have restored the water table. At any rate, running
across that field without getting your feet wet has once again
become a rare experience.

The wildlife has changed, too. There were never muntjacs
here twenty-three years ago. There are now. Nor, for that
matter, were there buzzards – although there were kestrels. But
the past five years have seen a revolution in the skies. Kestrels
have become vanishingly rare, while buzzards – presumably
sustained by a growing local rabbit population – are common.
I read recently that this is a nationwide phenomenon, although
no one knows if the two trends are linked. I'm ashamed to
admit that I'm not particularly bothered. Kestrels – athletic,
graceful and quick – are fine birds, but the buzzard – plumper,
greyer and grumpier looking – somehow seems to have more
about it that I can relate to at this stage in my running career.

Yet I'm pretty sure that, however much I enjoy a good
grumble among friends, I don't look grumpy when I'm
running. I may have done once – must have done, in fact,
in the years when I used to pound the pavements night after
night in pursuit of further marginal improvements in my
times and technique. But for the past decade – ever since that

moment of liberation in France – I have barely bothered about such matters.

It's not that I don't run hard or fast. I often do. But I no longer have the remotest idea of how long my runs take. I don't even wear a watch when I run, let alone check it when I start and finish. I suspect that many runners will see this as eccentric to the point of unacceptable weirdness – a bit like running naked. Yet the benefits, as I see it, have been huge and obvious.

If the satisfaction you get from your running depends directly on how close you can get to your best time for a particular distance, then once you're past the age of thirty or so, you are almost certain to experience a falling off in your satisfaction. The timing varies. Some of us peak quite late; some of us start quite late. Others are barely out of their teens when they reach their golden age. But most of us, at least by our forties, reach a stage where, even if we're not getting significantly slower, our chances of getting significantly faster are negligible.

When this happens, the satisfaction to be derived from timing yourself is limited. It's a useful tool, if you're determined not to give up a single percentage point of performance without a bitter fight. But no matter how single-mindedly you push yourself, raging against each marginal deterioration, the truth is brutally simple. If you were going to set any notable records in your event, you'd have done so by now. And the days when your morale would regularly be boosted by dramatic improvements and new personal bests are long gone.

If this applies to you, as it certainly did to me by the time I'd reached my mid-forties, then the watch becomes a tool not of motivation but of discouragement. You may derive some spiritual benefit from watching your performance deteriorate fraction by fraction. You may derive some physical benefit from continuing to push yourself right to your slowly contracting limit. But you won't be encouraged by it. And if you're not encouraged, then, in the long term, your running is likely to suffer.

In my mind's eye, I physically threw my watch away. In reality, I just stopped wearing it. It felt like a moment of liberation comparable to the one when I threw away my last packet of Winston in a flat in Wimbledon in early 1989 and ended a fifteen-year stretch of nicotine addiction. Stuff this for a lark, I said to myself. I don't have to wear these shackles. And that was that.

So it was with my watch. I didn't stop running fast. I didn't stop enjoying the sensations of speed, or the satisfaction of pushing myself, sometimes, to my absolute limits. I still raced occasionally, when it was convenient or friendly to do so. But I never again had a run from which the only satisfaction I took came from the knowledge of how long it had taken. I couldn't: I didn't know.

Looking back, I'm amazed that I didn't make this breakthrough sooner, but liberation often looks like that with hindsight. I'm also still amazed that it took me fifteen years to get round to giving up smoking.

What matters to me now is that I did it; and that, by denying myself the satisfaction of time, I forced myself into a choice: either to give up running, because I derived no satisfaction from it; or to find other satisfactions in it, and to enjoy them instead.

I chose the latter and the result has been, I think, my Fifth Age of Running.

If I'd ever imagined such an age to exist, I'd assumed it

would be a rather feeble shadow of the 'real' running I had done when I was younger. I was wrong. If anything, it's more vivid than anything that's gone before. Then, it was all about results, improvements, outcomes, marginal differences.

This is about running.

7

Back to basics

Much of the satisfaction we runners take from our sport is about self-conquest. You could have slumped in front of the television, but you made yourself go out and run, and you feel better for it. You could have stopped and walked, but you made yourself keep going, and now you're proud of yourself. You could have kept the pace comfortable, but you forced yourself to your limits, and now you're glowing with satisfaction. In each case, there's a pleasing contrast between the earlier you – the one who said, 'No, I can't do that: it will be too painful' – and the current you, who looks back and thinks: 'I've just done something that I thought was beyond me.'

Over the years, however, the surprise wears off. You know you're not going to quit; you know you'll run your best. It's as unremarkable as cleaning your teeth, and no more useful as a source of self-congratulation.

But nature is a different matter. It's hard to grow jaded by the challenges posed by the weather in the countryside. Rain, wind, snow, frost, mud, bogs, thistles, nettles, heat, flies, roots, hard ground, soft ground…there are so many possible sources of discomfort, varying daily, that it's impossible either to get completely used to them or to imagine a way of avoiding them all.

Here I am, for example, on another winter run. It is still night, by normal standards, as I squelch, about three miles from home, through a dark expanse of what I hope is just mud, looking for a gap in the overgrown hedge. I find the pale patch in the shadow, break my stride and feel my way through the overhanging branches and across the rickety wooden bridge. Giant brambles from the ditch beneath brush against my face as I pass, too gently to break the skin.

On the far side I pick my way along a thistly field verge, and then, beyond the next broken stile, there's just enough daylight to show a grey wasteland of coarse, tussocky turf, sloping away for hundreds of metres in most directions. I go bounding down the long, corrugated field towards Plumpton, wondering if I am really awake. The long, sprouting hedgerow on my right, silhouetted against the first glow of dawn, seems more painted than real, like a black and silver stage backdrop; while the scattered clumps of darker, denser turf – thickened by summer cowpats – give the pasture an unearthly cratered pattern, like the surface of the moon. There's no real chill to the air, no sense of impact as my feet strike the damp, spongy ground; and – apart from a vague sense of doggy breathing nearby – the world seems as soundless as sleep.

Halfway across the field, I'm struck by the thought that the little disused church on the edge of the village isn't there. Has it collapsed, or been abruptly demolished? Fifty metres closer, I discern among the fir trees the familiar grey shape of what you could easily mistake for an abandoned stone submarine – and I realise that I have been staring at the church all along.

Faint suggestions of colour have barely begun to seep into

the day, but Nutmeg, unleashed, is weaving wildly in front of me, pursuing what she imagines to be our real agenda. Her shaggy fur, usually a rich, gingery straw colour, seems drab and grey in the damp half-light. But last night's scents must be as vivid as neon to her.

In a dip in the middle of the field glows a giant puddle. You'd take it for a pond if you didn't know that it wasn't usually there: it's twenty metres long and mirror-smooth. A golden moon shines out of it, the only real colour I can see, clear as a vision of a smugglers' cove in a crystal ball, with a hint of cloud floating silently across its face in the reflected sky.

At the stile by the church, we turn westwards for home, and I look up to see the tallest, most perfect rainbow I have ever seen. I'm amazed, for several reasons. I'm amazed by its perfection: a hundred times higher in its arch than the mightiest cathedral, with each colour glowing rich and deep from end to end. I'm amazed by its proximity: another half-field or so, over that next stile, and I'll be touching it. And I'm amazed that it's there at all. I've noticed neither rain nor sunlight in the morning so far, and while I can see now that, from this perspective, it arguably is more or less daylight, it certainly isn't raining. Surely it isn't possible to have a rainbow without rain?

Then the rain hits us, crashing on our heads like the contents of a burst water tank. It's freezing, violent and overwhelmingly heavy. Instantly, we are drenched to the bone. How did I not see that coming? I'm not usually bothered by rain, but the iciness of this lot is shocking. A vicious wind has arrived with it, and my face quickly begins to ache as the high-speed drops bite.

I screw up my eyes, clench my teeth and try not to notice that, running uphill directly into the wind, I am barely going forward at all. There is, of course, nothing I can do about it, beyond lowering my face, getting on with it and resigning myself to the fact that this could take a long time. But self-pitying thoughts keep popping into my head. Can this really be good for a man of my age?

Over the next ten minutes, the wind redoubles in strength. Grey funnels of rain swirl up the far slope, from my right, like ghosts on an escalator. Then, for no clear reason, the rain turns to sleet. We follow the obvious route, up one hill and down another, on the same rough, uneven pasture as before, hugging the bare hedgerow irrespective of the fact that it is in the wrong place to shelter us. My teeth are starting to chatter. This is not the sort of weather you'd want to get caught outside in, I tell myself, especially if you were miles from home and weren't wearing much in the way of clothes; which, now I think about it, I am and I'm not.

Treacherous slush has already accumulated on the little wooden bridge in the dip. The brook beneath it is a gurgling torrent. Beyond, the field leading back up past the wood is freshly ploughed: sliced into thick chunks like giant, half-made chocolate bars. It's hard work negotiating the greasy surfaces of the partially frozen furrows; so hard, in fact, that I begin to feel mildly grateful for the pelting snow – which is what the sleet has become. At least I'm not overheating.

The wood itself provides a few minutes of notional shelter, although it's hard to discern much difference. I'm so shocked by the quantities of blizzard that machine-gun through the branches that I barely notice I'm now splashing through deep, muddy puddles that many people would consider impassable in anything but a 4x4. If I think of the puddles at all, it's just a small part of my brain focusing on landing my feet in the dead centre of each of them. That's the best way, I've found, to protect yourself from unexpected angles and slippery slopes: the middle is usually flat.

By the time we emerge, the world is white. The cold and wet seem suddenly secondary to the mesmerising monochrome landscape. Innumerable shades and fragments of white and grey shift and settle as I watch, while the snow piles noiselessly on wet turf and dark, bare branches. It feels strangely exciting to be here: as though I were witnessing that precise, rarely seen moment when winter takes the landscape in its grip – transforming it from fields on to which snow is falling into a proper snowscape.

There's something thrilling about the white emptiness, as pregnant with possibility as a blank page. It's also astonishing: I must have five square miles of Northamptonshire fields in my view, and I can't see a soul. The hidden sun adds the faintest tinge of rusty pink to the frosted black and white fingers of the trees on the horizon and the frosted black and white bristles of the dead thistle clumps that sprout from the white foreground. I don't suppose a morning like this would have looked any different if I'd passed this way fifty years ago.

The falling snow is still soft, but also thick and sugary, and so much of it has now settled that it no longer has any option but to freeze sooner or later – like moist fresh icing on a cake that will inevitably harden in the next few hours.

That image has no sooner come into my head than a flurry of childhood memories comes tumbling after it: of a nine- or ten-year-old me, standing in the kitchen with my mother, watching her ice and decorate the Christmas cake, sick with hunger and excitement, knowing that the glistening grey surface would before long be white and brittle; and that Christmas itself would follow soon after. And then – my head being what it is – one memory leads to another, until I am utterly oblivious to the blizzard raging around us. Instead, my head and heart are full of the remembered textures of life in a small Hertfordshire village nearly half a century ago: the cold houses, the long silences, the plain food, the unchanging cast of neighbours, the dull, reassuring certainties, the empty, neglected lanes.

When I do notice the weather again, my thoughts are coloured by these memories. The way the snow settles noiselessly on farmland hasn't changed since those days, but the world has. My parents' generation – they would both be nearly a hundred if they were alive – weren't afraid of weather, despite being far more exposed to its effects than we are. Their whole relationship with the physical world was different. They understood how things worked: their machines, their homes, their factories and, not least, the natural world around them. They knew how to make things, how to cook things, how to grow things – rather than just buying cheap packaged things that other people had made, cooked or grown for them. They looked after themselves, on the whole, without much help from anyone else. And it wasn't a big deal.

We might look back on that generation's lifestyle as unsophisticated. (What, no cappuccinos? No smartphones? No male grooming products? No foodie food?) But they endured two world wars and the Great Depression, then quietly got on with building the safe, stable, comfortable world in which I grew up. What, meanwhile, does our twenty-first-century sophistication really amount to? Most of us are pathetically dependent: on technologies we don't understand, fuelled by resources we don't have and paid for with borrowed money that no one in their right mind will want to lend us for much longer. Take away our oil, our electricity, our credit, our friendly satellites and telecommunications networks – or even just one of those pillars – and many of us would barely be able to function. Are we really so smart to have forgotten how to live in simpler ways?

And is it really that different with running? We are more sophisticated than any previous generation of runners. We all know the core concepts of sports physiology. Most of us are pretty clued up about the latest technologies in nutrition and kit manufacture, too, even though few of us really need the marginal gains such technologies confer. 'Motion control', 'forefoot cushioning', 'stability cradles', 'hydration', 'compression wear': is there a runner in Britain who doesn't speak this language? But what about the basics? What about the ability simply to go outside and, unaided by any kind of modern equipment, run happily across rough countryside for five or ten miles irrespective of the terrain and the weather? I suspect that many talented runners would struggle with such a simple challenge.

On a day like today, the difference in outlook is particularly stark. Previous generations might not have enjoyed being outdoors on a morning like this, but they would have made the best of it and then got on with their lives. That's what I'm trying to do now; yet to most modern eyes a run like this – with all this cold and wet and dirt and slipperiness – must seem close to insanity.

The thought makes me smile. What would my urban friends think if they could see me now? What would my colleagues in London think? I suspect that – if they believed their eyes at all – most of them would see me as, at best, some kind of crazed fitness survivalist, wilfully depriving myself of the protections of civilisation out of deranged obscurantism.

Perhaps they would be right. Perhaps the physical stoicism of previous generations has no place in modern life. After all, being unable to run without expensive running kit and a tame running environment is hardly a significant handicap, compared with, say, not being able to find your way without satnav, or not being able to do sums without a calculator. It's not as if there's a particular shortage of parks, pavements and gyms in which to train more comfortably.

But it's not just about handicap: it's also about loss. Ask anyone who has turned their back on takeaways and ready meals to rediscover the simple skills of basic cooking, or tried a camping holiday rather than a fortnight in a beach hotel. There's a powerful feeling of reconnection as well as empowerment when you rediscover simple skills; a sense of getting back in touch with instincts that are fairly central to what it means to be human. Without such reconnection, you are missing out.

Perhaps that's why I get such pleasure from my running these days. I am, in some sense, running naturally. Every day I experience sensations that would have been familiar to most runners in history. I feel the texture of the earth with my feet, and read the landscape with as many senses as I can activate. I experience hard, soft, cold, hot, firm, slippery, smooth, rough, heavy, sharp and more. I feel the wind and the rain and the baking sun; the winter and the summer; the night and the day. Each time I run I encounter the kinds of inconvenience and discomfort that come from nature rather than man. And, each time, there comes a point when I realise that they don't really constitute a reason for feeling sorry for myself.

I suppose you could call it self-conquest. But perhaps that's making too big a deal of it. All that's really required is to stand down my pampered, urban, indoor self and to wake up the basic *Homo sapiens* within, to whom storms and snow and puddles (or wind or rain or blistering heat) are no more remarkable – in fact, rather less so from an evolutionary perspective – than walls, doors and electricity.

I've done so thousands of times, and have been glad of it every time. And by the end of this run, too, as I shake the slush from my frozen feet and prepare to chip the ice off Nutmeg's undercarriage, I realise that, yet again, I've done it. I've prevailed.

No heroism or teeth-gritting were involved, just good old-fashioned getting on with it. Yet it feels miraculously good, as it always does. My brain and body feel detoxified, cleansed, recharged; it's almost as though I had restored myself to factory settings.

Or, more simply: I've discovered that there's more strength in me than I'd thought.

8

Playground Britain

A few minutes' walk from the offices of the newspaper where I spend part of most working weeks, there is one of those central London gyms that politicians presumably have in mind when they urge us to turn our backs on feckless obesity and 'join a gym'.

The Virgin Classic Kensington is as shiny and exclusive as the limousines that discreetly ferry diplomats and billionaires in and out of the gated enclave of Kensington Palace Gardens, just around the corner. There's a football-pitch-sized exercise space, a large swimming pool and a complex of changing rooms and relaxation areas so luxurious that I imagine that some members never get beyond them. It's not the most expensive gym in Kensington, but it wouldn't take many years' membership here to set you back the price of a small car.

At seven o'clock on a cold February morning, I counted fifty-three members working out on the main training floor, helped by half a dozen smiling, uniformed personal trainers and a handful of smiling, uniformed assistants and cleaners busy ensuring that no surface remained sullied by sweat for more than a few seconds. Not every member looked especially athletic, but compared with the tired, grey pastiness you'd find in a typical Underground carriage at that hour, the levels of youth, beauty and fitness on display were striking.

The members had plenty to motivate them, with state-of-the-art equipment for every possible kind of exercise, plus more than a hundred group classes a week, a special 'V-Cycle Studio', as much one-on-one tuition as they were prepared to pay for, and such extra attractions as a hydrotherapy area, a crèche, free wifi, Apple internet stations, complimentary phone chargers, Jacuzzi, sauna, steam room and relaxation lounge. The men's changing rooms have heated floors, wall-mounted televisions and hair-driers, free Molton Brown grooming products and shelf after shelf of huge, fluffy white towels. Rumour has it that the women's facilities are even more luxurious.

Few of us can afford this. (My own experience here was sadly brief.) But it is, I think, the kind of experience to which most other modern gyms aspire. It's not just the sense of being in a luxury spa. It's the palpable commitment to certain fundamental principles: cleanliness, comfort, safety, focus, results. So there are, for example, the usual safety notices, and the usual reminders to wipe down equipment after use, and containers of Oxivir Plus bactericidal spray with which to do so. Each of the 150 cardiovascular machines offers built-in multi-channel TV, iPod and iPhone dock, multiple training settings and digital monitors that keep you up to date with such data as, typically, calories burnt, exercise duration, distance covered, average power, average heart rate, maximum heart rate, calories per hour and 'performance index'.

This is exercise as it's supposed to happen in modern Britain: indoors and inward looking, controlled and clinical, using every trick in the book to minimise dirt, danger and discomfort, maximise fitness return on time invested, and dispel the inevitable boredom.

The modern fitness industry has become so good at this that the gym experience has ceased to be a means to an end – what you do to prepare for your real sporting activities – and become an end in itself: the object of exercise. 'Don't dream of the body you want,' says a notice on the wall of another gym nearby. 'Live the dream with personal training at The Gym.'

I am trying not to sound derisive, but a note of derision seems to creep into my words regardless. I don't know why. I've spent thousands of hours of my life in gyms and am as big a sucker for their gimmicks and luxuries as anyone. But the attractions of gym culture are as absurd as they are irresistible.

At the Virgin Classic Kensington, for example, the V-Cycles are fabulous: stationary bikes with screens and movable handlebars on which you can ride through a choice of exotic but virtual 'high-definition landscapes', the resistance varying with the notional terrain. Options include hills, desert, forest and parkland, and in each case intense concentration is required to steer through the hazards. My 'Highland' ride (complete with miserable grey sky) was so realistic I felt nauseous – at least until I thought of slowing down for the sharpest downhill corners. It's simultaneously inspired (what better way of preparing for a hard day's high-powered work than to hone your reactions with some high-speed mountain-biking?) and ridiculous – in the sense that users are paying good money to come inside and imagine themselves outdoors, in preference to the more modest option of simply remaining outdoors.

In 2012, 8.7 million people – one British adult in six

– belonged to a gym or health club, typically paying between £30 and £90 a month. Four times as many people exercise indoors, in gyms, exercise classes or yoga classes, as run outdoors. Most have good reasons for doing so. Not everyone is lucky enough to live somewhere where a rewarding outdoor exercise experience is readily available. There's a plausible case to be made that training safely indoors is the wise choice, if the alternative is dodging traffic and rapists, breathing exhaust fumes and battering joints on crowded pavements. And all of us, bar a few professional athletes, have to grab our exercise where and when we can. I often use gyms, when circumstances make it the only sensible option – and I happily concede that I benefit not just from the time saved and pollution avoided but also from the physical variation these sessions give me from what would otherwise be an unremitting diet of daily running.

What makes me uncomfortable is not so much the gym habit as the gym mindset: the underlying assumption that exercise is about consumption rather than pleasure, adventure or self-discovery: a bought experience rather than a natural one, in which the customer hands over money and expects to receive certain measurable benefits (comfort, convenience, weight loss) in return. That mindset is not exclusive to gyms.

I noticed this a few weeks later when – prompted by an overheard conversation in the Virgin Classic changing room – I took part in a 'mud race' in Wild Park, in the Derbyshire countryside near Ashbourne. The basic challenge sounded little different from what I do most mornings: a ten-kilometre run through rough, undulating grassland, taking in assorted swamps, woods and obstacles and getting indescribably muddy in the process. But the experience had been transformed by the tricks of modern marketing.

It had a brand name – Wild Warrior – and an entry fee – £50 – and 2,000 competitors, including several who, I was assured, were celebrities. There was an Event Village that included food and merchandise stalls, massage and physiotherapy tents, firework displays and a relentlessly upbeat commentator in wellies whose breathless ohmygods echoed across the valley all day. There was a mandatory twenty-minute safety briefing, and a five-minute Group Warm-Up before the start, and electronic timing chips and course maps and information leaflets. I recognised one face from the gym in Kensington, although only from a distance.

The race itself was tough, as you'd expect from any event that mixes the normal demands of running with intermittent but intense alternative challenges requiring the use of different groups of muscles. On this occasion, on an icy day, in a biting wind, with twenty of the sixty obstacles involving partial or total immersion in freezing, muddy water, I had to dig fairly deep to keep my muscles functioning at all.

I wasn't the only one struggling. Most of the water had been put there specially, but it had, in addition, been raining torrentially for weeks, and there were traces of sleet in the vicious wind. By the time the first two hundred of us had completed the first five-kilometre lap, the course was the kind of quagmire you'd associate with a bad year at Reading Festival. Runners were slithering and falling even in the gaps between the obstacles, and many seemed so disturbed by the lack of firm ground that they had slowed to a walk. I'd seen worse in my local fields, and made up for my middle-aged lack of pace by speeding up on the downhill stretches, overtaking fitter but more hesitant runners.

The obstacles themselves were significant but manageable: giant hay-bale hurdles, monkey bars, ditches full of burning straw, mud-filled tunnels to crawl through, waist-deep swamps to wade through and nets and walls to climb over or under. They removed any monotony from the running, without ever quite distracting the mind from the pain or the cold. Eventually, struggling with exhaustion on the second lap, I made a conscious effort to think about something else. I looked away from the course and out towards the jigsaw of fields and woods beyond Wild Park. The colours of the empty landscape had been washed grey by the cold, and I thought I saw snow on some of the more distant fields.

At what felt like the highest point in the park, I strained to see a skylark that was chattering excitedly above. But all I could see were the black, bud-tipped branches of the black, leafless trees on the field edge, bending and bowing like rubber as the wind tore at them. So I turned my eyes back to the northern horizon, searching for signs of the Peak District.

I'm not sure if I saw any or not. The wind was too fierce, blowing in gusts so strong that I imagined I could see them, traced in the sky by the swoops and swirls of the crows that were trying to fly in it. It made me think of the swooshes of blue and white in Van Gogh's *Wheatfield with Crows*, although I shouldn't think a mass-participation obstacle race was quite what he had in mind when he painted it.

Then the course bent sharply, breaking my view, and I realised that I had been running in the kind of dreamy, distracted autopilot mode that characterises my normal runs: too curious about my surroundings to fret about how fast I was going or how comfortable I felt. And, in the process, the race had stopped hurting.

It all seemed to go better after that, the biggest hazard being lapped or collapsed runners. The tunnels, swamps and walls felt like routine inconveniences rather than ordeals. None the less, I felt intense relief when I flopped over the final obstacle and staggered to the finishing line. I'd been soaking wet in an icy wind for well over an hour, and was feeling distinctly shaky. I was surprised to discover, later on, that I'd actually done quite well: thirty-fourth out of 802 people doing the ten-kilometre course. Perhaps I'd been helped by my period of enjoying the off-course natural beauty; or perhaps I was just more accustomed than most to the cold and mud.

But where you finished wasn't really the point. There weren't, as far as I could tell, any prizes. For most people the challenge was to complete the course. Many had run in teams or among groups of friends, and even the strangers among us had been offering helping hands to those who had fallen over or were struggling to get out of slippery tunnels or bogs.

Some seemed traumatised by the experience. I lapped one young woman who was curled in a ball on the ground, sobbing. 'Is she hurt?' I asked the friend who was holding her hand. 'No, she's just had enough,' she replied. But back in the Event Village there was a buzz of shared euphoria: from those who were thrilled that they had accomplished something that they had suspected was impossible, and from those who were simply thrilled that it was over.

It looked like a camp for survivors of a natural disaster. Filthy people huddled in clusters, trembling and wrapped in foil blankets. Some exchanged congratulations and commiserations; others, apparently in shock, were comforted by friends.

Non-racing spectators looked on in amazement as we hosed off the worst of the mud with cold water bowsers provided for that purpose. The water could hardly make us wetter or colder than we already were. Those who could find enough feeling in their fingers to unlace their shoes changed quickly into drier clothing in one of the barn-like buildings around which the Village was based. The rest of us just trudged back to the increasingly swamp-like area where we'd left our cars, casting envious glances as we passed a door marked VIP SHOWERS (reputed to involve hot water but available only to those who had paid £10 extra).

'Never again,' said a muscular, tattooed young man in the car park, teeth chattering. Like me, he was struggling to achieve the necessary transition from wet clothes to dry. 'Never again. It's just so bloody cold.' I thought he might cry. Nearby, an older man was complaining to anyone who would listen that he had lost one of his trainers in the big swamp on his second lap and had had to complete the course without it. 'I only had them a couple of weeks.'

Meanwhile, a more immediate truth was sinking in, and spreading visibly through the car park: the pain was over. The main thing that remained now was the rather exhilarating fact that we could say that we had done it.

Many hours later, back at home and putting my clothes through the wash for the third time in a vain attempt to banish the mud, I reflected with shame that I had gone to the event with the half-formed intention of sneering at it, with its branding and its goodie bag and its free Silicon Wrist Band and its medals for all comers. I had expected the competitors to be pampered urban gym-bunnies whose spirits would be broken by the first splash of ice-cold liquid mud, and a few probably had been. Yet what I'd also seen had been hundreds upon hundreds of people, from all sorts of backgrounds and with every possible level of fitness and outdoor experience, leaving their comfort zones, discarding sensible adult habits and, in the process, discovering depths of resolution and hardiness that they had either forgotten or, in some cases, never imagined.

In reality, most of the memories I took away from the Wild Warrior involved enthusiasm: of a team who ran in some kind of super-hero outfits (too muddy to identify more precisely than that), and who hollered like Tarzan each time they encountered a daunting obstacle; of the man who told me he'd been a seventeen-stone couch potato before he started doing regular obstacle races ('I could never get interested in exercise – but now I have something to train for'); and above all of the young woman, seemingly far too fat for this kind of thing, who sobbed with joy in a friend's arms at the finish of her single lap, endlessly repeating 'I can't believe I did it!'

'I can't believe I did it!' A fair chunk of the joys of running (and many of the joys of life itself) can be summed up in that phrase. We run, in part, because it helps us to find our inner hero, to conquer our little private Everests – and to discover retrospectively that, in our lower moments, we underestimated ourselves. If someone employs a certain amount of marketing and packaging in guiding people towards such discoveries, who am I to complain?

In the days that followed, however, I learnt a little more about the context in which such events take place. The growth of the obstacle racing industry in recent years has been so spectacular that many readers must have encountered it. Getting on for 200,000 people took part in such events in the UK in 2013; in the US, the equivalent figure was 1.5 million. *Obstacle Racing* magazine (launched in 2013) lists more than twenty races a month in the UK alone. Worldwide, the industry is worth $250 million; five years ago it barely existed. The story behind that growth is worth retelling, both because of what it tells us about the miracles of modern marketing, and because of what it tells us about modern attitudes to adventure.

It is, appropriately, a murky story. Its obvious starting point is 1986, when an eccentric ex-Guardsman called Billy Wilson (whose other claims to sporting fame include running in the first London Marathon as part of a pantomime horse) started a winter cross-country race at his farm in Staffordshire. Called the Tough Guy, this became an annual event: initially with just a few mud-related obstacles but quickly evolving into a full-blown military-style assault course of nearly eight miles. Regular hospitalisations, usually for broken bones or hypothermia, fuelled its notoriety, and photographs of mud-caked runners crawling beneath barbed wire sometimes made it to the 'fancy that' slots of national newspapers. Wilson was seen as a crank rather than a commercial pioneer. The takings went largely to two local charities. The wider world took little notice.

Then, in 2009, Will Dean, a twenty-eight-year-old Englishman studying at Harvard Business School, entered the school's annual business plan competition with a proposal for a mass-participation obstacle race. He lost, but he knew he had a winner because he'd done his homework: much of it in Staffordshire, where he had persuaded Billy Wilson to share the logistical and financial secrets of Tough Guy.

Wilson had cooperated in the belief that the project would focus, helpfully for him, on 'the feasibility and logistics of expanding Tough Guy internationally'. In fact, the final version that Dean eventually showed Wilson was subtly different from the one he submitted to Harvard, recommending a far more cautious, wait-and-see approach to expansion than the official version.

Shortly afterwards, in partnership with an old school friend,

Guy Livingstone, Dean – who had also studied the Strongman Run (estab. 2007) in Germany – set up his own event in the US. The first Tough Mudder was held in May 2010, in Pennsylvania.

Dean and Livingstone needed to sell five hundred tickets to break even. Thanks to clever use of an $8,000 marketing budget, they sold 4,500. Thanks to clever pricing, this meant they had $500,000 in the bank – before they'd even begun to pay for the actual event, for which the fixed overheads would in any case be negligible. It was, they realised, an even better business model than they'd imagined.

The subsequent story of Tough Mudder has been one of jaw-dropping growth. Revenues for 2010 totalled $2.2 million; for 2011, $22 million; for 2012, $70 million – all on minimal capital investment. At the time of writing Tough Mudder had thirty-five events worldwide; this was projected to pass fifty by 2014, with financial growth to match.

It goes without saying that Billy Wilson was not best pleased when word of Dean and Livingstone's success got back to him. The details of his displeasure will have to go largely unsaid, too, as both he and Dean are legally barred from discussing their dispute. Their out-of-court settlement in 2011 followed a lawsuit from Wilson, a counter-suit from Dean, and a storm of strong words alleged to have included at least one emailed threat involving beds and horse decapitation. The confidential settlement is reported to have involved a $750,000 payment to Wilson.

Nor is Wilson Tough Mudder's only enemy. Rival organisers in the US (some of whom insist *they* were first movers in the market) have complained about the company's aggressive marketing methods, from allegedly targeting Facebook users who 'liked' competitors' events to flying a plane over a rival race trailing the banner: 'THINK THIS IS TOUGH? TRY A TOUGH MUDDER'. One of these organisers, Joe DeSena, founder of Spartan Race, told *Outside* magazine in 2012: 'There's not a person on this planet I despise more than Will Dean.'

Yet quarrelling seems futile: there's enough money in this for everyone. Spartan Race (estab. 2010) made $30 million in 2012. Warrior Dash (estab. 2009 with a $5,000 investment) made $50 million. The UK market leader, Rat Race, had sales of £5.5 million in 2013, from a mixture of obstacle races and adventure races. And, with new ways of monetising the craze still being developed, few people believe that the limits of growth have been reached.

In this context, allegations of dirty tricks seem irrelevant. The staggering thing is how effective the clean tricks are. Spartan Race, for example, will not only charge you up to £50 to enter one of its UK events but will also allow a chosen few to pay an extra £38 a session to take part in specialist Spartan Race training camps (teaching such skills as water wading, coping with the cold, how to run on mud, how to fall without injury, etc.). Rat Race sells its customers its own branded kit and is moving into training programmes. Tough Mudder derives an increasing proportion of its income from sponsorship (by the likes of Bic razors, Dos Equis beer and Wheaties cereal) and from fees from would-be 'host towns' in out-of-the-way places (which, according to Tough Mudder's own analysis, can get a boost of between £1.3 million and £3.1 million to their local economies from a weekend-long influx of well-heeled obstacle racers).

It is, in other words, about marketing, monetisation and event management just as much as it is about sport or adventure. Will Dean has described Tough Mudder as 'a marketing company that puts on events', which succeeds because it manages those events with dazzling professionalism. The company is notable for the stress it places on corporate quality control. All new employees must enrol in the Tough Mudder University, which 'aims to replicate the Harvard Business School education of our founder and CEO'. They must also read *The Seven Habits of Highly Effective People*, by Stephen R. Covey, and *Getting Things Done*, by David Allen. Any resemblance to the corporate ethos of, say, McDonald's is not coincidental.

Branding, naturally, is a high priority. Customers are encouraged to describe themselves as 'Mudders', to wear distinctive orange headbands, to learn the Tough Mudder 'pledge', even to have permanent Tough Mudder tattoos – as more than 1,000 people have already done. All this maximises the return from the company's heavy use of social media. It has more than two million Facebook fans, and Dean thinks it may be Facebook's biggest advertiser; which is ironic, given the echoes of *The Social Network* in the company's back story, but does much to explain the exponential speed of its growth.

Yet none of this would amount to anything if the public demand weren't out there. Where did all these high-spending obstacle racers come from? The likeliest answer is that they've been there for years, waiting for someone to notice them.

Society in general has grown steadily more averse to risk and discomfort in recent decades: we all know that. But there has always been a minority that has reacted against this trend. That reaction prompted a mini-boom in the 1980s and 1990s in the world of extreme adventure sports, as the keenest recreational runners grew bored of marathons and sought alternatives. A handful (like me) discovered very local challenges such as traditional fell-running. Most wanted something grander. So extreme, heroic-sounding events sprang up to satisfy demand: triathlons (the International Triathlon Union was established in 1989); ultra-runs; multi-discipline, multi-day adventure races involving various permutations of running, cycling, sailing and kayaking. Many involved long-haul travel – for example, the five-day Marathon des Sables in the Sahara (which started in 1986), the Everest Marathon (1987), the Raid Gauloises (first held in New Zealand in 1989), the Eco Challenge (first held in Utah in 1995) or, more recently, the Ultra-Trail du Mont-Blanc (2003).

Kit manufacturers did well out of this and were happy to sponsor such events. But there was a drawback: only a tiny minority of more or less elite athletes had the ability, resources or technical skills (e.g. navigation, survival, climbing, kayaking, etc.) to compete at this level.

Then, about ten years ago, the smart money began to aim a little lower. Endurancelife, the people behind those Trailblaze boxes on the National Trails, were one of several start-ups that appeared on the scene in 2004. They started off by putting on a not-too-hard adventure race or two but went on to organise festivals, events and race-plus-campsite-plus-lecture packages that typically cost £95 a head, all aimed at recreational runners without pre-existing adventure expertise. Comparable British businesses that began life around this time include Detailed Event, Eight Point Two, Open Adventure and Running the Highlands; the latter's 'products' range from guided runs, talks and running workshops in the Cairngorms to an escorted six-day run through the Highlands that costs nearly £1,000 a person. And then there's a whole extra category of businesses – notably Lakeland Trails – that have sprung up in the past decade organising trail races, which combine the attractions of an off-road environment with the familiar comforts of a marked, supported, timed, professionally organised race.

I wouldn't categorise all these as Big Running (or, if you prefer, Big Outdoors). Many were conceived less as a way of becoming rich than as – to quote Neil Stewart, creator of Running The Highlands – 'a way of earning a living while doing what I enjoy'. But the businesses thrived none the less. They were giving the market what it wanted.

Few thrived as much as Rat Race, whose founder, Jim Mee, speaks with unusual articulacy of the moment when he worked out that the best way to turn adventure into a profitable business was, simply, to take the element of the unknown out of it. An events manager and mountain enthusiast who had been pondering ways of combining his enthusiasms, he started in 2004 by creating an 'urban adventure' challenge in the middle of Edinburgh. This mixed running with swimming, climbing and abseiling and more and was, by any standards, extreme; but, in Mee's words, it 'took adventure out of the wilderness and into the city'. Around three hundred serious adventure nuts took part, and, with sponsorship and media coverage, the event proved a moderate hit.

But the figures didn't make business sense. 'The work involved was vast, but the participant base was very small,' says Mee. 'People were showing an interest and then saying, hang on, I don't know how to kayak, I've never abseiled, I haven't read a map for ages.'

So he lowered the bar. A new breed of Rat Race events was born, offering adventure-based challenges in a safe, controlled environment. Some were simply runs in wild places – similar to what people like Running The Highlands offered. The game-changers were the obstacle races. These were events that – like that first urban adventure – required competitors to mix running with activities involving ropes, water, mud and climbing. But the levels of difficulty and danger were limited, expert staff were on hand in large numbers, and, although the locations were increasingly rural, the unpredictable hazards of the wilderness were excluded. For the less experienced would-be tough guy or woman – wanting the challenge of a new adventure but lacking the confidence to take on the wilderness alone – it was the perfect solution.

By 2013, Rat Race events were attracting 70,000 participants a year, and, in the meantime, an industry had been born. Rival British brands include Xrunner (the people behind the Wild Warrior), Warrior Run, Demon Run, Total Warrior – and almost any other permutation of those words that you can imagine; while the US giants are also increasingly gaining a foothold in the UK and Europe and beyond. In business terms, this is a market with barely any barriers to entry. All you need, if you fancy a slice of the action, is access to a bit of land; a few thousand pounds' worth of equipment; a respectable number of reasonably reliable helpers; detailed knowledge of one or two rival events; a decent insurance policy; the chutzpah to charge people £50–£100 a time for the privilege of, essentially, running, climbing, wading and getting muddy and exhausted in the countryside; and a bank account to put the profits in.

'You could say we've dumbed down,' says Mee (who at a personal level likes nothing better than to challenge himself in a seriously hostile mountain wilderness). 'We've lowered the barriers to entry and our customer base has broadened massively.' By 2013, Rat Race was putting on twenty-one events a year, ranging from a five-kilometre forest trail run to a two-day, twenty-mile obstacle extravaganza that cost

£150 to enter. Few of them were easy – or at least not if you approached them competitively. But none could be described as an adventure in the usual sense. 'It's a snapshot of adventure,' says Mee. 'It's designed for everybody.'

For the mud millionaires, this is the joy of it. Anyone can do it. Unlike a marathon or a triathlon, for which months of training are essential, an obstacle race requires little athletic prowess. It hurts less if you're fit, and you'll go faster. But you don't actually need any talent to immerse yourself in icy water or crawl through a tunnel of liquid mud. You just have to be prepared to do it.

And the delight, for many, is to discover that, despite their habitual assumptions, they are.

'It takes people out of their comfort zone,' says Sara Harvey, Tough Mudder's thirty-one-year-old UK Vice-President. 'People are often stuck in their rut: they're on the Tube, they're in the office all day. At the weekend they want to challenge themselves.' Or, as Guy Livingstone put it in 2012: 'Lots of people want to be a kid again. They love crawling through mud.'

You might wonder why they don't save themselves £50 and just go out and muck around in the countryside. But the price tag and branding may be part of the appeal. 'It's an adult adventure playground,' says Sami Black, Events Manager for Xrunner. 'But because it's tough, because it's a challenge, it's justifiable for adults. No one's just going to find a pile of mud and roll in it, or use the slide in a children's playground. But because you pay for it, and have to train for it, it seems OK.'

Countless people want to be liberated from the restraints of orderly urban existence. Most fear the complete liberation of a real wilderness adventure. Challenges that provide wilderness-style discomforts but retain the reassurance of slick, well-packaged event management are a lucrative compromise. It is, if you like, Adventure Lite.

And the moral? I don't know. Such businesses succeed because the demand is there; people enjoy these events and pay for them because they think it's money well spent. Adventure Lite satisfies a widespread craving among active people for new ways of testing, stretching and pushing themselves. It addresses widespread dissatisfaction with the dull conformity of modern life. And it avoids the risks associated with outdoor adventures of a more traditional kind. I've no reason to believe that any of the companies I've mentioned provides its 'snapshots of adventure' in anything but a highly professional manner, and it's certainly not for me to judge those who choose to spend their money buying these snapshots, any more than it would be if they spent it on eating out or buying clothes.

Yet I keep coming back to those multi-million-pound turnovers. Can it really be right for the great outdoors – part of our common heritage – to have been so monetised, and for so many ordinary people to have been persuaded that they need to pay to have outdoor adventures?

Perhaps it's a question of where you place the threshold of 'adventure'. There are, obviously, activities best not undertaken by novices without expert guidance and support. It's hard to dispute that, where rock-climbing, caving and kayaking are concerned, young urban fitness fanatics are often better off broadening their horizons in the safe environment of an adult playground than biting off more than they can chew in the real wilderness.

But getting muddy? Getting wet? Running through a forest? Messing about in a stream? Going out in the country-side at night? Do we really have to buy these experiences from Big Outdoors as well?

I know that most people live in cities; that hardly anyone absorbs the basics of outdoor self-reliance in childhood any more; and that events such as Wild Warrior will genuinely take many participants far beyond their emotional and physical comfort zones. But I also think that some perspective is needed. The world around us is less scary than it seems. Accidents happen in it, and the countryside has its dangers just as the city does. But putting yourself in someone else's hands – even if they're a trusted brand charging reassuringly expensive prices – isn't always the best way of safe-guarding your wellbeing. (Tough Mudder had its first fatality in 2013.) Sometimes it's better to take responsibility and learn to look after yourself.

Big Running wants you to run in a rut. It wants you to pay your big gym subscription, and to run in your big trainers and state-of-the-art running gear, and to venture beyond treadmill, pavement or park only for organised, sponsored, branded road races with entrance fees, goodie bags and changing facilities. Big Outdoors feels much the same about your adventures. If you insist on having them, just buy into one of our packaged adventure experiences and we'll do the worrying for you.

The message serves the sector well, allowing more people to get involved and, as a result, creating more customers for race places and merchandise. It also serves many customers well. Just as developing a conventional road-running habit is usually a positive thing for a person to do, so daring to try a packaged, sanitised adventure can, in many circumstances, be a life-changing liberation.

But don't let them tell you that that's the only option.

9

Slow Running

I've overslept. The sun is bright, and I am running so fast that the sound of my breathing deafens me to most other sounds. It's almost April, and the turf is soft as springtime. Dark buds shine on the tips of branches, and small birds – black flecks in the sun – dart and sing over the hedgerow. But all I can think of is that I am behind before I've even started the day. I might as well be running for a bus.

Nutmeg – who is perhaps best visualised as a much-miniaturised Highland cow with extra-short legs and no handlebar horns – is struggling to catch up after getting distracted in the woods. Her forte is stamina rather than speed (like a beagle), and I can't be bothered to wait for her to reach the big iron gate that I usually hold open for her at the corner of the woods. She barely slows down before squeezing under it, squirming through a shallow puddle and then resuming her flat-out running.

It occurs to me that Nutmeg could do a Tough Mudder in her sleep. Run through mud, leap through snow, plunge through icy water, climb fences, crawl under fences, get cold and scratched and wet, get tired, keep going – what's tough about that? It's what she does. It is, come to think of it, what every animal does in the countryside. So why is it such a big deal for humans?

Perhaps it's because we're so busy. I know I am. My head is full of things that I'll need to do as soon as I get back. I don't have time for obstacles. In fact, I'm going to have to do an even shorter version of this route than I'd planned. I push the pace further, trying to get the maximum training benefit from this limited outing. The fact that the run will be over even sooner as a result is an added bonus.

Then something inside me starts to thaw. The feel of the ground, the warmth rising from the grass, the scent of drying mud – it all blends to remind me that this is my favourite time of year, just a day or two before the clocks go forward. You can go for a run before work without having to start in total darkness, yet it's early enough in real terms for the wildlife still to be out and about. It is also that moment when a certain glow in the air makes you realise that, while you weren't looking, the world has been growing brighter: that it's nearly (if you're young) the school holidays and (if you're me) your birthday or (if you're not) Easter. Suddenly you remember what summer might feel like.

The rat-a-tat-tat of a woodpecker echoes sharply from the woods. I'm pretty sure it's the first I've heard all year. Does that mean winter is over? I slow down in spite of myself, deviating from my abbreviated route to trot quietly up the side of the wood and squint up at the treetops. But despite two more loud bursts of battering, I can't work out where the bird is. I never can with woodpeckers.

The air is warmer further up the slope: less sheltered from the sun, I suppose. The grass, flattened for so long by winter, is springing upright again, blade by drying blade; even the thistles seem to be bristling with new vigour. After so many bleak, pale, freezing weeks, the land is coming alive. This is happiness, I tell myself; this is life. Do I really have to cut this so short? Let's at least head up this hill and see what lies round the corner...

Another sound distracts me: a long, desolate, ululating bleat from somewhere behind me. I glance skywards to see a huge bird flapping heavily towards the northern horizon. Was that really only a buzzard? And, if not, what was it? But it's already put a line of trees between us. I'll just have to hope that it's still around when we pass back through that far field on our homeward leg.

Then, still looking upwards as I turn away at the top of the hill, I notice a bizarre pattern of jet contrails, ten or twenty of them, slashed in random patterns across the blue, as if the sky had been self-harming. Is this normal, I wonder? I don't remember seeing anything like that before; nor, come to think of it, do I remember hearing any aeroplanes. Perhaps it's something to do with the atmospheric conditions. Perhaps the jets in question passed over hours ago. The truth is, I haven't a clue: I'm an ignoramus where sky is concerned – which leads me into the thought that, on the whole, we runners pay remarkably little attention to the world above our heads. There are obvious reasons for this. Yet it's sobering to think how much must go on up there unnoticed, every day.

So now, jogging just a little slower than usual, I crane my neck to explore the world above me. Pinkish sunlight is glowing on the upper branches of the oak trees that punctuate the hedgerow at the bottom of the slope, lending a hint of gold to the edges of their sprouting dry green leaves. It looks warmer and more summery up there, although you'd expect the air to be colder. Rooks are wheeling above the largest oak, and I realise now that their caws are resounding through the empty air. Have I really not noticed them? And what exactly are they doing when they wheel? What's going on in the world, right now, from their perspective?

A fat bird – a dove, I think – flaps clumsily and suddenly across the middle of the field, in pursuit of who knows what urgent business. It's the only bird in sight that isn't above trees. Do birds fear empty spaces below them, I wonder?

Then I notice again the subtleties of the blue sky beyond them. Away from the vapour trails there's a fresh, almost wet quality to it, like new paint. But is it thick paint, slapped on quickly, or thin and watery? I can't decide: it changes as I gaze. An artist could go mad trying to identify all the different shades and tones in a clear sky. For the casual observer the mystery is joyfully beguiling. I am, I remind myself, extraordinarily lucky in the amount of blue sky I see, simply because I run first thing in the morning, when the sky tends to be at its most cloudless. Often, people moan about what a terrible grey summer we're having, and I wonder what they're talking about: it looked pretty summery to me, when I went out for my run.

I'm wondering if I can complete the rest of this run concentrating only on what I see above me when a stumble on an unexpected dip brings my eye lurching back to earth. I'm just in time to see a clump of dry mud in the long grass in front of me get up and hop, jerkily, across my path.

It is a hare, the size of a small dog, tawny and warm with life. It doesn't notice us until we are within talking distance: the wind is carrying our noise and scent away from it. Nutmeg, preoccupied by some other scent, shows no interest. The hare looks, thinks, straightens its long legs and lopes awkwardly towards the hawthorn hedgerow. It's a big, handsome beast; but I feel as though, if I chose, I could catch it.

There are people who claim to be able to run down hares. The art, an old poacher once told me, has more to do with cunning than with speed. You focus the hare's attention on an object upwind of it – a makeshift hat-on-a-stick is said to do the trick – and then sneak round behind it. I'd be tempted to try this, but I've no wish to cause gratuitous alarm to one of my favourite wild creatures. I've often fancied one as a pet – it would make a brilliant running companion – but hares are reportedly almost impossible to domesticate. (The only people I've heard of who have succeeded are Prince Rupert of the Rhine, nephew of Charles I, who reportedly trained one to follow him like a spaniel while he – and presumably it – was a prisoner in Lintz castle in Austria in the mid-seventeenth century; and the eighteenth-century poet William Cowper, who kept three, at least one of which was 'gruff and surly' and 'would not suffer the slightest caress'.) In any case, my local hares are effectively running companions already, doing their own thing in the fields, as Nutmeg does, while I do mine. I'd be amazed if they had any friendly feelings towards me, or could distinguish me from whatever other human beings intrude into their world; yet I still think of them as friends. I never catch sight of one without feeling my heart grow a little warmer. Such thoughts mark me out as an urban incomer. A true countryman sees a hare and wants to kill and jug it (a traditional method of slow-cooking that involves putting the marinated meat in a jug that is then placed in boiling water for three hours). Such thoughts also mark me out as, I think, a typical solitary runner, letting my mind take me where it wants while my feet think for themselves. Both mind and feet take me to some strange places, sometimes. It tends to be more rewarding than always being where I planned to be.

We wheel round and I see Plumpton Wood on the far side of the valley, sleeping all the way along the skyline like a giant dragon. There's a succulent roughness to its dark treetops that reminds me of broccoli. But it's the size of it that strikes me most, and the thought of the hundreds of acres of tangled undergrowth that lie sheltered beneath the protective filter of that forest canopy. It's too far to reach today, but I must remember to run out that way tomorrow, to explore.

We are now at the point where I had planned to turn for home. I can't bring myself to do so. I feel as though this run is helping me to shake off some encroaching spiritual sickness, and it seems reckless to cut it short. Look! Look at all those scraps of wool in the hedgerow, where sheep must have been cowering in the hawthorn for shelter during the colder weather. Look at the rough trunk of that ash tree, indifferent to winter and spring alike: what is it about its bark that communicates so unambiguously the heaviness and solidity of the wood within? Look at that heron, flapping up from the Plumpton fish pond like a pterodactyl. And isn't that a whiff of fox in the crisp April air?

The world seems so full of fascinations that it's like being in a gallery or a department store. I don't know where to look. I don't want to stop.

What was I in such a hurry about? Why am I always in a hurry? And I realise that even as I am thinking this – even as I have stopped hurrying – I seem to be running even faster than before.

At least, I think I am. Not having a watch, or more than the vaguest sense of the distance I am covering, I have no way of telling for certain. But Nutmeg is struggling to keep up again, and it certainly feels like fast running.

Will the speed be wasted because it will never be measured? Of course not. On the contrary: surely this is speed as it is supposed to be experienced? There have been times in the past when I have run quite fast on the track, but I can't remember when I last felt such a pure awareness of speed as I feel now. Then, my mind was always full of the ticking seconds and the battle to contain the agonies of oxygen debt and muscle fatigue. Now I'm at peace when I run. If I happen to be running quickly, I can enjoy it, rejoicing in being alive, strong and light-footed. I think back for some reason to the idea of 'fox-footing', and imagine myself skimming over the landscape like a fox. (Foxes can be cheetah-fast when they put their minds to it.) My feet and hands feel deft as a fox's paws, and I realise that my hands have formed gently into pointed paw shapes, wrists limp, with thumbs and middle fingers lightly touching. My whole body feels elastic and supple, while my strides are so fluid that I seem to be sprinting without effort.

And even when, a little later, we reach the corner of the field and have to slow and turn along the edge of a cattle-churned nettle patch, I can enjoy the change of pace, the fine balance of my cornering, the continuing delicacy and precision of my footfalls, and the simple pleasure of being a runner, running.

Skirting the field edge, absorbing the torso-shaking rhythms of the ridge-and-furrow waves in the tufted turf, I listen again to the sounds in the clear air: the caws of the rooks again, and the fanfare of a distant cockerel. There's no sign of that giant bird of prey I saw earlier, though; but maybe it will turn up later, or perhaps on another day. That's another thing I like about this kind of running: the possibilities.

Meanwhile, I wonder if, in my thoughts about speed, I might be on to something. You've probably heard of Slow Food, the movement founded in Rome by Carlo Petrini in 1986 as an antidote to fast food. It began as a local initiative but rapidly went global, as more and more people in the developed world responded to the idea that, by buying into the concept of convenience food and high-speed takeaways, we were depriving ourselves of nearly everything that made food magical. It's obviously quicker to grab a packaged sandwich than, say, to jug a hare; but if that's how you choose to eat you miss out on an entire world of culinary (and social) nuance. Think of it as haste versus taste.

A generation of future foodies was converted by Petrini's arguments, and seemed so satisfied with the results that a broader Slow Movement was born. Some of its manifestations were more convincing than others: Slow Parenting (the opposite of hothousing), Slow Travel (taking time to enjoy the journey rather than racing to the destination), Slow Gardening, Slow Cities, Slow Sex and so on. It's not complicated. Don't rush it and you'll get more out of it. Dwell in the moment, in this activity rather than the next one, or you'll be missing out.

And the thought that occurs to me now is: what about Slow Running? OK, it doesn't sound persuasive as a phrase. But isn't it a thing, none the less? What I am doing now is Slow Running: not because I'm necessarily running slowly – I suspect I'm not – but because I'm enjoying it, irrespective of time; focusing on the moment itself rather than trying to measure it.

I don't suppose it will catch on (and it's really just another label for what I have already described as the Fifth Age of

Running). But I like the concept none the less. I have no idea how slowly I run these days. Less slowly than many, I suspect, but more slowly than I used to. But I like the fact that it doesn't matter – and love the thought that, now I've stopped looking at running through the dark glass of clock-watching, I can now look clearly at the thing itself.

And if I am ever tempted to worry about declining performance, I can always reassure myself with the thought that, for most recreational runners, enjoyment is one of the very best ways of maintaining standards. If I carry on running like this every day for the next few decades – happily, healthily and uninjured – I'm going to be a spectacularly fast hundred-year-old.

IO

Out of bounds

There is a man who lives on the edge of Dartmoor who teaches 'wild running'. It sounds extreme, like white-water rafting, but it isn't.

Long-haired and tall, with a wispy beard, Ceri Rees runs in baggy shorts and minimalist shoes, with the casual agility of a hippie surfer. A nervous city-dweller might take him for a proper cave-dwelling wild man. In fact, he's a former elite athlete, now nearly forty, who grew up in Newcastle upon Tyne and lives today in a little terraced house on the outskirts of Totnes. His wilderness experience extends from the Alps to the Andes, Cumbria to Kenya. Yet what he teaches are not the hard-core skills of the mountains but the more basic art of running off-road, in nature.

It's a strange idea. If running off-road, in nature, is what humans have always done, how can it be an art? How can it need teaching? Yet even the most natural practices can be learnt, from swimming to sex. And in this case, as I found out when I joined Ceri for a wild run on Dartmoor, the educator has an additional role to play.

On a bright, windswept afternoon, Ceri led me through

the woods and valleys above Venford Reservoir, out on to the empty heights of Yar Tor Down, talking as we ran about what he does and why. I've run countless times on Dartmoor: Clare's parents live on its southern slopes. But this patch was unfamiliar, and there was something exhilarating about exploring it with Ceri. Picking our way through gorse and boulders, vaguely following a path of cattle-churned mud, we chatted away with barely a thought for the fact that what we were doing was 'wild'. And it struck me that, though he was younger, fitter and faster than me, in outlook we had much in common.

'It's sad that people are so suspicious about running in places like this,' he said. 'There's just so much more to moti-vate you here. I always come back feeling refreshed. At my age, my body ought to be getting weaker, but it's actually getting stronger.'

The path brought us to a fast-flowing, knee-deep stretch of the River Dart, which we crossed on stepping-stones. Then we scrambled up another muddy track through trees and small sloping fields, emerged on to a bouldered, gorse-peppered hillside and ran on sun-dried, sheep-cropped turf – Ceri leaping nimbly from tussock to tussock, me plodding patiently behind – up to a nameless tor.

Ancient slopes of moor billowed away from us, green and enigmatic, as far as the eye could see: grass, gorse, bracken, granite, woods, hills, valleys. There must have been a lane or two somewhere, buried in a fold in the landscape, but I couldn't see any. As for people, we seemed to have the entire area to ourselves.

'I often take people up this way,' said Ceri. 'But not nec-essarily this particular route. There are paths, but I just sort of go wherever feels right.'

In a marginally different life, Ceri might have earned his living from running on flat surfaces. He was a national cross-country champion as a schoolboy, represented Britain at various distances, dreamed of Olympic glory and made a habit of winning the half-marathons he entered. He studied sport science at Loughborough University, as many elite athletes do. Then he got bored.

'I hated the goldfish bowl ethos. I was sharing a house with eight athletes. We'd all sit around with bags of frozen peas applied to different parts of our anatomies, discussing our niggles and injuries. All people were really interested in was the outcome of their own personal athletic careers.'

So he drifted away, took up rugby instead – 'where at least you get proper injuries'; became a journalist and, later, a translator and occasional teacher; went travelling; lived in Scotland, Bournemouth, Basingstoke, Paris, Madrid and Buenos Aires; and, eventually, in his mid-thirties, settled down in south Devon. He was still running to a high standard, mostly off-road and, increasingly, in wild places. He was also enjoying it, more than ever. 'Going off for a weekend running in the mountains was the strongest expression of freedom I could think of. I'd go off in a camper van and come back feeling totally refreshed.'

One day, it occurred to him that other people might benefit from similar refreshment, even in a slightly tamer form. He'd been friendly in Bournemouth with a Zimbabwean asylum-seeker and marathon champion and had been struck by the way that running had kept him sane. 'By all logic, he should have been depressed. He wasn't allowed to work, he had to keep reporting to the police station, he'd been forced to leave his home country because of his politics and now he was treated like a criminal because his paperwork wasn't right. But he was still able to run, and that was his source of freedom. He trained really hard, but it wasn't a chore: it was the thing that made him feel alive. It made me look at running in a new way.'

So now, in Totnes, he tried to set up a social enterprise in which he'd take unemployed people for guided runs on Dartmoor, helping to give a structure to their day and a sense of achievement on which they could build. 'Running resets you. It gives you resilience. I wanted to share this.'

But it turned out that the people who embraced it most enthusiastically were barely unemployed at all, but, on the contrary, dynamic, professional types: people who, if they had problems, were already halfway to solving them. 'I thought: why fight this? I was obviously offering people something they needed, and it grew into a really lovely group, a bit like a family.'

Today, in partnership with another runner, Mark Brookes, he takes groups out two or three times a week, organises occasional off-road races (usually at night) and, when demand arises, does bespoke runs and 'wild running weekends' for individuals and groups. The weekends typically cost around £130 to £145 per person, excluding accommodation and evening meals. Bespoke runs vary from £40 to £90 a person, depending on length and numbers. The weekday outings include a Monday night 'movement awareness' session, at which runners are encouraged to focus not on time or distance but on the way they run: everything from stride length to breathing to the way it feels when each foot strikes the ground.

Ceri and Mark have a client database of up to seventy people, of whom perhaps a dozen are regulars. It's hardly big business – Ceri earns most of his living from being a supply teacher. But the biggest reward, he said, is the gratitude that people express towards him, for introducing them to a way of running that adds a new dimension to their life. 'A lot of people come along who you wouldn't necessarily have thought would need a guide. They've done marathons or half-marathons: they're quite confident runners. But somehow people don't feel the same confidence about stepping off the road. Sometimes it might be that they're not confident with navigation, or they're not sure how difficult it's going to be. Sometimes they just seem to need a bit of a push – a bit of external motivation.'

On a sunny afternoon like this, it was hard to see how anyone could find this landscape intimidating. The air was warm, the short grass dry and soft, the visibility perfect. But I've run on Dartmoor enough times to know how abruptly it can cease to be tame. A storm bursts, a wind whips up, the fog descends, and the gentle curves of grassland become an incomprehensible cat's cradle of indistinguishable slopes, booby -trapped with gorse and bogs, cold, confusing and distinctly dangerous. Even on a clear day, a momentary loss of concentration can lead rapidly to hopeless confusion: the shapes seem to shift as you move, until trying to plot your route by sight feels as if you were navigating a stretch of sea on the basis of the shapes of the waves. Could I have found my way back to safety from here, in a black Dartmoor downpour, if Ceri hadn't been here and I had slipped and sprained an ankle? I suppose so, but there was a time when I would not have been so confident. Even now, I was cautious enough to be carrying a map, compass and waterproofs in my bumbag.

I'd imagined that Ceri might have lots of specific tips about off-road running technique, but that didn't seem to be a priority: partly because, as a long-term 'wild runner', I wasn't really his target audience; but mainly because he doesn't really see himself as that kind of teacher. 'If anything, I'm a guide,' he said. 'A lot of it is just providing back-up and security. Dartmoor's a huge place but I know this corner of it like the back of my hand. People value that. You'd be surprised how intimidating many people find it, leaving the road, even when we're just running on unmarked paths.'

There's also spiritual guidance on offer. The Wild Running website describes the activity as 'a meditative experience' and continues: 'To run through nature not only stretches the limits of the body but also the mind... You rarely return the same as when you started out.' If it sounds a touch pretentious, it is also true.

As we strode back down across the open moor towards Meltor Wood, weaving between somnolent brown cows and letting gravity do most of the work, Ceri talked about the relationship between stride patterns and the optimum positioning of one's centre of gravity. The interest of the discussion came less from the words used than from the necessity to focus absolutely on what I was doing in order to make sense of them. In addition to savouring the warm, springy grip of the dry turf beneath my feet, I was playing with stride lengths and body positions, comparing the feel of different movements, thinking about what I was doing not in terms of outcome ('How long will this run take?') but in terms of, simply, what I was doing.

It felt highly satisfying, and when Ceri used the phrase 'mindful running' to describe his Monday-night sessions, I thought: yes, that's exactly what I'm doing; and, now you mention it, exactly what I had in mind when I coined the less felicitous concept of 'slow running'. Never mind the outcome. Run in the moment; if the moment is in nature, run in nature, too. Focus on what you are doing and where you are doing it. You will rarely return the same as when you started out. (Much later, I learnt that a handful of people in the UK teach 'chi running', which is running in accordance with the mindful principles of t'ai chi – although there doesn't seem to be much interaction with nature involved.)

'The trouble with all that,' said Ceri, leading me back across the river and into the woods, 'is that it got a bit of a bad name in the 1970s. All those dodgy gurus. It's a pity really. But I think if you start talking about "enlightenment through running", people just say, "*Oh yes?*"' His tone of voice captured perfectly the scornful cynicism that down-to-earth people traditionally deploy against proponents of spiritual enlightenment.

So he and Mark focus instead on providing a practical service: guiding runners safely into unfamiliar places, sharing their enthusiasm and leaving people to find their own enlightenment. 'I find we don't really need to tell people what they can get out of this,' he said, on the long uphill run-in back to the reservoir. 'They tend to find that out for themselves, and tell us.'

My legs were tiring by then, but it was hard not to be galvanised by Ceri's enthusiasm as he danced with no apparent effort between boulders and gorse bushes, light-footed as a goat; and I found it all too easy to believe his claim that 'I never feel tired after a wild run, no matter how far I've run'.

But in that case, I asked, red-faced and spluttering as we finally reached the reservoir car park from which we had set out, why doesn't everyone do it?

'I don't know,' he said. 'I think a lot of people would like to. Sometimes it almost seems as though they just want someone to give them permission.'

I I

Spring in my step

I don't notice the lambs until they are almost under my feet. I have been running with my eyes half closed, trying to focus on the sounds of the morning, and, as a result, have been oblivious to most other aspects of my surroundings.

The idea occurred to me just a few minutes ago, when I opened the front door and was struck by the cascade of individual birdsongs that greeted me, palpable as the warmth from an opened oven. There was something both uplifting and reassuringly familiar about the pattern of songs – ringing, distinct and bright as sunlight – which made me wonder if all rural mornings sounded like this, or whether this particular set of harmonies was unique to my garden.

Common sense suggested that, although the basic line-up of birds must be much the same in most parts of Britain (just as the line-up of instruments is much the same in most orchestras), different times and places must sound as distinct as different symphonies. But it had never occurred to me before to listen attentively as I ran.

My first conclusion was that there was a huge difference between the background twittering in the garden and that in the lane outside, barely twenty metres beyond, where the overhanging trees gave a platform to a host of additional birds. In the garden I was aware of perhaps half a dozen voices – blackbirds, tits and I've no idea what else – along with the rattle of a woodpecker already at work on our neighbour's tall pine. In the lane, especially at the place higher up the slope where the shadows turned to sunlight, it felt like a wall of sound: dozens of different voices, each echoing and resonating and, presumably, interacting with the others. It would be sentimental to describe the effect as harmonious – but it certainly wasn't discordant.

Now, in the first field, the sound thins with each stride away from the lane. By the middle of the bowl-like depression halfway across, the symphony has subsided into chamber music, with half a dozen voices dominating – rather as they did in the garden, except that this is a different combination of voices. The sound is quiet enough for me to hear the mewing of my cats, Thelma and Louise, who often come with us for the first few hundred metres of a run. (They're amazingly fast but quickly run out of stamina, at which point they protest loudly and give up.)

Then, as we climb the slope towards the far side of the field, I realise that there are sheep in it: a dozen or so shabby ewes standing around, with some of the smallest lambs I have ever seen outdoors lying in huddles nearby, white as plum blossom, their little black feet tucked neatly under their tiny chests. They stare at us in wonder, while their mothers fuss around them like plump, ill-kempt kindergarten teachers.

The lambs seem so delicate that I half wonder if Thelma or Louise might think of them as potential prey. But they haven't followed us this far and, in any case, the mothers seem highly protective. One of them, deciding that Nutmeg and I

have come too close, comes bustling up to us and makes a
rather comical attempt to butt me as we approach the stile to
the copse.

I suppose it is possible to see young lambs without smiling,
but I find it hard to imagine doing so. I don't know if it's
their innocence or their novelty or the way that, when they're
a little bit older, they will gambol around like idiots on the
green grass, but somehow, invariably, like daffodils, they
always surprise me with hope: an unexpected reminder that,
whatever else is wrong with the world, there is always springtime, and life hasn't stopped renewing itself yet.

Spring optimism distracts me as we cross the next field.
The air has an oddly viscous, temperate quality, as if moisture
evaporating invisibly from the earth were somehow softening
the light. The grass seems a brighter green than it has been
recently, the sky a richer blue, and there's a sticky blackness
to the shadows beneath each leaf on the distant hedgerow. A
mile and a half to my left, the edges of the roofs of Canons
Ashby seem less distinct than usual. In fact, the whole landscape seems softened, as if the whole centuries-long process
of its erosion by human use had somehow become visible.
Then I remember that I'm meant to be listening, not looking
– and I realise that, again, the background music has changed.
Even if I close my eyes, I can sense that the sky is broader
than before: the bird calls are less numerous but echo further.
And then, when we reach the far side and continue alongside
the hedgerows beyond the footbridge, a denser sound resumes.
I lack the knowledge, or the aural discernment, to identify
each call, but the complexity is still thrilling – like the voices
of a London street market – and distinctive, in the way that
the sounds of a London street market are distinct from those
of a street market in a foreign city.

I wonder if I would be able to tell where I was if someone led me blindfolded round this route. Probably not: I haven't paid enough conscious attention over the years to the field-by-field variations in the soundscape. (It might also be confusing if farmers unexpectedly moved livestock from one field to another.) Yet I am beginning to enjoy glows of sub-conscious recognition as I notice the way that different patterns of sound are already associated, somewhere within my mind, with different parts of this familiar route.

My eyes are still more or less closed when a gradual increase in volume tells me that we are approaching Grumbler's Holt. I open them to avoid mishaps with low-hanging branches but continue to focus, as far as possible, on what I can hear. The path beside the wood itself is relatively muted, as if the trees were muffling the sound; as for the forbidden world beyond the broken fence, I listen in vain for rustling in the unseen recesses of virgin undergrowth. But I do eventually hear a stark, crow-like sound echoing among the highest treetops, and from somewhere in the background – I can barely tell from which direction – throbs the muffled cooing of doves.

In the field beyond, the voices grow brighter and clearer again. Rooks are circling and barking above an isolated oak tree, but there's also a confusion of voices broadcasting from the wood's edge. The noise is not as dense as in the hedgerows earlier – more like voices on a village green than those in a street market – but there's still something fascinating about the mingling: each call with its own message, yet each contributing to a brilliant, intricate whole.

There are other sounds among the birdsong: occasional bleats, reminding me that there are some older lambs a couple of fields ahead (time to put Nutmeg back on her lead); a distant murmur of traffic, so faint that, like a ringing in your ear, it is either there or not there depending on where your attention is focused. There is a cockerel, too, crowing from somewhere down in Plumpton. I wonder if that sound has only just come into earshot, or whether it has been there all along and I have failed to notice it.

The more I think about it, the more ashamed I feel to be so unobservant. Has all this really been passing me by, day after day? And, if so, what else have I missed? I suspect, though, that most of these sound impressions will have been having their effect on me anyway, if only at a subconscious level, contributing to the sense of refreshment I feel after running. And, of course, I do notice some of the sounds I hear, sometimes. If I ran with headphones (as 55 per cent of British runners now do, according to a 2013 report by *Men's Health* magazine), all of this would pass me by, always.

Studies have shown that we tend to run faster when listening to music, if the tempo is suitably fast and the mood suitably motivational. For many runners, that's a conclusive argument for never venturing out without headphones. Others say that they find training too boring without music to distract them. I disagree with both arguments. If running bores you, find a more interesting way of doing it. As for speed: even if I did bang out some faster times as a result of having a high-speed playlist plugged into my brain, I doubt it would really make me fitter, in the long term. On the contrary, I suspect that the resulting disengagement from the environment would demotivate me, making my runs less interesting, my sense of immersion in nature less rewarding and, eventually, my reasons for keeping up my running habit less compelling. Rural running is rewarding largely because of the rich stream of sensory input you constantly receive from your surroundings. Why filter out a whole layer of it?

I am distracted from these reflections by another field of lambs, a month or so older than the previous lot. They're plumper and woollier than the little ones, with a curiously dodo-like shape to their puffed-out chests. Our intrusion fills them with unease rather than wonder. Some seem tempted to approach us; others edge uncertainly away, as if waiting for someone else to lead a panicked flight. Their mothers seem barely interested, glancing up and, in a couple of cases, summoning their offspring with peremptory baas, before resuming their grazing – rather as parents outside school continue to chat to fellow parents even after the children they're waiting for have emerged for collection.

The comparison catches my imagination, and before I know it I am detecting echoes of school in every aspect of my sheep encounters. The different fields are like different classrooms, each containing a different age group. There's a new intake every year, and each new set of arrivals will steadily progress through the age groups: from wide-eyed innocents, overwhelmed by it all, to woolly puppies, messing about and boisterous, to stronger mini-adults, whose bulkier frames only partially disguise the insecurities within. As a casual observer, I watch their progress with detached interest: warm but not protective, as if I were looking at pupils at a school my children used to go to. If it saddens me to think that the little ones I saw earlier will soon be gawky, unruly adolescents on the verge of 'leaving' altogether, that has less to do with concern for their ultimate (culinary) destiny than with a more general regret at the implacable passage of time. Each new cycle begins with boundless hope and ends with something less. I expect teachers feel something similar, as the generations pass through their classrooms.

A sudden hiss of flies brings me back to reality, alerting

me to a heap of fresh horse dung on the grass. Is there a horse nearby? Sure enough, I eventually spot a distant mounted figure beyond the hedge on the skyline. Once again, I'm struck by the sheer depth of information that the countryside offers up to those who pass through it. In this case, a sound a few feet away has alerted me to a sight several hundred metres away. What else could my ears tell me, I wonder, if I really learnt to use them, as a blind person does?

Not long afterwards, I change direction in the corner of a field and hear immediately a soft breeze roaring gently in my ear. I had no idea before that there was any wind at all. Now that I hear it, though, I know also that I am running into it, and, as a result, look out more carefully than before for wildlife up ahead. This heightened attention yields no sightings – it's too hot, I think. (The hotter the morning, the earlier creatures disappear.)

But I do notice one unmissable whiff of what I think is fox – which prompts me to think: maybe one day, when I've learnt to listen properly, I should start training myself to smell properly. I'll always be an olfactory dunce by Nutmeg's standards, yet perhaps even a human being could in theory learn to find his way around a familiar route by smell alone.

I'm still exploring this idea – trying to work out if there's something fruity about the lush grass-scent I inhale as we cross the big penultimate pasture; struggling to unmix the notes of bark, resin, mould and earth that I notice as we pass through the old copse (does it smell *insecty*?); being reminded by a pungent aroma of drying wool that there are lambs in the final field – when Thelma and Louise burst out on us from behind the last bent hawthorn tree. Thelma almost knocks Nutmeg off her feet as she barrels into her. Then, fresh from forty minutes of mucking about in the long grass, the two cats sprint off ahead of us, pausing twice to look back mockingly. I'm smiling at their transparency – even the most brazen schoolboy cheats usually make a little more effort than that to disguise their dishonesty when they pull the old hide-behind-a-tree-until-they-come-back routine – when another olfactory perception almost stops me in my tracks.

On this short stretch of lane, which hasn't had so much as a pot-hole filled in it for more than two decades, all other smells are masked, first, by a sickly trace of diesel exhaust (presumably left by the van I heard passing a few minutes ago) and, secondly, by a faint but unmistakable scent of tarmac: acrid, tarry, permanent and, once I sense it, impossible to ignore.

The observation is sobering. How many thousands of times have I run this way without noticing this obvious aspect of my environment? But it's also instructive. Perhaps it isn't surprising that my understanding of the runner's place in the countryside should be so at variance with the typical road-runner's view: a road is almost the opposite of a field. When I run, my senses are bombarded with input from the rural environment – no matter how clumsily I attempt to decode that input. But a runner on a busy road, with headphones on and, let's assume, with dark glasses as well, with the sounds, sights, scents and general menace of road traffic all around, is almost entirely cut off from the countryside's sensory cacophony.

From the road, the fields I run in must seem to offer no more interest than a pretty arrangement of shapes and colours – like a picture. From out in the fields, meanwhile, the road-runners I occasionally glimpse on the far side of a distant hedge appear so removed from what's really going on around them that, as far as I'm concerned, they might as well be running indoors.

No wonder we see things differently.

12

Roots

Someone in a nearby village organised a cross-country race, to raise money for Help for Heroes and the local church. A landowner made his fields available, the event was advertised with flyers and postings on running websites and the whole of Adstone turned out to help. 'A certain amount of arm-twisting's been involved,' a friend confided. It seemed ungrateful not to enter.

There were fifty or sixty runners. A few were locals who didn't usually do this kind of thing but were being good sports. Most – from their kit – appeared to be members of running clubs, including a couple of local ones. My heart sank. Nearly all looked younger, leaner, fitter, more muscular and more focused than me. Several wore what looked like Olympic-inspired bright orange spikes; the rest wore trainers.

The ten-kilometre course wound in two undulating laps around wide field boundaries and muddy paths and could hardly have been kinder to run on: soft, relatively smooth and (except on the second lap) not especially muddy. I plodded off near the front, enjoying the scenery. I can never entirely shake off my competitive instincts when I race, but

I was broadly resigned to being overtaken by dozens of younger, more driven runners. But after the third or fourth overtaking, it all went quiet behind me.

It was an utterly different quietness from that of my usual runs. I could hear my breath rasping, feel my stomach teetering on the edge of nausea from my unaccustomed sustained speed and sense the grunting and crashing footsteps of the faster runners ahead. There were marshals aplenty to say hello to, breathtaking views and, as long as I didn't push myself too hard, a gathering sense that I might get round this without undue pain. Halfway through the second lap, some of the frontrunners began to drift back to me.

'This isn't my kind of race at all,' gasped one as I passed him. 'Not like a normal 10K race.'

I don't know, I said. I don't normally run 10K races.

'You're sensible,' he said. 'This is the last time I do this.'

By the time I reached the finish, there were (I think) only five people in front of me. I was knackered but, primarily, astonished. I forgot to check my time – I was too surprised at my position – but I know it wasn't fast. (Another runner pointed out to me early in the second lap that 'Mo Farah would have finished by now.') And the question immediately presented itself: how did a middle-aged devotee of Slow Running end up beating scores of younger, fitter, keener, shinier-kitted club runners?

As the rest of the field staggered up to the finishing table – one, two, five, ten, fifteen minutes later – a possible answer emerged.

'That was murder,' said one man in a Silson Joggers vest.

'I've never known anything like it,' said a mud-caked woman with mirrored sunglasses.

'I'm not trying that again,' said a shaven-headed man, bent double with exhaustion.

People had, it seemed, been freaked out by the terrain. Not all of them (and some, obviously, had taken it in their stride better than I had). But for most people, to go by the post-race chat, it had been too muddy, too rough, too scary to risk going fast on. A few complained that they hadn't been able to follow the course markers because the rough ground had demanded so much of their attention. 'I think some of them might need counselling,' joked a high-visibility car-park attendant.

Everyone perked up soon enough. I even heard one runner saying that she had enjoyed it. A couple of junior races followed, the hardcore athletes left and the running gently gave way to the more traditional business of village get-togethers: raffle, refreshments, cake stall, tombola. A respectable sum was raised for the good causes.

Yet the question stayed with me: why had so many people disliked these innocuous conditions? It wasn't like one of those obviously difficult mountain races that I've sometimes done (for example, during a blizzard in the Black Mountains a few months earlier) when an older fell-runner expects to get a bit of an advantage over younger, fitter athletes with less mountain experience. On the contrary: the rough turf was soft, the air crisp, the mud shallow; the ups and downs were gentle and the views breathtaking. I'd expected the post-race talk to be about how glorious it all was.

But rough turf and shallow mud are, of course, no longer everyday underfoot occurrences. We live in an urban age. Ninety per cent of the British population live in urban areas (that is, in towns or cities). And although, paradoxically, nearly a sixth of the British population might reasonably describe themselves as rural – in the sense of living in country towns, villages or hamlets – there's an important caveat to that. Getting on for two-thirds of those 9.5 million country-dwellers are newcomers, having migrated from city to countryside at some point in the past forty years. You could, if you like, talk about Britain being two nations: one urban, one rural. If so, you would have to count the vast majority of us as being urban. And those of us who have transplanted our urban roots into the countryside have, not surprisingly, brought urban attitudes with us – including attitudes towards running.

Most of us learnt our hobby on pavements or in parks; the more gifted may have done so on tracks as well; a few in gyms. A handful of the more talented will have experience of what's known as 'cross-country': that is, of racing on a marked, undulating track on smooth grass. But barely any of us, wherever we live now, will have started out as rural runners. Indeed, I'm not sure most of us know what the phrase 'rural runner' means, or if it even has a meaning in the twenty-first century. The real gulf is not between town and country but between present and past.

Yet there must, surely, have been a tradition of rural running once, in the days when Britain was a predominantly rural nation?

If you seek an answer to this question in books and libraries, one of the first things you notice is that, right up until the early twentieth century, authors used scenes of daredevil 'wild' running as liberally in their fiction as modern thriller writers use car chases.

From Edmund Spenser's *The Faerie Queene* (1590) to James Fenimore Cooper's *The Last of the Mohicans* (1826) and H.G. Wells's *The Invisible Man* (1897), the set-piece foot chase, usually in wild places, was a staple of adventure writing. Many of the scenes remain evocative, and it's worth quoting a few, simply to remind ourselves how wide that gulf between past and present is. Our ideas of running-related excitement generally involve scientifically trained professionals in hi-tech kit, or Lucozade-gulping marathon runners pounding well-marshalled tarmac. Here, by contrast, is Robert Louis Stephenson, describing his hero's life-or-death dash from pursuing soldiers in *Kidnapped* (1886): 'Now we ran among the birches; now stopping behind low humps upon the mountain side; now crawling on all fours among the heather. The pace was deadly; my heart seemed bursting against my ribs; and I neither had time to think nor breath to speak with...'

Here is Thomas Hardy, who had rural running scenes in half a dozen of his early works, in *Desperate Remedies* (1871): 'The path...was ploughed up with the rest of the field... The thaw had so loosened the soft earth, that lumps of stiff mud were lifted by his feet at every leap he took, and flung against him by his rapid motion, as if it were doggedly impeding him, and increasing tenfold the customary effort of running.'

And here is John Buchan in *The Thirty-Nine Steps* (1915), with his hero on the run from both the police and a sinister secret society in the Scottish Highlands: 'I was in a wide semicircle of moorland, with the brown river as radius, and the high hills forming the northern circumference. There was not a sign or sound of a human being, only the plashing water and the interminable crying of curlews...I felt the terror of the hunted on me...Crouching low in the runnels of the bog, I ran till the sweat blinded my eyes. The mood did not leave me till I had reached the rim of mountain and flung myself panting on a ridge high above the young waters of the brown river...'

Such scenes are imaginary, but they were not drawn from thin air. Pre-twentieth-century running was a sport of rural adventure. Hard evidence to back this assertion is thin – no one much bothered to record non-aristocratic leisure pursuits until about 150 years ago – but the clues are there if you look for them. Written references appear from the seventeenth century onwards to 'foot races' being held, usually for bets, at village shows and festivals. References to children playing 'hunt the hare' and 'hunt the fox' go back even further. (It's conceivable that Shakespeare referred to such a game around 1600, when Hamlet, telling Rosencrantz and Guildenstern to lead him to Claudius, says: 'Hide, fox, and all after.') Then, from 1800 or so, the landscape itself begins to feature as well.

A few reports refer to fell races: a fairly specialised, local tradition. Others describe 'hare-and-hounds' contests in rural boarding schools, in which a human 'hare' or 'hares' would run off ahead, choosing their own route across rough ground and leaving a trail of scraps of paper. After a suitable interval, the 'hounds' would set off in pursuit. The first hound to catch the hare was the winner. Nineteenth-century novels that make reference to such activities include *Tom Brown's Schooldays*, by Thomas Hughes (1857) and *The Way of All Flesh*, by Samuel Butler (published posthumously in 1903 but written between 1873 and 1884). There's also a famous paperchase scene in *The Railway Children* (1905). Such works may tell us little about life beyond the ruling classes, yet they do give some sense of the texture of the age. Butler has a hero who thinks nothing of 'a run of six or seven miles cross-country', although it does leave him 'crimson with exertion' and 'covered with dust'. Butler was educated, and learnt to run, at Shrewsbury School, where a game called 'The Hounds' was established by, probably, 1819. The school keeps written records – Hound

Books – going back to 1831, describing events in which two 'foxes' with a head start laid a paper trail over anything up to fourteen miles of Shropshire countryside, using all kinds of cunning to confuse and elude the pursuing 'hounds', who would cry 'view halloa' when they sighted their quarry. The fastest hound would eventually achieve a 'kill'.

The earliest record of an organised adult paperchase is from 21 March 1868, when a group calling itself the Thames Hare and Hounds staged an impromptu event from the King's Head in Roehampton to replace a cancelled Thames Rowing Club steeplechase. Similar events followed rapidly, and by the late nineteenth century there were paperchases in most parts of Britain, with the practice increasingly being taken up beyond the boarding-school-attending classes. The 1898 edition of the *Badminton Library of Sports and Pastimes* estimated that one athletics club in four was 'a Harriers or Hare and Hounds club'.

But then something happened. The golden age of paper-chasing was also the period in which modern athletics of a more conventional kind became established. The Amateur Athletic Association was founded in 1880, while 1896 saw the first modern Olympic Games. Paper-chasing was already falling by the wayside when the nation's toughest young men went off en masse to the Great War. By the time the survivors came back, the craze was almost over. Challenges involving feats of hardiness in north European mud had probably lost much of their appeal; and running, like everything else, began the slow process of urbanisation.

Yet the appeal was certainly there once, and it's fair to assume that the Victorian equivalent of today's recreational road-runner might well have been a paper-chaser. Wondering how such a runner's life might have compared to mine, I trawled briefly through an archive of nineteenth-century

Northamptonshire newspapers and found dozens of accounts of paperchase events, over distances of up to twenty-five miles, reported in sufficient detail to convey both the flavour of the contests and the interest that they must have held for participants and non-participants alike: 'Some stiff ploughed fields and some difficult ditches caused the followers to progress slowly' (1879); 'The hares...were sighted by the hounds, who were thus enabled to save two miles' (1898); 'Several water-jumps were included, some of them being rather stiff' (1898). Hounds are described as 'scrambling at fences and jumping in and out of ditches in the most undignified way' (1871), and a fast pace is described as leaving 'little jumping power in a man's legs' (1871). Legs and lungs are only part of the equation: success also depends on having the agility and nerve to leap stiles and ditches boldly, and the grittiness to crawl swiftly under or over natural obstacles ('belly-hedging', as the Shrewsbury boys called it), the resilience to shrug off bruises, scratches and falls, and the resourcefulness to deal with unexpected hazards (such as angry bulls). Above all, there is a sense of unpredictability. Starting the contest is no guarantee that a runner will even find the finish, let alone reach it. 'Owing to losing the trail,' says a typical report, 'one or two competitors failed to keep the course.' You can imagine the displeasure that such inconveniences would cause in a public race in the twenty-first century.

There were mentions of other kinds of racing, too: handicaps, where runners started at different times according to past form; and steeplechases, or 'foot grinds', where runners had to race from point to point but could choose the routes by which they got there. Other sources, such as the Thames Hare and Hounds club's official history, describe contests on 'the roughest, boggiest parts of Wimbledon Common' (including the notorious Dismal Swamp); a contest in which a competitor was 'delayed by a morass at the bottom of a ravine'; another involving 'waist-deep black mud'; and another in which the course went through 'a very wide and deep part of the ancient Hog's Mill River'. But the gist, in all cases, was the same. The events involved a significant degree of adventure, and it would have been hard for anyone to take part without real mental engagement with the landscape.

The key to such contests was unrestricted access to suitable land – including 'heavy ploughed land', brooks, hedges and ditches – which was easier then than it is now, especially for the privileged. Even so, misunderstandings and disputes were common. At Shrewsbury, for example, the schoolboys regularly caused trouble by finding ways of trespassing and, indeed, of making mid-run diversions to local pubs. Eventually the school authorities decided that enough was enough. The free laying of trails was banned and foxes were made to strew their paper along pre-ordained routes. Dr Benjamin Kennedy, author of the celebrated *Kennedy's Latin Primer*, was one of the first teachers to try to enforce the ban. The boys responded by laying a trail with shredded copies of his *Primer*.

I can see their point. Cross-country runs are all very well – and the Shrewsbury ones are notorious for the range of challenges they pose – but they're not the same as a genuinely unpredictable adventure, where slackness of thought and faintness of heart are as big a handicap as weakness of legs or lungs. This often used to bother me in the days when I ran for the bloodhounds. Yes, it was fun and absorbing and sometimes exhilarating. But imagine how much more exhilarating it would have been if I could have chosen my own routes, pitting my brain against the collective intelligence of the pack, rather than following an agreed route, chosen for the benefit of farmers, landowners and horseback followers. The potential drawbacks to such an approach, in a land crowded with people, cars and jealously guarded private property, are obvious. None the less, it would have been fun to try it once.

Is there a place for such no-routes-barred games in modern Britain? I suspect not. (But I'll return to that question later.) Meanwhile, it's pretty plain to me that something significant has been lost: something that we might do well to rediscover. The default relationship between rural runner and rural land-scape has changed. Once we were happy to run through all and any of it. Now we are all at sea if we leave the road.

You could say that we've become soft, but I don't think that's fair. The boom in obstacle and adventure races shows that there are plenty of people who relish challenges that expose them to all manner of hardships and indignities. But while man-made obstacle courses such as Tough Mudder and Wild Warrior offer many of the same physical hazards as wild countryside (although nothing so dangerous as bulls or belly-hedging), they do not require us to engage with nature: to adapt our sporting aims to a landscape with its own pri-orities. The challenge has been tamed; and the wildness, as in so many other areas of life, has been filtered out.

This seems a pity: not because there is anything to be ashamed of about being an urban 'incomer' (which as often as not means someone whose rural ancestors were forced off the land by enclosures), but because runners who persist with an urban mindset in the midst of the countryside are con-demning themselves unnecessarily to an altogether more limited version of their hobby than is actually available to them.

13

Slippery when wet

This is what they tell you when you take up running for the first time (most of this comes verbatim from www.nhs.uk, but most running magazines or websites will tell you much the same):

- See your GP before you start running.
- Make sure you buy a good pair of running shoes to reduce the risk of injury. Thick cushioned shoes are best. Get advice from a specialist retailer.
- Set yourself a goal. Whatever your level, setting goals is important for staying focused and motivated.
- Plan your runs. Work out when and where (the exact route and time) you're going to run and put it in your diary. Then stick to your plans.
- Keep a diary of your runs. Note down each run, including your route, distance, time, weather conditions and how you felt.
- Use running music to motivate yourself.
- A good pair of running socks can prevent blisters and is a wise investment at the start.
- Wear reflective or high-visibility clothing to reduce

the danger from traffic, especially if running at night.

- Consider using a carbohydrate sports drink to provide additional fuel: aim for 750ml fluid per hour of running.
- Use a running app to find, record and share your favourite running routes.
- Stop if you feel short of breath, dizzy or unwell.

They don't say anything about mud. Or cows. Or puddles. Or a dozen other subjects you might want to know about if you wanted to do your running off-road, in the countryside.

This is what I wish someone had told me when I first moved to Northamptonshire, to save me from having to work it out for myself, through trial and error, over several decades:

- Use your runs to explore. There's no better way of getting to know your local countryside, through trial and error. This may make it hard to monitor your performance in terms of time and speed. It doesn't matter.
- A local Ordnance Survey map will cost about a tenth of the price of a pair of new running shoes and will do infinitely more to enhance your rural running experience. You might want to splash out on a compass, too; and perhaps even learn to use it. If you're new to an area, try to develop a detailed and accurate sense of the lie of the land, as well as getting to know where all the footpaths, bridleways and other rights of way are. If possible, learn which land is whose, and how different fields, paths, woods and streams fit into other people's lives. Think of it as a new relationship, between you and your local countryside. The more you put in – especially in those crucial early years – the more you'll get out of it in the long term.
- If you want to keep a running diary, write down what

you see. It will be a lot more interesting to look back on than a list of times and distances.

- Falling over won't kill you. It won't even hurt you. (Actually, it might. But less often than you'd expect. And you'll usually get better.)

- Your biggest injury risk is a sprained ankle. The thicker the soles of your running shoes, the greater that risk will be. Thin-soled or minimalist footwear is best (see Chapter 16). Or, if you have really weak ankles, there's no rule to say that you can't run in high-ankled walking boots or something similar.

- Use the first five to ten minutes of your run as a warm-up. This is absolutely not recommended by experts, but in practice most rural runners will have to negotiate plenty of gates, stiles and narrow paths and lanes before they reach the kind of open countryside where they can run at full speed – so why not put that phase of the run to good use?

- There is no rule to say that you can't get muddy, or get rips in your clothes, just because you're an adult.

- If you feel cold, or wet, you're probably just not running fast enough. None the less, it's a good idea to have at least one windproof garment to cover your torso. Keeping the wind out is much more important than keeping the rain out. If you go running on a wet day, you're going to get wet.

- In remoter areas, where mountains or large areas of moor are involved, it's irresponsible not to take safety seriously, and you should carry windproof and waterproof top and bottom, and a hat, and a survival bag, and emergency food, as well as map, compass and whistle.

- In normal countryside, you'll have little need for specialist kit. If in doubt, take that windproof outer garment, even if it spends most of its time wrapped around your waist. Otherwise, just wear clothes that are comfortable to run in, easy to wash and not too expensive. The risks of damaging clothing are greater off-road than on.

- If you want to splash out on an extra bit of equipment, buy a whistle. It won't cost much, it will fit in the tiniest pocket and yet it will be incredibly useful in the unlikely event that you need to call for help while out in the middle of nowhere. Much more useful than special running socks or a silicon wristband.

- The other safety precaution you can take, if the countryside you're planning to run in seems intimidatingly wild and unknown, is to make sure someone knows roughly where you're going. That way, the search party will know where to look for you if you don't come back. But bear in mind, too, that the sort of dangers runners tend to fear – muggings, sexual assaults, dog attacks – are statistically far more likely in cities than in empty fields.

- Don't fight gravity. Going uphill, take small steps and wait patiently for the top to come. Going down, don't hold back. The faster you go, the less likely you are to injure yourself.

- Don't fight mud. A bit of sliding around is easily absorbed into your running motion. It may slow you down, but think what a good work-out it's giving you. Mishaps (i.e. falling over) tend to occur if you try to change direction suddenly, or try to slow yourself down too abruptly. Just remember that you're on a slippery surface and enjoy the skidding rather than trying to resist it. Going downhill, let the slope dictate the direction of your descent.

- Don't wear headphones. Most people do – but dare to be different. Being unable to hear what's going on around you puts you at greater risk from all sort of dangers, from traffic to raging bulls. It also deprives you of a whole layer of the rural running experience. You might as well wear blinkers, or run with a clothes peg on your nose.

- Don't run in blinkers. Or with a clothes peg on your nose.
- Have a strategy for dealing with mud when you get home. If your clothes are caked in the stuff, just putting them straight in the wash will result before long in a clogged-up washing machine, while shoes have a tendency to rot if you just leave the mud on them until the next time. If possible, therefore, give everything a pre-rinse, outdoors. I'm lucky to have an outdoor tap with a hose attached (also good for the dog). But a bucket is better than nothing. Unless you're the dog.
- Running in the countryside will probably bring you into contact with animals. Not necessarily wild ones, which will shun you, but farm animals and pets. Pets, or rather dogs, are probably the most hazardous. My rules for dogs are (a) to make friendly noises to them, (b) to keep your hands to yourself and (c) if in doubt, to keep your gaze fixed on them until you're at a safe distance. The latter is easier said than done but seems to work. It's also worth looking around for sticks, which you're more likely to find lying around in the countryside than in a city. A long one can be useful for keeping a hostile animal at a distance. And a short one? Well, you can always try throwing it and see if the dog runs off to fetch it.
- Farm animals are discussed in greater detail in Chapter 14. As a basic rule of thumb, sheep of all kind are safe; horses are safe unless startled; cows are generally harmless unless you have a dog with you, but cows with calves can be aggressive even to the dogless, and should be treated with

great care; bullocks can be dangerously frisky and should be discouraged from stampeding after you; bulls should be treated with extreme caution as a matter of principle, even though any bull you encounter in a publicly accessible place will probably be docile. The greater your awareness of what your local livestock is up to, the easier it will be to make any necessary route adjustments. Remember: you can beat a sheep in a fight but not a cow or a horse.

- Wild animals can be assumed to be safe – not because they necessarily are, but because they'll keep out of your way. But don't get into a fight with a badger. Or a fox. (Or, I suppose, a rabbit, if you meet one that wants to fight.)
- If you are interested in seeing wildlife as you run, run early in the morning, before the day has heated up; or, if that's not an option, in the evening twilight.
- The other key tip for wildlife-spotting is to look in the direction the wind is coming from. Or, more sensibly, wait until you are running into the wind and then look ahead of you. If your scent and sound are blowing back behind you, it's possible that any wild creatures up ahead won't notice you.
- Bear in mind that, unless you're a big landowner, or lucky enough to live in a National Park, you're likely to be running on other people's land. The existence of rights of way across the land doesn't give you rights to the rest of it, and you should respect the Countryside Code, details of which can be found at, among other places, www.naturalengland.org.uk. (Key points: leave gates and property as you found them; follow paths unless wider access is available; leave no trace of your visit and take your litter home; keep dogs under effective control.) It is also only fair to consider what the landowner – as

likely as not to be a farmer – is trying to do with the land you're running on. For example, might he prefer you to run gently around those sheep, rather than sticking exactly to the path and causing a stampede?

- If you're unused to running on rough surfaces, doing so in the countryside might give you blisters, especially if you're wearing traditional trainers. The best solution? Ignore it. The pain won't damage you and you'll end up with tough skin in the affected spot. Alternatively, get a needle and thread (the thinner the better) and pull them through the blister, drawing out the fluid painlessly and leaving in place plenty of protective skin.

- There's a lot to be said for gloves, whatever the weather: not just for keeping your hands warm but to protect them from accidental injuries. If you fall over, as you will from time to time, you'll instinctively (and usefully) put out a hand or two to break your fall. The resulting wounds can be incredibly irritating and slow to heal, because most of us use our hands so much in everyday life. If you can't manage thermal gloves, socks – not necessarily clean – are perfectly adequate.

- If your hands still aren't warm enough, one winter trick which works well (although I don't expect many readers to try it) is to break the ice on a puddle, bucket or barrel of frozen water and immerse your hands in it for a few minutes. If they don't fall off, they'll be warm for the rest of the day. Especially in thick socks.

- Puddles: don't pussy-foot around the edge of them. As previously discussed: the edges are the slipperiest bits, at the most dangerous angles; the centres, by contrast, are flat. Aim for the dead centre of each puddle. You'll get splashed, but you won't fall over.

- Nettles: they sting. Get over it. It won't kill you. And remember: if you don't rub the sting, or touch it in any way, the poison won't be released, and the irritation will be gone within a minute or so. (The tricky thing is remembering not to touch it for hours afterwards, even though you're no longer aware that it's there.)
- Thistles: they scratch. If possible, avoid them. Otherwise, get over it. But bear in mind that the really big, savage thistles can also inflict catastrophic damage on your clothes and shoes.
- Brambles: they scratch worse than thistles; and, sometimes, carry traces of bugs or viruses from other creatures they have scratched. Best to clean any such wounds thoroughly as soon as you get home. Then get over it.
- If you particularly dislike being stung or scratched, wear leggings. But bear in mind that brambles, nettles and thistles are at their worst in summer, when leggings may feel too hot; and remember, too, that, unlike legs, leggings tend not to mend themselves after being ripped.
- The other hazard of summer is insects. You rarely get bitten when you're moving, but you may accidentally swallow one, or get one in your eye. Learn to recognise the kind of places (shadowy, damp, near trees or near livestock) where insects congregate, and take appropriate precautions: for example, by lowering your eyes and trying to keep your mouth closed.
- Don't underestimate the hazards posed by trees. I often run with a hand or two held out in front of me when there are low-hanging ones around, especially when the light is bad. But what I'm really paranoid about are roots. They're so easy to overlook, when you're running along a woodland path, yet even the flimsiest, least conspicuous

root can exercise a deadly and unyielding grip on a trailing foot, with painful consequences. So pay attention, pick your feet up and remember that that's another reason to have a hand held out in front: to break your fall.

- Don't trust wooden structures. Stiles, bridges, fences, tiger traps, path edges: no matter how inviting they look, unless you have thoroughly tested them before, DON'T TRUST THEM. Wet wood, often lubricated with moss, mould or lichen, is the slipperiest surface in the universe; and one of the least pleasant to slip on (there are usually unforgiving edges involved). Wood that looks dry often isn't. Even when dry, wooden structures that are out in the countryside in all seasons and weathers rapidly become unstable. Very few running mishaps result in such painful or long-lasting injuries as overconfident approaches to wooden structures. Just slow right down for a few strides and, if possible, find something to hold on to as you go. It will add a second or so to your time. So what?

- Oh yes, and don't trust the ground on either side of wooden structures either – in case you were thinking of leaping over one. If it's a stile, or a bridge, or a gate, or a hunt jump, or whatever, it will, in effect, be the entrance and exit to a field. The ground on either side will be much trodden and thus probably churned up, slippery and generally untrustworthy. Just relax, take that extra second and speed up again when you're on the other side.

- Electrified fences, generally recognisable by the rubber insulators with which the wires are attached to the posts, are often found where livestock are kept. The pulses are mild and regular, and for humans who know what to expect they are usually no big deal (especially if you're the kind of human who has childhood memories of putting a nine-volt battery on your tongue to see how long you could keep it there). For animals, though, they can be terrifying, so if you're running with a dog take care that it doesn't get tangled up in one, as Nutmeg did once. She was traumatised for hours. That is, on reflection, the one aspect of a Tough Mudder that she would struggle with: the Electric Shock Therapy obstacle, where you run through an area of dangling, live electric wires.

- Snow, so hazardous for runners on roads, is actually rather pleasant to run on when you're properly off-road. What's underneath it is rough and soft rather than smooth and hard, so you can relax and enjoy the extra cushioning. Just bear in mind that, as with mud, abrupt changes of direction are unlikely to end well. And it's worth knowing that, if large parts of your route are very icy, smooth-bottomed shoes grip better than studded ones, because there's more of them in contact with the ground – whereas studs act like the blades of skates.

- Storms aren't usually a problem for rural runners, if you don't mind being wet and buffeted. Think of it as a free Jacuzzi. It's not as if you're going to slip on a hard pavement. But it's always worth being alert with at least part of your mind to the dangers of falling trees and branches, and to the risk of lightning. So: when passing trees, keep ears and eyes open for potential hazards. If you see a branch that looks dodgy, think what your exit route will be before you pass it. Don't be tempted to shelter on the leeward side of big, old trees. As for lightning, I'm afraid there's no answer to this. If there's a proper thunderstorm, with lightning, get indoors as soon as possible. And don't shelter under a tree.

- If you feel short of breath, dizzy or unwell, don't stop.

Or, rather, you can stop if you like. But bear in mind that there won't be any public transport to get you home and that, if you're going to be ill, the middle of a field isn't an ideal place to do it. The alternative – which you'll probably prefer in the end – is to keep plodding on, as slowly as necessary, until you've reached some kind of civilisation again. It isn't unheard of in the countryside to knock on a stranger's door in an emergency.

I could go on. But let's leave it at that for now. To rural readers, and perhaps to many others, most of those tips will have seemed obvious to the point of banality.

Yet the very ordinariness of this advice intrigues me. Once upon a time, perhaps just a single generation ago, all of this would have been common knowledge. Everyone would have known how to deal with farm animals or read a rural land-scape. And everyone would have had some sense of how to deal with the discomforts of outdoors.

For example (to throw in another top tip that has just occurred to me): if you come home with frozen toes, you need to thaw them out – typically by running a cold tap over them until they can feel that it is cold – before letting them anywhere near warm water. Otherwise you will experience excruciating agonies and, possibly, chilblains. Even when I was a child, half a century ago, everyone knew that. Now it's the kind of arcane trivia that gets aired on *QI*. And to my children, to whom I am constantly trying to impart such knowledge, it's the kind of advice that's entirely pointless. They know a far smarter solution: don't get your feet cold in the first place.

They are, however, missing out.

14

The Box

There's a field about two miles from home where I'm often surprised by a thrilling sensation that I'm running very close to the sea. I'm not sure why: we're about as far from the sea as it's possible to get in Britain. Perhaps it's because the prevailing wind has to pass over a series of exposed, dew-soaked fields on its way to this point, giving it the moist flavour of a sea breeze. Whatever the explanation, the illusion always fills me with renewed zest for life, just as a real sea breeze does.

But the zest lasts longer on some days than on others.

One bright May morning, we emerged from the woods into the undulating field in question, caught the scent of the imaginary sea, and sprang joyfully up the slope, enjoying the softness of the ground: the grass crisp, the soil not waterlogged but moist enough to be springy, the sunlight illuminating the delicate clusters of golden seed-heads that floated above the shorter grass like spray. After a few minutes, a sharp pain alerted me to the sprouting of a new crop of thistles. Actually, the pain wasn't a total surprise. Nutmeg, still on her lead, was already hanging back and the thought had been starting to form in my mind that fresh green mini-thistles might be the reason.

Thistles are easy to deal with, once you know they're there. You just avoid them. But Nutmeg, who is guided by smell rather than sight, hasn't mastered that, so I had to more or less drag her along the relevant zigzags.

Not long afterwards there were nettles, which, again, were young, small and particularly vicious. Nutmeg ignored them, while I tried to pick my way between them, with limited success. But I did remember not to touch the stings. At some point in the next minute or two, I forgot them – but not before reflecting that, if I ever had nothing better to do or to spend my money on, I really ought to enter Billy Wilson's summer Tough Guy event, the Nettle Warrior. As the name implies, nettles are involved. They've yet to kill anybody.

The next field had white sheep scattered right across it. The sight seemed curiously bracing, like white horses on a mildly choppy sea. Shortening Nutmeg's lead slightly, I navigated a clever zigzag path through the biggest gaps and was gratified to reach the far side without disturbing any of them. The pleasure I took from this was arguably excessive, but it took me years to develop that skill, and I'm proud of it. The knack is so intuitive that I can barely describe it. You just develop a feel, over time, for the way flocks arrange themselves – and, often, for the role in that arrangement of the ground beneath them or the elements above. I've learnt, as a sheepdog does, what responses my lines of running will evoke, and to sense which individuals within the flock are most likely to trigger a panic. Thread the right line, work with the flock rather than charging blindly through it, and they will barely notice that you've been there.

It's hard to imagine a skill with more limited applications, but it's still an acquired accomplishment, and I sometimes wonder if I should put it on my CV. It's also important, for the rural runner. A full-scale sheep stampede poses no threat to human wellbeing but can be hazardous to the sheep themselves, and a watching farmer would not be impressed by a runner who set one off.

Cows, such as those in the field after this one, are a different matter. They're as tough as young rhinos, and it's for your benefit, not theirs, that you need to treat them with respect. Most are docile, but things can get complicated – and dangerous – once anyone goes above walking pace.

These ones, about twenty-five mothers and young calves, were grouped right by the gate by which I'd been planning to enter the field. We could probably have barged through them safely, but then we would have been running with them behind us, which is precisely what you don't want to do. Herds of all descriptions have a tendency to follow a running creature, and cows are quick to build up potentially lethal momentum. So we improvised a diversion that involved going to a different corner, climbing across a barbed-wire double fence, fighting our way through a thicket of nettles and brambles and then entering the field at a point where the cattle might not notice us.

I was feeling quite hot and bothered by now. Scratched, stung, tormented by flies (which tend to attack the moment you slow down), I felt as though I'd been in a rather unpleasant fight – and we weren't even halfway through our run. Maybe I should have stuck to the road.

We sneaked as quietly as we could along the far side of the field, but had gone barely ten metres before the first cow noticed us. After twenty metres, the whole herd was ambling after us. After forty, they were stampeding. I took the emergency step of charging back towards them, shouting and waving my arms. It was enough to stop them in their tracks and, eventually, send them back where they came from. We then trotted very slowly towards the stile in the far corner, trying to give the impression that we weren't moving. When we were halfway there I noticed that one of the beasts had failed to retreat and was looking at us intently. I also noticed that it was a bull.

We edged away more slowly than ever, and I tried to make it clear through my body language – don't ask me how – that I had no interest in his harem. We reached the stile without incident. I always treat bulls with respect, because an angry bull can kill. But short-tempered bulls are not supposed to be kept in places where there are public rights of way, and I've never yet met a bull that wasn't placid.

I can't say the same about cows, especially if they have calves and you have a dog and there is no bull to act as a calming influence. Out and out attacks are rare but do happen: around sixty people are injured by cows each year in the UK, and on average at least two will be killed. In twenty years of rural running I've never felt in serious danger, but I have encountered some degree of aggression on perhaps half a dozen occasions. My golden rules are as follows:

(1) If you have a dog and you come under attack, let it off the lead. The cow is almost certainly more interested in the dog than in you, and the dog is almost certainly more agile than the cow.

(2) Don't run away. Back away slowly towards an escape point, if there is one nearby, but don't run. Keep your eyes on your aggressor, and at all costs stay on your feet. (This applies to confrontations with most animals, including humans.)

(3) Better still, counter-attack. It may not always work

with humans, but a cow will almost invariably back off if you charge towards it rather than standing meekly while it charges you. Close up, jostle, barge and punch as you see fit. You won't hurt the cow, but you might succeed in giving the impression that you're in charge. Cows aren't known for their courage or independence.

This counter-attacking rule applies even more infallibly to bullocks. I wouldn't quite go so far as to say that they are harmless. If you panic, run away or fall over, things can turn nasty. If you don't, however, you should be fine.

As it happens, there were bullocks in the next field but one: the big, rough, sloping one that backs on to Plumpton church. This particular group were barely more than calves: half as bulky as they might have been but twice as frisky. We improvised another diversion, hugging the hedgerow furthest from them, but they spotted us before we were halfway round, and caught us up while we were still fifty metres or so from the exit stile. I stopped them in their tracks with a counter-charge, but each time we resumed our course they rapidly worked up a new mini-stampede. It seemed to be the only available strategy: twenty steps forward (mainly downhill) and fifteen steps back (uphill), for as long as it took. It was, if nothing else, good exercise, especially as each bout of fifteen uphill steps was taken at a fairly aggressive sprint. I've been through this ritual many times, and I'm sure it's been good for my fitness. The secret, as I see it, is to identify the bullock that's leading the charge (there's always one) and punch it hard on the nose. You never actually get close enough to land that punch, but if the intention is genuine enough then the bullock will always back down. And once the stampede leader loses his nerve, the rest of the herd will do so, too. There's no more moral fibre in a bullock than there is in an adult cow.

By the time we'd finished running that particular bullock gauntlet, my doubts about my fields-are-better-than-roads philosophy had returned. This was ironic, because I had begun the run feeling rather pleased with myself about my enlightened approach to rural running. My self-satisfaction was fuelled by the memory of a car journey to Oxfordshire the previous morning. We had passed a succession of brightly clad road-runners, each on a relatively busy road, two out of three wearing headphones, one wearing sunglasses and all three wearing the glazed expression of people whose main concern was to keep up the pace and rhythm. This struck me as grotesque. Had none of them noticed the fresh green countryside around them? Were they really so blinkered that they weren't tempted by the footpaths, bridleways and fields on all sides – preferring to limit themselves to traffic, exhaust fumes, tarmac and the sound of familiar music?

Now those complacent thoughts came back to me. The three miles – at most – that Nutmeg and I had covered so far that morning had taken probably half as long again as they would have done on roads. We'd suffered nettles, thistles, brambles, barbed wire and flies, and repeatedly been exposed to potentially life-threatening bovine danger. Was it really so obvious that the road-runners I'd scorned the previous day were the misguided ones?

Instead of answering this question, I forgot it. I didn't mean to: it just slipped my mind. We were running now on the rough, springy turf of a cattle-free field. Birds were singing, the scent of unseen blossom was in the air and I could almost sense the grass growing in the sunshine. Happiness spread through my being like warmth. Within minutes, it was as if none of the morning's difficulties had taken place. I could both hear and see a soothing breeze gently ruffling the heavy-leaved treetops up ahead. If I put my mind to it, I could discern a distant hum of traffic. I didn't feel the slightest urge to be running amongst it.

It probably helped that Nutmeg had remained unperturbed by our altercations with the local livestock. My previous running companion, a Labrador called Hawthorn (still alive at the time of writing but far too old to run any more), used to bark ferociously when cows or bullocks attacked, which rarely calmed the situation. Eventually, I learnt to release him at the first sign of trouble, and he, in turn, learnt to scarper.

With horses, however, it was the other way round. Any we met would be happy to make friends with Hawthorn and he with them. Nutmeg, on the other hand, is liable to be freaked out by them, probably because we encounter them only rarely. Luckily, her standard response to such shocks is flight rather than fight.

As a runner, I have two rules for dealing with horses. First, never overtake a horse without warning. If it hasn't heard you coming, and you suddenly appear, at speed, in the corner of its eye, it will panic. So call out well in advance until the rider, at least, is aware of you. The other rule, for when a horse or horses can see you coming, is simply to show your back. I suspect that this is unscientific nonsense, but I once heard it from a self-described horse-whisperer and it has always worked for me – so far. The idea is that, if a horse can see another creature running towards it head on, it may feel threatened. But if you appear to be approaching obliquely, laying yourself open to easy counter-attack by exposing your side or back, then you can't be attacking. So when I run towards a horse I always twist my torso until the back of one shoulder is visible from the front and I seem, from the horse's perspective, to be looking at it over my shoulder. A few friendly words never go amiss either. It may, as I say, be nonsense, but my one other piece of horse lore – that a horse puts its ears forwards when it's happy and backwards when it's not – suggests that it works.

That's probably enough animal advice for now. None of it is based on expertise, just on experience – and I strongly advise you to work out your own policy on such matters. Developing a working understanding of the farm animals – and farmers – with whom you share the countryside is a vital part of the rural runner's experience. That experience will vary for everyone, but the underlying point applies everywhere. The countryside isn't just an amenity for runners. It's a complex organism that has evolved over the centuries in conjunction with human society. Agriculture is part of the fabric of the landscape, and if you don't engage with it you won't really be engaging with the land you're running on.

I suppose that's also why I like running with a dog. Not everyone does, or is lucky enough to have regular access to countryside where it is possible to run freely with a dog in a natural environment. Some simply dislike dogs; others like them but find them disruptive to running. I've always felt that any disruptions are outweighed by the rich extra dimension that a four-legged companion adds to the rural running experience. I'm not just talking here about the average dog's cheerful can-do approach to the hazards and discomforts of the land, nor about the motivating power of the dog's relentless requirement to be exercised every day; nor about the broader benefits of sharing an important part of your daily routine with a loyal and enthusiastic companion. It's more that the dog provides an extra way of understanding your surroundings:

an extra pair of eyes and ears, a different world-view, and a nose a million times more sensitive than yours.

I like it best when there is no livestock around and Nutmeg is running free, pursuing her own agenda but also keeping close to the focal point of the running pack, as dogs do. I can sense, indirectly, what she is sensing; and she, in turn, must have a vague impression of my more cerebral observations. There is something therapeutic about engaging with the thought processes of another species. That, I'm told, is one of the attractions of proper fox-hunting: trying to second-guess the fox (although I don't quite understand why it's necessary to kill it as well). Running through the same few square miles of countryside, week in, week out, I gradually build up a sense of which creatures are living where and when and where I'm most likely to spot them. The older I get, the better I get at reading such signals – tracks, for example. But it's interpreting Nutmeg's behaviour that teaches me the most. I can't smell what she can smell, but I can notice much of what is being revealed to her at the level of scent. Alone, I am as blind to that information as she is to the information I glean from looking over hedges and into distant fields. Together, we see something closer to the full picture.

But that's just what running with a dog means to me. It's equally possible to take a more familiar modern path and turn the activity into an act of consumption, by buying into the canine sub-sector of Big Running (Big Walkies?). If that approach appeals, a quick visit to www.canix.co.uk should have you sorted out in no time – just make sure you have your credit card handy. The website offers not just pages and pages of technical and safety advice and details of 'Cani-cross' races but also the chance to buy a whole range of specialist gear for running dog-owners.

I looked it up after driving past a runner on a main road who had a husky attached to her waist by some kind of lead, leaving both her arms free to pump vigorously while the dog ran on ahead. Items on offer that afternoon included the Euro dog-running harness (£38.30), which you attach to your dog and then, via a CaniX Line (£34.04), to your 'top-of-the-range' fleece-lined and padded CaniX running belt with integrated bungee and sewn-in stainless steel lightweight quick release, removable leg straps and high-visibility reflector strip (just £97.87), which you could accessorise with a CaniX running vest (£38.33), CaniX running shorts (£9.37), a Running With Dogs sticker (£3.19) and a CaniX Coolmax hi-tech black sports cap with CaniX logo incorporating a 100 per cent Polyester Coolmax© fabric sweatband, mesh ventilation panels, 360° Hi-Viz binding and Rip-Strip™ size adjuster (one size; £19.57). No doubt it will all have got more sophisticated by the time you read this.

Meanwhile, if you don't want to be seen as a heartless cheapskate towards your dog, you might want to buy some Toughtek dog booties, to protect it from getting its paws muddy. These are just £8.51 for two, although I wouldn't have thought that that would be enough for the average four-legged friend. And then, since you've ploughed so much money into the thing, you'll probably want to spend a bit more on joining the running-with-dogs 'community'. In 2013, membership of CaniX cost a very reasonable £27.50 for your first year, while entry to CaniX races was an additional £16–£19 a time.

Alternatively, for anyone who's worried that even that might be a little bit too rugged and adventurous, there's always the option of spending between £870 and £7,795 on a Fit Fur Life dog treadmill. Sammy French, an entrepreneurial runner, breeder and trainer based in Haslemere, Surrey, originally developed this for rehabilitative veterinary use, but recent marketing has emphasised the benefits for general canine fitness, weight loss and 'pre-show conditioning' ('Gain optimal appearance . . . Avoid lengthy grooming during bad weather . . .'). Celebrity enthusiasts include Pudsey, 2012 winner of *Britain's Got Talent*; and James Caan, who invested £100,000 in the company after Sammy took the concept to *Dragons' Den*. Apparently the treadmills are better than walking for ensuring that your dog builds up muscle evenly. I'm not sure that they can be quite so good for mental stimulation, though.

But it all depends on your prejudices. Once again, mulling these matters over for much of the latter half of that May morning run, I tried to think dispassionately about the relative merits of field, track, road and treadmill. As I did so, I wondered if I was becoming a rural running snob. I had leapt to the conclusion that all those road-runners I'd driven past were misguided; I had decided no less unthinkingly that it was self-evidently absurd to buy your dog running shoes or make it run on a treadmill. Yet what right did I have to be so superior?

Presumably there were people who would look at me now and think it equally self-evident that the absurdity lay in a different direction. Look at me: muddy, sweaty, stung, scratched and numb-toed (I'm not quite sure how that last one happened); keeping a little corner of my mind alert to the risks of attacks by farm animals; absent-mindedly passing Nutmeg's lead from one hand to the other every now and then; gazing up at the treetops, then sniffing curiously as I wonder if the foxy whiff I've just noticed in the air is the same scent that Nutmeg's been excited about for the past few minutes; almost falling over as a muntjac bursts out of a pathside thicket and scurries away like a super-squirrel (foxy? Nutmeg must think I'm a moron); and then, a mile or so later, accelerating way beyond my comfort zone as Nutmeg tugs off in pursuit of another scent, slowing down only when she darts under the barbed-wire fence on my right and tries to inspect what I realise (from the white lamb's bones outside it) is probably a fox's lair... By the time we get home we'll both require serious hosing down – and as for what they're discussing on this morning's *Today* programme, I haven't a clue. I'm too busy wondering how long those bones have been there – at least until I'm distracted by the sight of a plump, buzzardish bird hunched at the top of a distant tree...

You can see how such an approach to exercise might strike some people as uncivilised. And perhaps, at heart, that's what distinguishes my kind of running from... well, the other kinds of running. It's partly about surfaces: tarmac versus grass, park versus ploughed field. But it's also a question of more fundamental temperamental preferences. Smooth or rough? Urban or rural? Packaged or raw? Civilised or uncivilised? Most people will incline towards one set of choices or the other.

Of course, there's no law to say that these have to be either/or choices. You can enjoy the countryside but still enjoy and live in a city. You can enjoy the comforts of civilisation but still get a thrill from roughing it occasionally. With running, however, there seems to be a psychological barrier to sampling the 'rough' side at all – as if it were a choice between conventional running and eccentric, wrong-side-of-the-track running.

Is it the mess that deters people from the rough option: the mud and the scratches and the getting lost? Perhaps – but all runners get messy to some extent, so I doubt that it's just that. Instead, I wonder if there might be another factor at work as well: namely, the inescapable magnetism of Big Running.

Whether it's Trailblaze and its £61 a year for the privilege of running on freely available National Trails, or Tough Mudder and its commercialisation of common-or-garden mud and cold water, or CaniX and its branding of taking the dog for a run, there's something reassuringly civilised about a brand, about handing over money and receiving in exchange something packaged and labelled and new; about reverting to our familiar identity as consumers rather than free and self-sufficient human beings. It reminds me of what Ceri Rees said about people wanting someone to give them permission to step into the unknown. Buying a branded product or two seems to take the risk – the wildness – out of the process.

So it is, for example, that most people would think twice – for fear of being considered laughably eccentric – before whipping off their clothes on the spur of the moment and having a quick dip in a nearby river or lake, simply because they were hot and it was there. But call it 'Wild Swimming' – a phrase coined in 2008 by assorted publishers and soon-to-be-bestselling authors, notably Kate Rew and Daniel Start – and no such stigma would attach. Suddenly we are talking about an altogether more formal kind of leisure activity that involves seeking expert advice (get one or more of half a dozen books in the Wild Swimming series), buying equipment (you weren't thinking of going in without a wetsuit, were you – or managing without the Wild Swimming app?), making every possible risk assessment (if in doubt, consult a medical practitioner) and, not least, giving a name to the activity that makes it sound like a proper sport with rules and a governing body. It's almost as normal as paying to go to an indoor swimming pool.

The reassurance is illusory, of course. Lakes and rivers are made no safer by a label; nor is running, wherever you do it. But the craving for normality remains: the normality of the kind of running that everyone else does, the kind of gyms that everyone else goes to, the kind of kit that everyone else wears. Even when we do try running in an unfamiliar rural environment, we reach instinctively for the comfortingly familiar embrace of the running industry: the same brands, the same eye-watering price tags.

And I think what I'm proposing, in preaching the gospel of 'wild' or 'natural' running, is that we try to free ourselves not just from the tyranny of road and gym but also from Big Running's embrace. Yes, it's seductive. It's also disempowering. And while breaking free from that stifling relationship remains a frightening prospect – just as it is to break free from any relationship or behaviour that has achieved the status of normality – that doesn't mean that our lives wouldn't be richer if we succeeded in doing so. It's just a question of summoning the resolution to run into the unknown...

Those, at least, were the thoughts that were going through my head as Nutmeg and I came panting and grunting into the final muck-flecked sheep field at the end of our run – at which point I was amused to see a gang of young rams loitering under the same untidy oak tree where we'd seen them when we set out nearly an hour earlier. They were still glowering at us suspiciously, still waiting uneasily for someone else to take responsibility for what to do next; their body language – half fearful, half threatening – still that of a gang of teenage boys at a bus stop. They're just like us, I thought. And then I thought: no, that's not quite right. We're just like them.

It's natural, for all of us, two-legged or four-legged; and it applies to, among much else, running. Moving away from the safety of the herd, or staying put when other members of the herd are moving away, tends on balance to be more frightening than tempting. It's all too easy – for runners – to reach unthinkingly for the comforts of convention and consumption. If nothing else, that seems to be what most other runners do.

I think of it as The Box: like one of those big, irresistibly designed boxes that Big Running's products come in, complete with guarantee, registration card and at least one glossy leaflet full of hi-tech gobbledygook. Ideally, Big Running would like all your running experiences to come, metaphorically at least, in such boxes – that is, to be branded, designed, packaged, marketed and paid for. But they don't have to.

And what I'm suggesting, even though I'm not quite sure what it means, is that it can be quite rewarding to try Running Outside The Box.

15

Down in one

There is a ring of steel around Cooper's Hill, five miles outside Gloucester. The usual car parks are closed, with police roadblocks on the lanes leading to them. Police cars also guard key laybys nearby, while others patrol the busy main roads, warning off anyone who tries to leave a car on the verge. It's a bit like trying to get into central London on the day of Margaret Thatcher's funeral.

The nearest place you can park without harassment is two miles away. A long line of pedestrians traipses back along the main road towards the hill. There's no pavement, and several people observe that the restrictions' net effect on road safety seems to have been negative.

Others are talking about cheese. Will there be any? Will it be real? Will it be Double Gloucester? And (several times) has there ever been such a crass example of police heavy-handedness?

The past forty-eight hours have been abuzz with rumour and counter-rumour. The main facts are undisputed. For at least two hundred years, and probably much longer, an annual 'cheese-rolling' race has been taking place on Cooper's Hill. Local daredevils race down the vertiginously steep slope after a rolling cheese that usually weighs eight pounds (in modern times – some of the older ones weighed four times as much) and which can reach speeds of up to 70mph. The winner keeps the cheese. Except that, this year, there may not be any.

Reports emerged over the weekend of a visit by the police last week to Diana Smart, in the nearby village of Birdwood. Mrs Smart, eighty-six, was warned that, if anyone was injured in this year's race, she, as supplier of the cheese, could be held responsible as an 'organiser' of the event and sued for damages. A subsequent statement by the family suggests that this is a risk that Smart's Farm cannot afford to take: 'Any litigation could completely destroy our business, and it would not be in our interests to continue.'

The police insist that they haven't banned the cheese: they've merely warned the Smarts of a legal liability that has nothing to do with criminal law. They have issued similar warnings to other people who might be deemed organisers. Yet the people closest to the event insist that there aren't any organisers.

There used to be, but the official organising committee dissolved itself in 2011, unable to find a satisfactory way of dealing with an intensifying tornado of public liability and health and safety issues. The event has continued regardless, without official orchestration; which hasn't made it obviously healthier or safer for anybody.

This year, inaccurate rumours that the event has been banned have led to a surge of public interest. Notwithstanding the police blockade, getting on for 5,000 people have made their way to the hill on foot, many walking all the way from Gloucester. I speak to several people who have come more than a hundred miles to get there. 'We'd never heard of it until yesterday,' says a young woman who's driven down from Stafford with a friend in a forty-year-old Fiat 500. 'We heard they were trying to ban it,' says the middle-aged father of a family from Coventry. 'So we thought we'd better come and support it.' They're not the only ones.

A long uphill trudge through the woods from the road brings us, eventually, to Cooper's Hill itself. Most of the pilgrims cram themselves into the narrow spaces up the sides of the main slope, between a flimsy fence and the woods on either side of the clearing. A few, including me, continue to the top of the hill.

It is, by any standards, a dramatic hilltop, surrounded by trees on three sides but with an awe-inspiring view to the north, right across the Vale of Gloucester to the Malvern Hills. Yet the view that causes sharp intakes of breath is not ahead but down. It's not quite a cliff, but it's the next best thing: a ninety-metre slope whose gradient allegedly averages 1 in 2 (although my calculations put it nearer 1 in 1).

I imagine that, if you took an Olympic-sized ski-jump ramp, replaced the snow with thick, rutted, crumbling mud, and then covered the whole slope with tangled, knee-deep grass, you'd get pretty much the same effect. Here, though, the idea isn't to ski down it before soaring into a giant void of mountain air. Instead, we are supposed to sprint down it, then somehow slow ourselves down on a ten-metre patch of flat grass before crashing into a lethal looking combination of wire fence and spiky hedge – or, if we're lucky, getting tackled by one of a line of local rugby players (not organised, I emphasise) who just happen to be waiting at the bottom.

I say 'we', but it's far from clear who will be doing the sprinting. A spindly fence divides the hilltop from the slope, with a gap in the middle of it and a hand-painted banner

– saying 'Brockworth Thanks You' – strung across the gap. (Brockworth is the nearest proper village to Cooper's Hill.) A harassed looking thirtysomething man called 'Chris' – not his real name – guards this gateway. 'We're only allowing 15 people in each race. Otherwise, if someone gets hurt, we might get sued.'

I thought there weren't any organisers to sue.

'There aren't,' he says. 'But we still don't want to get sued.'

Is there going to be cheese?

'Oh yes.'

Where from?

'Well...Let's just say, it's here. There's a sort of underground.'

Chris, who's from Brockworth, has a can of beer in one hand and a small megaphone in the other. Most of the Brockworth lads on the hilltop seem to be carrying beer cans, apart from one, dressed as a pirate, who swigs from a large flagon of cider. 'You'll need a bit of this,' he says, offering it. 'Helps you stop thinking.'

But I am thinking. I'm thinking, first of all, that the slope looks steeper in real life than it does in photographs and video footage.

I'm also thinking about the video footage itself: sturdy young men bouncing down the hill like rag dolls; bodies tumbling, flailing, skidding and crashing; rips and bloodstains appearing from nowhere in jeans and hoodies; injured non-finishers limping away in shock. I've winced less watching boxing matches.

I'm thinking, too, that everyone else on the hilltop is at least fifteen years younger than me. Most are thirty years younger. They'll heal quickly enough, if anything goes wrong. What about me? One of the joys of my 'slow running' philosophy has been that, in marked contrast to my Fourth Age of Running, I seem to spend next to no time injured. Do I really want to go back to the bad old days of moping in bandages for weeks, unable to run? For a fifty-three-year-old, a typical cheese-rolling injury could take months to heal...

Last but not least, I'm thinking that, assuming there are the usual three men's races, a limit of fifteen people per race will leave most of these would-be runners without a race.

There's a while to go before the start (generally agreed to be midday), so I put my mind at rest with a couple of practice runs: one tentative, one medium-paced. It's not as bad as it looks. Or, at least, I've been down worse, in the mountains. True, the hillside is badly eroded, with holes and ridges and miniature cliffs hidden in the long grass. In some places the turf gives way beneath your feet; in some it clings to them; in some it does neither. But, on the plus side, there are no rocks to land on if you fall; and I find that I can get down quite quickly with no greater mishap than a little controlled skidding. How I'll manage going flat out, with flying bodies all around me, remains to be seen. But at least I know that the slope itself is manageable.

Back at the top, as midday approaches, the crowd of would-be runners is growing bigger and rowdier. It's an odd mix of tourist hotspot and football crowd: getting on for two hundred people now, mostly male, still decades younger than me and, in many cases, considerably drunker. The 'tourist' element includes people from Japan, New Zealand, Australia and the USA, including several in fancy dress (a panda, a ninja, a Stars and Stripes morph suit); the football crowd tendency is largely local. A youth who seems a little unsteady on his feet starts a chant of 'Let's go fucking mental', which peters out fairly quickly. Cans, fruit and abuse are thrown in various directions. A TV helicopter passes overhead and is greeted with rude and derisive gestures. Then the unsteady young man shouts skywards: 'This is Brockworth. You'll never take this away from us. This is all we've got!'

Meanwhile, minute by minute, the crowd is pressing closer to the starting gate. Those of us near the front are being crushed and pressed downhill. The flimsy fence bulges under the weight, and Chris becomes increasingly stressed in his attempts to persuade people to get back. The potential for disaster is obvious, and I feel more alarmed by the prospect of being crushed by a combination of massed humanity and gravity than I do about racing down the hill. But it's hard to blame the organisers, because there aren't any. Once again, the net effect of the health and safety crackdown seems to have been to expose the public to more danger.

I'm wedged against a young man from Gloucester who had been planning to chase the cheese but has been put off by the TV cameras. He's in the final months of a marketing degree and is worried about finding a job after he graduates. 'What if I get on television and an employer sees it?' I say that, if I was an employer, I'd actively welcome someone who had the guts and gung-ho spirit to chase a high-speed cheese. But that's not how he reads the job market. 'It's basically impossible to find a job as it is. I can't take any risks.'

And then . . . Well, after that it all goes downhill. After much jostling and arguing, and further alarming surges from the crowd behind, fifteen runners are chosen to line up for the first race. The cheese is released – although it turns out that it isn't a real cheese but a 'safe' foam substitute, which trickles halfheartedly down most of the hill. There are several fallers but no spectacular prangs. The man in the morph suit

– a twenty-seven-year-old Colorado estate agent called Kenny Rackers – is declared the winner and is mobbed by cameramen.

A second race follows, using a second 'cheese'. A thirty-year-old Australian, Caleb Stalder, takes the cheese. The mid-race carnage is more alarming this time, and one faller – the unsteady youth mentioned earlier – takes several minutes to get back to his feet. Then comes a ladies' race, won by sixteen-year-old Lucy Townsend from Brockworth; a children's race; an uphill race; and a third downhill race, which is won, to great acclaim, by Ryan Fairley, a twenty-three-year-old builder from Brockworth. Again, at least one faller needs extra time – and help – to get off the hill.

Back at the top, tempers are fraying. The entire crowd, along with the starting line and most of the fence, has slid a yard or two downhill, and with each advance the downhill pressure of gravity intensifies. People begin to slip under the fence to get to the starting line. An increasingly fraught looking Chris – helped by another unofficial organiser called 'Sara' – pleads with people to get back. He also tries cajoling, shouting, gesticulating and swearing. Some take no notice; others try to comply but are unable to move. One or two seem to forget that no one has actually paid to take part and that Chris is no more answerable to them than they are to him.

A third 'non-organiser' arrives: a man in rugby kit whose *nom de fromage* I don't catch. Further races are promised – as many as necessary – which calms things a little. All the 'cheeses' have been used up, but one of the winners is persuaded to lend his. Not that it particularly matters, since the cheeses roll so badly anyway. A fourth race sets off. Once again there are some spectacular falls in the mid-section, where the contours draw people into a bottleneck on the right-hand half of the course. I'm given a place on the starting line for the next race.

But there's a delay. One of the fallers hasn't got up. He isn't completely motionless, which is reassuring, but he seems to have a problem. Then he holds up one of his legs and gasps ripple through the crowd: the foot is pointing in completely the wrong direction.

I'll cut the rest of the story short. The man has to be helped off the hill – obviously – and – naturally – great care has to be taken not to injure him further. But the degree of care is breathtaking. Barely fifty metres of grassy slope separate him from the nearest bit of road (once the police have reopened it). None the less, around two hours and forty minutes elapse between the unofficial first aid person's arrival on the spot and the victim's eventual departure in an ambulance. By then, by one count, eleven emergency vehicles have been involved (one ambulance car, two ambulances, three fire engines, a fire and rescue car, two 4x4 ambulances and two police cars). Around forty-five specialists have taken part in the 'rescue', many of them helmeted, using an array of ropes and harnesses to prevent anyone from falling over. No possible risk has been taken with the safety of anyone involved.

In the meantime, seventy or eighty people who would like nothing better than to put their own safety at gratuitous risk by racing down the hill have reluctantly accepted that they won't get the chance to do so. A handful try to race unofficially down the other half of the slope, to the fury of the emergency services. Others complain loudly. Chris goes home – or, at least, downhill – in disgust. The rest drift off to cars, friends, homes or, in many cases, the pubs of Brockworth and Gloucester.

It's hard not to seethe with frustration at not having had

the full-on cheese-chasing experience that I'd anticipated; but, equally, I have no cause for complaint. In fact, I feel ashamed to have felt even momentarily aggrieved. What was I expecting? A slickly managed event? The guaranteed satisfaction of an upmarket leisure experience? A goodie bag? Not being organised – not having any organisers – is, in this instance, the whole point. If you want professional event management, you pay £100 to enter a Tough Mudder.

The more I think about it, the more inappropriate my frustration seems – implying a sense of entitlement that epitomises the runner-as-consumer mindset that I've spent much of this book criticising. No one advertised the cheese-rolling, or asked the likes of me to come along, or charged us money for doing so. It was just a local event, put on by local people for their own enjoyment as it has been for generations. The rest of us are curious outsiders, barging in. If weight of numbers has marred the occasion, whose fault is that?

Meanwhile, there is frustration among the locals, too. 'When I was first involved, we used to set it up in the morning, take the afternoon off and then come back in the evening for the races,' Robert Seex, a local farmer who acted as MC for the cheese-rolling for twenty years and was also active as an official organiser, tells me later. 'But gradually the numbers went mad. By the end, it was a right royal pain in the neck. The last year we organised it, we had traffic queuing back to the motorway.'

That year – the last time an official cheese was rolled – was 2009. According to police, 15,000 people tried to come and watch, although only 5,000 made it to the hill. Nearby lanes were largely impassable and nearly a hundred £70 penalty notices were issued for illegal parking in the area. Eighteen people were injured, of whom ten were spectators. You didn't have to be a health and safety professional to see the problem. The difficulty was knowing what to do about it.

The volunteer organising committee was bombarded with demands from police, the local authority and its then insurance company, including: a 'defined area', with fencing, for spectators; a traffic and parking plan, including road closures; and some kind of limit to the numbers attending, which would mean ticketed attendance. How this was to be financed was anyone's guess – especially since Brockworth locals objected furiously to the idea of having to pay anything to attend their own generations-old event.

'People said we had to have this, that and the other,' says Robert Seex. 'By the time we'd added up everything we needed to make it workable, we were looking at a fag packet figure of £250,000. There was no way we could make that back on gate receipts. We'd have needed a sponsor, and we couldn't get one in time. So we chucked it in.'

'On the plus side,' says a former cheese-chaser called Stephen Gyde, 'now it's officially stopped, no one will ever break my record.' Stephen, a fifty-two-year-old Brockworth-born labourer who recently moved away for the first time in his life to nearby Cheltenham, won a total of twenty-one cheeses between 1976 and 1991, including two clean sweeps (in 1980 and 1991) when he won all three races. 'I quite like cheese,' he explains. 'I just used to share it with my family and eat it.'

He attributes his success to a combination of hardiness and cunning. 'My work used to keep me fit, and I used to play rugby as well. But the secret was starting in the right position and then finding the right path to follow.' (If you're thinking of trying it, the preferred route is down the right – although recent erosion of the left-hand part of the slope means that most runners now try to squeeze into the same narrow bottleneck.) 'Also,' he adds, 'I was always sober when I did it. A lot of people used to get drunk and then break their legs. I never had worse than a few scrapes and bruises.'

Was that really all there was to it? 'Well, the other thing was that, when I was younger, I was always in trouble. I got fit being chased by the Old Bill. We used to have a thing called the Donkey Derby, too. We'd race up Ermin Street, jumping over all the hedges. If you did that nowadays, you'd be charged with criminal damage. In those days the policeman would just give you a kick up the arse.'

Drink and disorder have always helped lubricate cheese-rolling, to the obvious unease of the respectable classes. Reports from more than a century ago mention all–night revelry, 'ruffianism' and the use of the occasion to settle 'village feuds, grudges and personal quarrels' with 'sanguinary and prolonged fights'. The unruliness never quite went away, and since 1999 it has been deemed more prudent to start the event at midday – rather than early evening – to reduce the scope for pre-race drinking.

It's a familiar story. Look at any ancient 'mob' sporting event – Shrovetide Football in Ashbourne, Derbyshire, or the Hare Pie Scramble in Hallaton, Leicestershire, or the Haxey Hood in Lincolnshire – and you'll see a similar mix of themes: origins lost in the distant past; a vague association with the assertion of common people's land rights; and an attitude to health and safety that reflects the values of a rougher era, when pain and injury, though harder to treat, were somehow more easily borne. Such traditions have been kept alive by popular demand, tolerated rather than encouraged by the ruling classes; increasingly, they survive without official organisers. And, increasingly, the powers that be wish to tame them. Whether or not they are wise to indulge that wish is open to debate. Traditional wisdom suggests that one day a year of uproarious misrule can be a valuable social safety valve. But then who listens to traditional wisdom these days?

Meanwhile, the Cooper's Hill cheese-rolling has an additional difficulty. Journalists have been writing about it for a century or more and television cameras have been coming since 1952. The publicity has drawn visitors and contestants from all over the world. Fame, widely considered the ultimate blessing of modern life, has proved an insidious curse, creating a problem that may not have a satisfactory solution.

For locals like Stephen Gyde, the Cooper's Hill cheese-rolling remains primarily a local tradition. 'It meant a hell of a lot to Brockworth. Everybody used to meet up – even people who'd moved away used to come back. We'd go to a cider farm and get a gallon of scrumpy.'

He is sad to think that it may have reached a point where its long-term survival cannot be guaranteed. 'A lot of things have changed and changed for the worse,' he says darkly.

'Years ago it was mainly local people. Now people come from all over the world. I don't mind people coming: everybody deserves a chance. But it's too big. And all this health and safety stuff is ridiculous. People should just be able to organise things, and people who want to take part should just be able to sign a bit of paper saying, "I'm taking part at my own risk – if anything happens to me it's my fault."

'When's enough going to be enough? Nobody's going to be able to do anything soon.'

He may be right. But, then again, perhaps it depends on where and how you do it. On my way back to the distant car park after the cheese-rolling, I work off some frustration by running down through the woods on the side of Cooper's

Hill. Drifting off the path, I savour the challenge of the slope, the treacherous surface and the daredevil obstacle course set by the trees. It's almost as reckless as cheese-rolling, and some walkers on the path gawp in amazement as I crash past. But three little girls playing some kind of hide and chase game among the trees barely look up. They are, I realise, doing much the same as I am. So why aren't I as happy as they seem to be? Because, all the same, I can't say that I've 'done' cheese-rolling.

'It was on my bucket list,' Kenny Rackers told the television cameras after winning the day's first cheese. I suppose it was on mine, too: my list of things to tick off; things to say that I've done before I die. But is that really the only thing that matters: being able to say you've done something?

It's certainly a major part of many runners' motivation. We push ourselves because we want to be able to say that we've done a half-marathon, a marathon, a sub-three-hour marathon, a sub-sixty-minute ten miles, a four-minute mile, a Tough Mudder. That's why we want our T-shirts, our medals, our race photographs: to prove that we've done it.

It's an understandable urge, yet the older I get the more futile it seems. Living for outcomes rather than experiences works only if you avert your eyes from the inevitable final outcome (death). The precious things in life are moments: the experience itself, not the tweeting or posting about it; the doing, not the having done.

I have, for what it's worth, run down Cooper's Hill, on cheese-rolling day, twice. I don't think that counts as doing it properly, but in retrospect I'm glad of that. If I really want to chase cheese – rather than just be able to say that I've done so – I'll just have to keep going back until I get a chance. Or I could buy some Double Gloucester, get some friends together, find a steep slope, chuck it down and chase it. Either way, I already feel that I've brought back something valuable from Cooper's Hill: a new resolve to seek pleasure in running itself, rather than the bragging rights it confers.

Perhaps, in essence, that's what the Fifth Age of Running means: not ticking off achievements but doing things for their own sake. In fact, it's hard to think of a better definition of natural running. Never mind targets. Simply decide what kind of running will bring you most joy – and then just do it.

16

Nature's way

Sometimes I wake in the black of the night, cold with fear. Premonitions of despair overwhelm me, and I lie sleepless for hours, heart thumping. Yes, my life is full of undeserved good fortune. But it will take only one routine catastrophe – one simple bereavement, one everyday sacking, a bad accident, a major illness, natural disaster, war – and my cosy life will collapse. I and those I love will be defence-less against the casual cruelties of the unfeeling universe. Such catastrophes strike millions of times a day, across the planet, and the rest of us barely notice; hundreds of millions are tormented by such cruelties at any given moment; all of us succumb in the end.

How bleak the world seems; how imminent disaster. Even when I remind myself that countless daytime rationalisations have exposed such worrying as idiotic, the chill lingers. I try to sleep, but waves of fear return, like toothache.

I awake early after one such night, feeling bleak and grey as death. It is Saturday. Work has kept me away in London all week. I got home around midnight, so cold from my motorbike journey that it took an hour to warm up enough to go to bed. Then I lay awake half the night anyway, fidgeting and fretting.

It is all I can do to force myself out of the door for a run. If Nutmeg wasn't demanding it, I wouldn't bother.

I plod stiffly up the back lane, limbs half asleep, eyes half closed. The day, in so far as I am aware of it, seems pale and joyless, like cold tea. The back of my head feels as though it had been wheel-clamped.

I am still pondering the feasibility of somehow combining the act of running with going properly back to sleep when we reach the gate into the first meadow. I yawn, open it — and the world explodes into colour.

The field is shining like an early morning sea: each sharp blade of shin-high grass silver-edged with icy droplets. My sleep-cold soul recoils at the thought of it, but it is too late. Nutmeg plunges forward, dragging me with her, and the shock of the fresh dew sends shivers of life through my drowsy legs, galvanising me into alertness.

In front of me, beams of sunshine stream through the groping tendrils of the far hedgerow to bathe all the colours of the meadow in brilliant light. The rough field is luminous with variety. Strands of rogue grasses scorned by sheep stoop knee-high above the grazed green stuff, their intricate seed-heads heavy with dew and brightened from brown to dazzling gold by refracted sunlight. I must be imagining it, but it feels as though the colours are singing, harmonising with a chorus of birdsong that for some reason I haven't noticed before.

We wade through the shimmering waves of grass, and bright dew drops spray around us. I feel utterly, miraculously awake. The air is sparkling, like a silent firework display, with a thousand simultaneous silvers, golds and greens, and it seems as though heaven itself is blazing through the ragged hedgerow, whose dark-leaved trees – hawthorn, blackthorn, dog rose, hazel – wave in the mild breeze with gently bowed heads, silhouetted against the shining morning like distant saints.

As my lungs fill with the fresh scent of a June meadow, my heart fills, too, with forgotten joy. This is what has been missing from my recent life: the colour, the detail, the texture, the incomprehensible complexity of nature, inexhaustibly refreshed each day. The world has its faults, but each night ends with day, and hope floods in when morning has broken.

The further we run, the more the night's bleakness recedes. It's not that the fields we are passing through are necessarily beautiful: I imagine that connoisseurs of views would consider them dull. But there is so much to be curious about. Who's in that tree? Who made those prints? Who broke that branch? What makes the water gather halfway down this field, rather than at the very bottom of the slope? Never mind that the answers aren't important. Curiosity is life's rocket fuel.

'I have rarely met with two o'clock in the morning courage,' said Napoleon. He must have had precisely such nocturnal cowardice as mine in mind: the human heart reduced by sleep to its infantile, vulnerable essence. You certainly won't meet any two o'clock in the morning courage in me.

But seven o'clock in the morning courage? Now that's a different matter. Send me out for forty minutes or so of running through the fields, making full use of a body that has taken aeons to evolve, absorbing a million little details of the corner of the universe that actually surrounds me, and by the time I'm halfway through I'm ready for anything. Troubles? Bring them on. We're only helpless if we choose to be helpless. That's the miracle of humanity: resourcefulness; resilience; defiance; heart.

I suppose it helps that you're boosting your morale with a

little achievement, which is part of the appeal of running – and part of the additional appeal of running in rough countryside. If you've jumped a ditch, or splashed through an icy puddle, or shooed off some bullocks or run up a hill, or simply been out in the fields while most other people are still in bed, you can't be the total no-hoper your night fears implied.

There's also a boost to be had from the act of taking the plunge: into the weather, or into the discomfort zone created by aching muscles or joints. All runners know this; but, again, there's an extra boost when what you're plunging into is the muddy otherness of the natural landscape, rather than the sensible lines of the man-made environment.

It's a bit like taking the first hit of a contest in a contact sport. You can't quite remember what it's going to be like – but it's never quite as bad as you thought. Then, plunge taken, you find yourself absorbed by more immediate matters. In a broader context, it's hard not to feel encouraged by this. The world may be full of threats and sorrow, but it's also unimaginably rich in interest, consolation and beauty. And so, perhaps, are you.

On this particular morning, I am especially aware of the ground beneath my feet. Everything about it – the springiness, the sudden density of the bright green grass emerging through last year's pale, flattened tangle, the indefinable sense of crisp-ness, the slight warmth underfoot, the fact that it is moist but not slippery – seems perfect for running. The air feels alive with the sense of soft, young vegetation, and it is hard to believe that this ground can be having any impact at all on my joints. This is despite the fact that (again, in contravention of mainstream expert advice) I'm not wearing running shoes.

Instead, as usual, I'm wearing what my children call 'froggy feet' – a phrase that will suggest more to some readers than to others. It is – to explain briefly – a long time since I ran in footwear with more than the thinnest of soles. For fell-running I used flat, uncushioned shoes with rubber studs (Walshes), and in recent years I've done nearly all my running in Vibram Fivefingers – one of several brands that allow you to do what is popularly known as 'barefoot running'. These are, in effect, rubberised socks or foot gloves, barely thicker than rubber washing-up gloves. There are five individual toes on each one, but no cushion, midsole or heel. Common sense suggests that they will be considerably more painful to run in than conventional trainers. In fact, if you run on the balls of your feet, as nature almost certainly intended, the shock absorption is provided by the complex structure of your feet. Landing on your heels, which is what conventional trainers encourage us to do, is so uncomfortable as to be almost impossible.

There is, I admit, something frog-like in the design, but this indignity is more than made up for, in my view, by their intense comfort. I love having so little between me and the ground: it makes today's run feel like an utterly different experience from those I've done recently in different conditions (waterlogged, say; or frozen iron-hard), and suggests a sense of connection with everything that is happening nearby, from seeds germinating in the earth to wild creatures weighing up the pros and cons of venturing out of their lairs.

Barefoot running has grown in popularity in recent years, but mainstream opinion still disapproves of it. 'A good pair of running shoes that suit your foot type will reduce the risk of injury,' says the NHS. 'Get advice from a specialist running retailer... The shoes' shock absorbers weaken over time, increasing your risk of injury. It's advisable to replace running shoes every three hundred miles.' 'Shoes with good cushioning

will...reduce the impact of running on your body,' says www.
runningforbeginners.com, 'and stop you getting nasty blisters
and injuries that poorly cushioned old trainers can encourage.'
And so on. It's hard to believe that anyone with the slightest
interest in running is unfamiliar with such received wisdom.
Yet I'm not convinced that it's true.

I've been a barefoot runner ever since I read Christopher
McDougall's 2009 bestseller, *Born to Run*, which includes
(among much else worth reading) a devastatingly clear dem-
olition of the case for conventional trainers. I don't propose
to examine these arguments in detail, but I will digress briefly
to summarise a dozen key points.

(1) Every year, vast numbers of recreational runners
are injured. McDougall quotes a range of between 65
and 80 per cent; the wider barefoot running lobby has
settled on a figure of 79 per cent; polls of *Runner's
World* readers in the US yield a range of 60 to 66 per
cent. The lowest estimates I've found come from two
comprehensive reviews of major studies: by W van
Mechelen in 1992, which puts it at between 37 and
56 per cent; and by R.N. van Gent et al. in 2007,
which found a range between 19.4 and 92.4 per cent.
But even 19.4 per cent would be shocking, given that
this is not a contact sport; every runner knows that
injuries are a major fact of running life. The last time
I looked, Sweatshop, the running store mentioned in
Chapter 2, sold fifty-six different products for runners
to treat their own injuries with.

(2) The cumulative probability of any given runner
still being a runner in ten years' time is just 0.71 (for
men) or 0.56 (for women), according to a 1995 study
at the National Center for Chronic Disease, Prevention

and Health Promotion. The same study found that nearly a third of runners who give up the sport cite injury as a reason.

(3) Most of these injuries (between 50 and 75 per cent) will be, in Van Mechelen's words, 'overuse injuries due to the constant repetition of the same movement'. These repetitive strain injuries typically affect knees, hamstrings, Achilles tendons, plantar fascias, iliotibial tracts and lower back. Since the 1970s, when cushioned trainers were introduced, there has been no decrease – and in some cases a significant increase – in the proportion of runners suffering from such injuries. (There has, of course, been a huge increase in the absolute number of such injuries, and in the number of recreational runners.)

(4) The more injuries runners have suffered, the more they have been prepared to pay for hi-tech shoes to protect themselves. But getting on for half a century of scientific innovation, in an industry that's worth nearly £10 billion a year, hasn't alleviated the problem of running-related injuries at all. McDougall cites a 2008 paper by Dr Craig Richards of Australia's Newcastle University demonstrating that there was not a single evidence-based, peer-reviewed study to support the claim that running shoes make you less prone to injury.

(5) There is also evidence that runners who use the most expensive trainers are more vulnerable to injury than those who use cheap ones; and that those who use worn-out trainers suffer fewer injuries than those who use new ones.

(6) Most technical developments in trainers since the

1970s have essentially been about limiting injuries or compensating for the forces that cause them. It's possible, however, that they are part of the problem rather than the solution. Bill Bowerman, founder of Nike, also created the concept of jogging: a supposedly undemanding, low-impact version of running in which, in contrast to sprinters, runners land on their heels before taking off from the front of the foot. No one ran like this before Bowerman (a) started marketing cushioned trainers that made it possible and (b) published *Jogging*, the 1967 book that started the running boom. But many sports scientists now believe that the heel-first running style actually causes injuries. This implies that Bowerman simultaneously created a product (cushioned shoes) and a previously non-existent demand for that product (from injured heel-striking joggers crying out for more 'protection' from injuries).

(7) Many expensive conventional trainers lack stability on rough ground. The thicker the cushioning, the more likely you are to go over on your ankle (as you would be if you ran in platform shoes). I've no statistical evidence to support this statement: just decades of first- and second-hand experience – and a rough understanding of the laws of physics.

(8) Runners – any runners, even the same runners switching between different kinds of footwear – are more than twice as likely to strike the ground heel-first when running in cushioned running shoes as when running barefoot. Worldwide (according to a study by Hiroshi Hasegawa et al. published in the *Journal of Strength & Conditioning Research* in 2007),

around 75 per cent of habitually shod runners are heel-strikers.

(9) We need heels to stand, to walk and, arguably, to run slowly. We don't need them for full-out running: that's why you rarely see heels on the blades used by amputee athletes. (But it's a good idea to let your heel touch the ground after your forefoot has landed, to load energy and prevent overstraining the calf.)

(10) With 26 bones, 33 joints, 107 ligaments and 19 muscles and tendons (in each one), the human foot, used correctly, is a natural shock absorber of extraordinary sophistication. The human heel isn't.

(11) In terms of nerve endings, the bottom of the foot is one of the most sensitive body parts of all, right up there with lips, genitals and fingers. Presumably nature intended us to feel the ground in some detail.

(12) Experienced barefoot runners appear to strike the ground with less impact when running barefoot than those who habitually run in trainers do when running shod. (But simply dumping the trainers won't initially reduce the impact: you have to adapt your style, which takes practice.) One theory is that we may strike the ground harder in trainers to compensate for the fact that the cushioning prevents us from feeling the ground as we would like to. In other words, the feet are seeking feedback.

I can't prove that switching to barefoot running reduces a runner's risk of repetitive strain injury, and there are plenty of reputable sports scientists, coaches and, not least, runners who insist that it doesn't. But I'm certain that it has worked for me, and I know that there are thousands of other barefoot runners out there who say that it has worked for them.

But that's not why I'm a barefoot running enthusiast. For me, it's not about health: it's about comfort, and satisfaction. Barefoot running feels better. It feels better even on tarmac (once you've retrained yourself to run in a natural way), while off-road there's simply no comparison. Grass, tracks, mud, stones, root-strewn woodland paths – they're all perfectly comfortable to run on, if you don't slap down on your heels; and the more I run on them, the more in touch with them I feel. My feet give me feedback: about temperature, moisture, weather, wildlife, crops, weeds. I'm not aware of any scientific evidence to support the assertion that the feet can feel the shape of the ground before they touch it, but that's certainly how it seems to me. Going back to running with thick shoes would be like...well, like having a shower with your raincoat on, as the old saying has it.

I suppose that, as a runner who distrusts Big Running and believes in doing things simply and cheaply, I really ought to run with completely naked feet, rather than using a product with a price tag on the wrong side of £80. I'm afraid, however, that my feet aren't quite tough enough. There are too many thorns and stones and other sharp objects where I live, and, indeed, where most people live. A foot glove won't give you complete protection, but it does greatly reduce the risk of tiresome puncture wounds.

I wouldn't use my Fivefingers on serious mountains – fell shoes are much better at gripping on steep, wet surfaces. But you can certainly use them on small, dry mountains. Shortly after getting my first pair, I spent a week on holiday in Provence and tentatively tried them on the rocky paths on the foothills of Mont Ventoux. My first impression was that I would never be able to run flat-out downhill while wearing them: the fear of landing on something agonisingly sharp would always restrain me. Then, picking my steps carefully on a slow, tentative descent through a forest on a narrow trail of sharp-edged rocks, I found myself face-to-face one morning with a little, furry, humbug-striped wild boar piglet. I stopped to stare at it, and two of its siblings came out to take a look at me. As the vague thought formed in my head that such vulnerable youngsters might well have a protective parent or two nearby, there was a crashing in the undergrowth. I took one look at the approaching blur of brown...and I can now say with confidence that it *is* possible for a barefoot runner to run flat-out down even the stoniest, steepest path.

What's slightly harder than adapting to barefoot running yourself is to persuade fellow runners who are unfamiliar with it that such a choice of footwear is sensible. The implication is that pretty much everything they have been told by the running industry is wrong – and that shoe manufacturers, shop assistants, magazines, gait analysts and multi-million-pound advertising campaigns have all been selling them the footwear equivalent of snake oil. Understandably, they are reluctant to accept this; and if they don't accept it, then, logically, my choice of footwear must be bonkers. I'm not interested in getting into arguments about this: I'm a runner, not a shoe expert, and I'm not on a mission to convert anyone. Yet I can't help being amused by the shock, verging on disapproval, that people sometimes express when they see what I have on my feet. It is as if I were running naked.

This is, interestingly, a similar reaction to the one I get from some runners when they realise that I run without a watch, or any other means of monitoring my performance. It is, again, perceived as a kind of indecency.

But it's not just me who's eccentric in this respect. The history of athletics is full of notable athletes who preferred to run barefoot, from Abebe Bikila to Zola Budd. And there's a growing awareness among sports scientists of the benefits of the practice. Dr Mick Wilkinson, Senior Lecturer at Northumbria University's Department of Sport, Exercise and Rehabilitation, is one of the more eloquent. 'The true benefit of minimal-shoe and barefoot running comes from the feedback received through the feet,' he told me. 'This is useful to prompt changes in technique so that we can learn – or relearn – the skill of running in such a way as to respect the mechanical structure of the body as evolution has shaped it. It is not about shoe versus barefoot: it is about skilled versus unskilled movement. And the quickest way to learn a skill is when you have plenty of feedback about when you are doing things right and wrong. That is how children learn locomotion.'

Nor is it just a running thing: Robert Macfarlane, in his absorbing study of paths, *The Old Ways*, argues that there is a 'connection between barefootedness and awareness' that is relevant to walkers, too. He cites the pioneering work of the Scottish naturalist Frank Fraser Darling, whose studies of red deer were transformed when (in Darling's words) 'I went barefoot, and after a fortnight of discomfort, I had my reward. The whole threshold of awareness was raised...' He began to perceive the landscape as the deer perceived it, and our understanding of the behaviour of herds in the wild has never been the same since.

Macfarlane, a prolific walker and adventurer, goes barefoot experimentally rather than habitually, selecting surfaces that don't seem to pose too great a threat to his (completely) naked feet. Perhaps he's mad, too, but his writing seems profoundly sane to me – not least in this summary of the benefits of direct contact between foot and ground: 'I remember the terrains over which I have walked barefoot differently, if not necessarily better, than those I have walked shod. I recall them chiefly as textures, sensations, resistances, planes and slopes: the tactile details of a landscape that often pass unnoticed.'

The appeal of 'barefoot' running is much the same to me. It's less about injuries, or running motion, than about contact with the landscape. It's about natural running – which is, I suppose, the phrase that best sums up the kind of running that I believe in.

Natural running is about far more than footwear. It's also about where you run – the obvious point being that rough surfaces require irregular movements that are far less damaging than the endlessly repeated uniform movements of road-running; and the scarcely less obvious point that running in nature will refresh and re-energise you mentally as well as physically. And it's about how you run. If you focus on the act of running itself – the movement in the moment – rather than the outcome (time, result, medal, etc.), you will not only open yourself to infinitely more mental stimulation. You should also find it easier to run with a natural, flowing movement – correcting imbalances in your action and posture – which, again, should reduce your risk of injury.

I've been pondering these matters for a while when the homeward stretch of our run brings us into a field of knee-high grass so overshadowed by trees that the sun has yet to reach it. The wetness is overwhelming: the residue of an overnight downpour that has barely begun to evaporate. I struggle through it, bringing a knee to my chest with each stride, while Nutmeg leaps pluckily in my wake. The moisture at foot level feels icy, reminding me that it won't be all that long before yet another summer is behind me. By the time we reach the far side, my toes are distinctly numb.

This reminds me of a minor drawback with barefoot running: it's not ideal for winter, or even, in some respects, for cold June mornings. Snow, ice, frost, even very cold water: they all lead inexorably to toe chill. This is not a big problem. No shoes guarantee you warm, dry feet when you run in snow, and at least with Fivefingers you get to impress your neighbours by leaving a frozen trail of barefoot footprints. But frozen feet are not among running's joys and I can't deny that, in the worst of winter, minimalist footwear increases your chances of ending up with them.

I put up with this because, actually, it's not so bad. You're conscious of the cold for a while, and then you stop feeling anything. It's only when you get home that real agony becomes a possibility. If the feet heat up too quickly – in hot water, or warm water, or even, sometimes, in the ambient warmth of a centrally heated house – you experience indescribable torture as the feeling returns, nerve ending by nerve ending. It's the worst pain I know. And the need for a post-run shower or bath makes it hard to avoid.

Luckily, there's a solution. Or, rather, there are two. The first, if you've half an hour or more to spare, is the traditional approach of reheating the feet very, very slowly: first wrapping them in dry socks, then allowing them to adjust to the warmer indoor air, then immersing them in what your taps consider to be cold water, until they have recovered enough sensation to feel that the water is cold; and then adding hot water, ridiculously slowly, until the water is warm and your feet feel normal again. It should then be safe for you to have a hot shower or bath.

The simpler solution is to have a cold shower or bath. It's less crazy than it sounds.

First: immersing yourself in cold water isn't difficult. It

can come as a shock if you're not used to it, but, I repeat, it isn't difficult. It doesn't require any special talent. You just do it and survive. And, if you make it a habit, you soon realise that it's no more 'agonising' than, say, swimming in the sea.

Secondly, it's good for you: not in the traditional sense that it's character building, but in the simple medical sense of making you healthier. Cold water immersion has been linked with a huge range of health benefits, from improving circulation and aiding muscle recovery to protecting against antioxidants, correcting hormone levels, boosting the lymphatic system, promoting weight loss (by increasing the metabolism), preventing dry skin, aiding sleep and reducing depression. The evidence is clearer in some cases than in others; but it's overwhelmingly convincing when it comes to the effect on your immune system. Cold water immersion dramatically reduces your susceptibility to colds and other common infections. (If you look it up, you'll see that some scientists believe that the real explanation is that hot water immersion *increases* your susceptibility. But for practical purposes it comes to much the same thing.)

You could probably argue that taking cold showers is character building, too, but I don't want to over-labour the point. What I will say, though, is that, like barefoot running, it works for me, on many levels. It's years since I suffered the agonies of reheated frozen foot. I can't vouch for its long-term effects on my character, but I've a strong subjective sense of the morning morale boost it gives me. You need to be in a positive frame of mind to get into a cold shower, and once you're in one you tend to remain in one for quite a while (the frame of mind, not the shower). You also get an extra morale boost when the shower is over. As for the health benefits, I'm married to a teacher and until very recently had two school-age children. Bugs and viruses come into our household on a depressingly regular basis. I escape two-thirds of them.

So there you have it: barefoot runner; watch-free Slow Runner; cold shower nut. Can my experiences and views really have anything to teach the normal, non-eccentric recreational runner? I'm not sure. Sometimes I think about it, and about the sheer number of people whose views on such matters are diametrically opposite to mine, and I begin to suspect that it's me – and not received running wisdom – that's crazy.

But then, glowing from my cold shower and looking out of the window at what seems to me like a gloriously crisp morning, I think again of all those banks of runners I've seen (and trained with) in gyms over the years. Presumably many of them were there again today, pounding away on treadmills, headphones in, top-of-the-range trainers on, before pampering themselves in hot showers and emerging, teeth gritted, into what they probably still consider to be another miserable British morning. Their idea of a sane approach to running involves spending gratuitously large amounts of cash on non-essential kit and facilities in the middle of an economic downturn in which throwing away money unnecessarily should, rationally, be considered the behaviour of a lunatic. Mine involves using a minimum of equipment, toughening up a little bit, getting back to basics and making the most of nature – one of the dwindling number of good things in life that are still free.

And I'm supposed to be the one who's mad?

17

'On, on...'

In a rough hilltop car park overhung with trees, a dozen runners are loitering and chatting by their cars. Far beyond them, the sun is slipping down into the east Devon hills. The Otter Valley, in between, is bathed in a silver glow so bright that I can barely make out the runners' faces.

It hardly matters. I'm looking for a friend called Graham Harbor, but I have no idea what he looks like – Graham being (for me) a member of that twenty-first-century sub-species: the electronic friend. Our paths crossed years ago, online, and we have kept in touch. But this is the first time we have attempted to meet in the flesh.

He has promised to introduce me to his lifelong passion: hashing – a form of running that, he tells me, is about as far as it is possible to get from the regimented orthodoxies of Big Running. 'It's probably a bit surreal if you're used to running clubs,' he's warned me. 'Competitive running is frowned upon. New shoes are laughed at. You'll need a torch and a change of clothes. Hashing routes tend to find mud and water at some point on the trail. We tend to change in the car park and then drive to the pub.' I'm looking forward to it. First, however, I must find him.

Initial inquiries aren't promising. 'Graham? Does anyone know a Graham?' The question is passed from runner to runner. Then someone says, 'Oh, you mean Gromit.'

That's a rule of hashing. No one uses their real name. No one can explain why; but that, I soon discover, is another rule of hashing: it's a sport rich with apparently random customs.

Gromit turns up a few minutes later. He's a compact, cheerful looking man, forty-one years old, in a T-shirt and floral beach shorts, with a ten-year-old son in tow whom he introduces as Ferrari. Both are wearing head torches, which seems odd, because it won't be properly dark for a couple of hours yet; but this is, it seems, essential. 'You'll see why,' says Gromit.

More cars arrive as we talk, and runners spill out of them. The dozen-strong cluster grows quickly to a crowd of nearly fifty. There's an even mix of men and women, and a lack of uniformity in appearance that suggests a wide spectrum of ability. It's not just their physiques – which range from the wiry to the … well, not so wiry – or their ages – which range from eight to at least sixty-eight. It's also their kit. Some seem dressed for extreme mountain racing; others favour baggy shorts or flared jog-pants. Several wear T-shirts bearing what I think of as their 'hash tag', although no one else uses that expression: I notice a Bogof, a Back Banger and a Flying Fokker. Footwear includes trainers, trail shoes, fell shoes and what looks like a pair of football boots.

But everyone seems to be enjoying each other's company, and by the time a woman called Grand Mattress tries to call the crowd to order the rumble of chatter is sounding like a crowded bar – which isn't, I'm told, inappropriate. It doesn't help that someone else is trying to shout above the din as well – 'Any more orders for food at the pub?' – or that several of the half-dozen dogs in attendance are joining in the clamour.

'Right,' says Grand Mattress eventually. 'Rambo's laying the trail. The on-down is at the Red Lion in Sidbury. It's good to see a big crowd here tonight. Do I see any virgins?'

A couple of us who have never hashed before are introduced and welcomed, to raucous laughter, along with one 'near virgin' who had her first hashing experience a few days earlier. Someone mutters a dark warning about 'down downs' for virgins in the pub afterwards.

Then Rambo, a quietly fit looking man in his late fifties, adds a few gnomic words of his own, the gist of which seems to be that 'There will be two long-short splits' and 'There are a lot of checks and back checks' and 'I suppose the long is about five miles'; and, again, 'The on-down is in the Red Lion'. It doesn't mean much to me, but it animates the onlookers, who respond with groans and cheers at appropriate moments.

Then someone shouts 'On, on', and the hash begins.

A hash, I have since learnt, is a run, the purpose of which is to follow a trail. It's a bit like fox-hunting, but without the fox, or the horses, or the hounds. It has its roots in the paper-chase games discussed in Chapter 12, but has evolved in its own idiosyncratic way. Its founding fathers were some British expatriates in Kuala Lumpur – generally listed as Alberto Gispert, Frederick H. Bennett, Cecil H. Lee and Frederick Thompson – who in 1938 agreed to start spending their Sunday mornings running after a man-laid trail. The Malay authorities required organised gatherings to be registered, so the law-abiding expats gave their group a name: the Hash House Harriers. 'Hash House' was their nickname for their club, the Selangor. (Accounts differ as to whether 'hash' refers to a popular item on the breakfast menu or to what they felt the club's cooks usually made of all their meals – or even, in some versions, to what was smoked there.)

The practice caught on, and, as those involved moved on to other outposts of what used to be the British Empire, it caught on more widely. The name went with it, along with the rules that those first hashers had light-heartedly laid down when they registered themselves:

'*This Association shall be known as the Hash House Harriers ... Its objectives are:*

> *(a) to promote physical fitness amongst its members*
> *(b) to get rid of weekend hangovers*
> *(c) to acquire a good thirst and to satisfy it with beer*
> *(d) to persuade the older members that they are not as old as they feel ...'*

The rest is a rather specialist branch of sporting history. The hashing habit has spread like a slow virus through parts of the world where British expatriate communities are found. It's reckoned that there are now around 100,000 hashers worldwide, distributed among 2,000 hashes in, altogether, 130 countries – although most activity is concentrated in those parts of the globe that used to be coloured red. These numbers include around 250 hashes in the UK. All figures are approximate, though, because anyone who feels like it can set up a hash whenever they want to, organise it however they like and, if they choose, let it die from neglect without informing anyone. There are no rules, no central authority or franchise – just a shared tradition whose catchphrases include: 'The first rule of hashing is that there are no rules'. I suppose you could see it as a classic 'soft' network, held together only by a loose set of ideas that different people interpret in different ways: a bit like international terrorism but based on bonhomie and *joie de vivre* rather than psychopathic hatred.

The Otter Valley Hash House Harriers (often abbreviated to OVH3) is, I'm told, one of the more serious-minded groups – which tells you something about the others. Like most hashes, OVH3 styles itself as 'a drinking club with a running problem', although not all members would identify with that label. There are some able runners among them: Gromit has drawn my attention to several – Rambo, Cousteau, Mini Bah, Mad Max, EJ, PDQ – who have serious credentials in the worlds of long-distance fell-running and orienteering. But the object of the hash is not to prove how good you are. Indeed, I am warned more than once that 'it's not a race'.

That's fine by me. Any temptation to surrender to my racing instincts is negated by the fact that I can't work out which direction I'm supposed to be running in. The hares have left a trail of sporadic marks on the ground, none more than six inches across, at intervals of perhaps thirty to fifty metres. These look like chalk but are, I'm told, flour. They come in different shapes, each with its own meaning. An arrow means 'this way'. A circle means 'check' – that is, the trail continues from here in some direction, but you'll have to look around for another mark nearby to tell you which direction. Actually, you'll have to find, usually, three arrows in a row to confirm that you've found the real trail and not a false trail. A circle with a cross inside it means: bad luck, this was a false trail, you'll have to go back and find where the real trail branched off. I think this is a 'back check'. The fact that we're in a muddy forest, with fifty runners and assorted dogs crashing around in the fading twilight, makes it far from impossible that a key flour mark may have been obliterated by ill-placed feet. Obliteration can also be caused by rain – which, patently, is not unknown in these parts. In the event of such mishaps, explains Gromit, 'it all gets a bit more interesting'.

The pack splits almost immediately in half, with the slower runners following a short trail and the rest of us the long one. Our trail takes us sharply downhill, on a narrow forest path that soon becomes a mudslide. Shortly before the bottom someone shouts 'Check' (I think), and we skid to a chaotic halt. At least, the half-dozen runners around me do. I'm not sure what's happened to everyone else.

Then people start going, and coming, in different directions – apparently scanning the area for clues – until someone shouts 'On, on' and sprints up into the trees on our left. Others follow, each shouting 'On, on' as they see the next mark. One runner – I think it's Big Jim – uses his foot to make a break in the flour circle in the direction in which the trail is heading. The runners who have been checking in other directions come puffing back to the mark, then head off in the right direction, guided either by the break in the circle or by the chorus of 'On, on' from up the hill.

I won't attempt to describe the entire hunt. I barely understood it at the time, and if I transcribed my impressions accurately it would be incomprehensible. But part of the appeal is obvious. It allows runners of very different standards to share the same adventure, each experiencing it in a slightly different way according to ability and inclination. The keener and more energetic you are, the further and faster you run: scurrying off in this direction and that in search of the trail, eyes peeled for chalk marks, then doubling back to rejoin the main pack when your line of pursuit goes cold. Those who prefer a more leisurely approach can just plod along behind, letting others do the real hunting but enjoying the scenery and the company. It's a bit like taking an energetic dog for a walk.

That last comparison is complicated, though, by the

presence of real dogs in our pack. These lope along happily and, in some cases, at a more sensible pace than some of the runners. They take some interest in the hunt, but generally seem to be pursuing their own agendas. 'They do seem to make suggestions sometimes,' says Mad Max, a small, wiry man in his sixties who is loosely accompanied by a yellow Labrador. 'But not enough to spoil the fun.' They also have their own hash tags. Mad Max's dog is called Lethal Weapon II; she's named after his previous dog, Lethal Weapon, who liked to charge through crowds of hashers, mowing them down with the giant branches she insisted on carrying between her teeth.

No one gets mown down on this occasion, although several people fall victim to tree roots and mudslides, which are hard to judge in the fading light. There are several long stretches of steep, thickly wooded slope where tangled, spiky, rust-coloured undergrowth conceals the deep mud beneath, and it's a struggle to watch your footing and your direction of travel at the same time. After a couple of checks and one long back check ('That's a bit sneaky, Rambo,' shouts an aggrieved voice), I give up trying to work out what's happening trail-wise and just jog along gently in the middle of the pack. Someone – I think it's Mini Bah – tries briefly to explain the lie of the land to me, but there are too many abrupt changes of direction for me to compile a coherent mental map.

In one place the forest breaks and we can make out the grey smudge of Ottery St Mary across the valley, wisps of white mist clinging to its roofs like cobwebs, as if it were an illustration in a book of fairy tales. Then we're back in the grey-brown underworld of forest again, with its shadows and bird calls and scents of damp leaf mould, dry bracken and dead and drying wood. A voice behind tells me helpfully that Ottery was the birthplace of Samuel Taylor Coleridge. At least, I think this was directed at me. When I turn round to see who spoke, I fall over.

Coleridge, of course, was yet another creative giant who used to stimulate his thoughts with long perambulations through the countryside. (In later years he used opium for the same purpose, with mixed results.) I wonder if he ever walked here; and, if he did, if he was too busy thinking poetic thoughts to keep his eyes open for tree roots. I suspect not. It's focusing on tree roots that keeps your mind empty for the poetry.

One odd thing about the hash is that the vagaries of the trail and the landscape constantly vary your position in relation to the other hashers. It's like being at a party where the floor keeps shifting. One moment I'm talking to Mini Bah, Cagney and Grand Mattress (who, it seems, isn't really called Grand Mattress, which is just an honorific title indicating that she's in charge of the hash, but should really be known as Free Wheeler) about the joys of fell-running and the mystery of Mr Grand Mattress's bad back, which is keeping him from running; the next we've drifted apart and I'm in a bunch that includes Mad Max and Huey, talking about the Grizzly, a notoriously tough local trail race in which several of the hashers have recently competed.

Then we emerge from the woods on to a wide slope of rabbit-cropped turf, where we all stop for a 'regroup'. Bogof, who's probably the least athletic looking of the bunch, seems as fresh as clean laundry. 'I pick the direct routes,' he explains, with a twinkle in his eye.

'That's the sea,' says Rambo, who has rejoined us, pointing to some grey roofs in the valley with a grey cloud steaming around them. 'That's Seaton,' he clarifies, 'down there, and that's the sea beyond it. At least it would be, if we could see it.'

The last stragglers arrive. Water and jelly babies are shared. People stand and sit in clusters, enjoying the rest, the sea air and one another's company. It's a strangely uplifting sight: fifty ordinary people, muddy, happy, sodden-footed and at ease with themselves, relaxing in the middle of what most people would probably consider a rather weird form of evening's entertainment. The really weird thing, to me, is the thought that anyone might prefer to be indoors watching television rather than be out here with us.

It also strikes me that, in contrast to a 'proper' running club, no one seems to be talking about races or injuries or personal bests or new kit. Instead, conversation covers such topics as someone's holiday plans, some major garden works, a mutual friend's health problems and an obscure incident of drunken excess at a party – in short, the kind of ordinary things that ordinary people talk about everywhere.

The hubbub of chatter is so loud that it's impossible to tell if there's any background sound of waves, or even seabirds – although there does seem to be a rather fed up owl hooting in the woods. But there must be sea somewhere, because the sea mist is still creeping up the steep slope of gorse below us. Some girls are arguing about where the sun is. I'm not certain, but wherever it is, it's sinking, and the colours are leaking from the hillside. Then the cries of 'On, on' ring out and the hash resumes.

Those of us following the long trail head down into the grey valley, snaking in single file through the gorse. The mist rises to meet us, and by the time we reach the woods below we are in a world of shadows. A faint twittering of birds can be heard above the crackling of feet on bracken, suggesting

that, somewhere, it must still be day; but down here it's definitely evening. There's just about enough light for running,
but not for spotting flour marks, so people begin to switch
on their head torches.

Within minutes, they're all on, as the lights destroy everyone else's night vision. I'm not normally a fan of torches, but
if you're looking for indistinct white smudges in the undergrowth in twilight they're pretty indispensable. Even with
them, we struggle to find the trail. But no one seems to mind:
the keenest runners just have to do a lot of futile rushing
around. I've long since given up trying to do more than tag
along, pleasantly aware that, with no sun and countless abrupt
turns, I have once again lost all sense of direction. All I know
is that there are trees, roots, shadows, mud and tangled undergrowth, and a reassuring scent of moss and leaf mould, and
the insistent footfalls and heavy breathing of a largely unseen
human pack, going about its benign business around me.

After a while, entirely by accident, I find myself relatively
near the front, running alongside a thin, ginger-haired man
in his forties called either EJ (his hash name) or (in real life)
Tim Gent. 'I used to be a serious competitive runner,' he tells
me. 'I'd race every weekend. I didn't win much but I always
did quite well. But after a while you just think: "I've done
that." It ended up always being me and the same four or five
runners doing more or less the same times. It was the same
every time. The order would vary, but that was all. I didn't
want to spend the rest of my life doing that.'

These days he races only occasionally. 'I'm doing a lot of
orienteering, which I enjoy. And I do this. You run in nice
places and they're a good bunch of people. The rest of the
time I just run for pleasure. You might as well enjoy doing
it, because you're not going to get any faster – although you

can always do a harder session if you're worried about your fitness.'

This reminds me that I have no idea how far we've run or how long it's taken. But I'm beginning to feel the tiniest bit heavy legged, and I'm not disappointed when someone shouts 'On, in', and Big Jim, who's running alongside me now, explains that 'On, in' means that all that remains is a straightforward run-in of about a mile back to the start. Matching Big Jim stride for stride is no easy matter (the clue is in the name), and by the time we reach the car park I feel that I've had a good work-out.

It's pitch-black by now, which is probably just as well. Fifty steaming runners strip off the worst of their muddy clothing, half concealed by cars and each other; hastily replace it with something cleaner and drier; and drive off to the Red Lion, a mile or so down the road.

The on-down is tamer than I've been led to expect. There's a limit to the amount of mayhem a group of fifty relatively exhausted people can cause when crammed into a small West Country pub. Half the conversation consists of 'Excuse me' and 'Mind your back', and it would be hard to organise drinking games without a PA system. Instead, people settle down to their pints and their meals in as civilised a fashion as space and personal hygiene permit. I'm gradually learning to match hash names with faces, but it's hard to keep track (Shameless, Mini Bah, Car Loss, Mrs Baldrick, Jelly Baby, Ferrari, Strappo, Cousteau, Drop Off, Forget-Me-Not, No Name, Doris, Troy, Huey, Free Wheeler, Spocky Bits, Cold Bits, Brambleballs, Legs Akimbo ...) Many of the names have stories behind them, some more repeatable than others. Examples include Huey (threw up after his first hash), Mini Bah (got carried away in a hotel), Car Loss (couldn't find his car) and – although not present this evening – Dumbarse, who arrived at his first hash saying that he was determined not to do anything stupid, 'so that I don't end up with some dumb-arse name'.

You get the idea. In many hashes, the puerile humour seems more important than the running, with drinking games a close second. Check out the endless hashing sites on the internet and you'll see what I mean. Indeed, you'll risk being overwhelmed with 'fnarr fnarr' names – Purton Perverts, Pissed Up Pensioners, Mountin' Sheep – and double entendres and tales of drunkenness and crudity. Overseas hashes, in particular, place great emphasis on the saloon bar rituals. One runner I know who travels a lot to cities where hashing thrives describes it rather coldly as 'fine if you've got that amount of time on your hands'. Another friend, a keen runner who works in Hong Kong, dismisses his local hashers as 'tossers' who 'just jog a bit and then drink heavily'. If you hate beer, it's possible that hashing isn't for you; and there are clearly some US hashes that could prove irritating to those who don't like drinking songs with obligatory hand gestures.

A substantial part of me feels that, if I'd wanted to spend most of my evenings in the same handful of favourite pubs, endlessly repeating the same jokes and rituals with the same friends, I'd have stayed in the rut I was in before I started running. But it would be ridiculous, and missing the point, to be judgemental. The point of hashing is that people can make of it what they choose. It's about running for pleasure and for company rather than performance; and the role that drinking, rituals, double entendres and anything else play in that process is entirely a matter for the individuals concerned.

In any case, it's hard to see anything rut-like about the Otter Valley Hash House Harriers, where the sport's arcane social codes seem incidental to the evening's real business, which is simply a group of like-minded people, of disparate ages and backgrounds, getting together to share a common enthusiasm for rural running and one another's company.

Everyone I speak to in the Red Lion enthuses about hashing, but it clearly means different things to different people. For some (such as Free Wheeler) it's a once a week light relief from more serious training. For others, it's the only sport that matters. Gromit, for example, runs not only with the Otter Valley H3 (on Thursdays) but also with Ashburton (on Tuesdays, along with his wife, three sons and three stepdaughters) and, sometimes, with Teign Valley (Mondays), South Hams (Wednesdays) and – 'when there's a full moon' – Devon Lunatics. (Many hashes have a full-moon theme.) Bogof, similarly, hashes with Teign Valley and Ashburton as well as Otter Valley. It's a struggle sometimes to get away in time from his work, at a post office in Torquay, but he thinks it's worth the effort, and his fellow hashers seem to appreciate it. Ashburton gave him a 'Hasher of the Year' trophy, which doubles as his toilet seat.

For Mad Max, who has travelled widely over the years, it's a way of meeting like-minded people wherever his work happens to take him. 'I first came across hashing in Bahrain,' he explains. 'I was in this hotel and suddenly I bumped into an old colleague in the foyer. He said: "Are you here for the hash?" I thought: "What have I got myself into?" But it turned out to mean going for a run and then going back to the bar. There were a lot of down-downs that night.

'There are big differences from hash to hash, I think the British ones tend to be a bit more sober than some of the expat communities. Mind you,' he adds, 'some of the Scottish ones are pretty hard-core. There's one near Aberdeen that I've done. Oh dear...'

Much of the talk in the pub is about future hashes, which can only happen if the hare-raiser – usually Doris – succeeds in recruiting suitable 'hares' to lay the trails. Everyone is expected to do their bit, as long as they know what they're doing – which is a rarer qualification than you might expect. The most satisfying trails are laid by people who understand the landscape in question intimately, and can anticipate how the pursuing hounds will react to it. They also need to be clued up about which land they have the right to roam on and what is out of bounds, as well as practical issues such as car-parking, regroup points and the need to keep well away from busy roads. Above all, they need to be persuaded to commit to laying the trail in a particular place on a particular date. 'The trick,' says Bogof, who is hare-raiser for Ashburton, 'is to ask people when they've had a couple of drinks – but not when they've had so many that they won't remember the next day.'

There's no sign of any memory loss tonight – the drink-driving laws and the prospect of work the next morning put a brake on the drinking. In fact, I'm beginning to suspect that, for many, the boozy talk is largely bravado. But I think it may be a rather important kind of bravado: the language through which hashers assert that they run in pursuit of pleasure, not of personal bests. Or not the usual kind of personal bests. A few weeks later, Gromit tells me proudly that he has just done the Salcombe Marathon, a multi-terrain coastal race of (thanks to landslides) nearer twenty-eight miles than 26.2. The course passes several pubs on its way from Slapton Sands to North Upton. 'We stopped for a pint at fifteen miles and another at twenty-three miles. It was great fun, and two pints beats my previous PB of one and a half pints!'

If you're steeped in the values of Big Running, you may

feel queasy at the thought of such an accomplishment. Yet it is, I think, an admirable one, which has less to do with beer per se than with a defiantly happy-go-lucky approach to life and running.

It echoes, too, some rather different kinds of running that have been growing in popularity in recent years. You may, for example, have come across Park Runs – an international series of organised, free-to-enter five-kilometre events, which make as big a deal of the community and companionship they offer as of the actual race – or, more recently, assorted urban 'night runs', such as the women-only We Own the Night ten-kilometre run, the Energizer Night Run, or the Electric Run series, which aim to combine the characteristics of a race with those of a party. Lights, lasers, installations, glow-sticks, smoke machines and high-tempo dance music feature heavily. These are as metropolitan and modern as hashing is muddy and old-fashioned, but the emphasis on the social side of running – the party rather than the performance – is much the same.

There is, of course, a crucial difference. These new events are Big Running's version of companionable running. Park Runs are sponsored by (among others) Adidas and Lucozade Sport; the 2013 We Own the Night was sponsored by Nike and *Elle* magazine. Visit the websites for either and you'll be left in no doubt as to the vision of running being sold. Contestants in We Own the Night were offered not just a 'six-week personalised training programme' and a Nike fitness app to track time, distance, pace and calories burnt but also the opportunity to buy a whole 'collection' of fashionable and expensive running kit. And signing up for a Park Run without repeated exposure to the sponsors' messages requires considerably more digital ingenuity than I possess.

This is running as consumption; the runner cultivated as

a valuable customer. The fact that such events are 'completely free to enter' (as several people have breathlessly enthused to me) seems unremarkable, given what contestants are expected to spend on sponsors' products in the long term, and the fact that, er... running is free anyway.

But my sneering is neither here nor there. What matters in this context is not the commercial motivation behind such events but the trend that makes them succeed: the public appetite for a way of running that is about 'us' rather than 'me'.

And in this respect I think it might be me who deserves to be sneered at. For it has, I now realise, been far too long since my running was about anything but me. In fact, there was a time – somewhere in my Fourth Age of Running, when all that mattered was squeezing out every last drop of my athletic potential – when I turned my back, deliberately and shamefully, on the human side of my sport.

It wasn't all my fault. Some of my best running companions moved away; others succumbed to injury and age. But there was also a half-conscious realisation on my part that running with friends slowed me down. Better to do most of my running alone, I decided, than to risk compromising my training with too much faffing about and waiting for people to catch up.

In terms of my approach to running at the time, it was a wise decision. Perhaps, at some level, it made sense on human terms, too: much of the spiritual refreshment that comes from running or walking through natural environments depends on being alone and undistracted. But I doubt, looking back, that it enriched my life. They say that no one ever looks back from their deathbed and says: 'I wish I'd spent more time at work'. Nor, I suspect, do many people say: 'I wish I'd knocked another half-second off my PB'. On the other hand, 'I wish I'd made more time for my friends' must be one of the most frequently-expressed regrets. Running rewards us in many ways, and we are short-changing ourselves if we forget that our running companions may be the most rewarding of all.

My most vivid memory of my hashing debut had nothing to do with either the run or the pub. Instead, it was a quiet conversation in the car park with a tall, hollow-cheeked man called Dirtband, who stood back slightly from the other runners. We got talking, and before long he told me, in a slightly apologetic voice, that his son, Tom, had been killed a few months earlier, in an avalanche in Scotland. Three of the friends he was walking with, in the mountains near Glencoe, were killed with him. He was twenty-eight.

Dirtband's voice tailed off. Then he said: 'The only thing that's been helping us to get through this has been all the warmth and support we've been getting from the amazing group of people in this hash.'

18

The brown stuff

You can't be a rural runner for long without noticing the limitations of the word 'mud'. There are so many contrasting varieties – each with its own consistency, depth, colour, smell and effect – that it feels ridiculous to be expected to use the same bald three-letter word to describe them all. The Yupik people of central Alaska have at least fifteen words for snow, while the Inuit are reputed (unreliably) to have dozens. You can see why they might need them. Shouldn't we British have a comparable number of mud words?

Those of us who feel strongly enough about this to look into it are taken aback to find that, in fact, we have, or used to have, a vast repertoire of such words. The Second Edition of the *Oxford English Dictionary* lists more than sixty, and there are plenty of local dialect words beneath the official radar. The Sussex dialect is said to have more mud words than any other – there are at least thirty in the Reverend W. D. Parish's 1875 dictionary – although I'm not sure why: I think of Sussex as a well-drained, chalky county. Thomas Sternberg's *The Dialect and Folklore of Northamptonshire* (1851) mentions at least a dozen from my own county, although I may have missed some.

Tot them all up and we must have getting on for a hundred words from those sources alone. My favourites include *clag* (mud entangled in sheep's wool), *clart* (sticky dirt), *drownings* (boggy fens), *galls* (wet and moist patches of land), *gubber* (black mud of rotting organic matter), *plash* (a giant puddle), *quag* (a bog or swamp), *rile* (liquid made muddy with disturbed sediment), *sadland* (earth saturated with water), *slab* (wet or slimy matter; ooze or sludge), *slamp* (wet, boggy earth), *slather* (thin mud), *slumgullion* (mud in a mining sluice), *sleech* (mud deposited by a river), *slub* (soft, thick, sludgy mud), *slurry* (mud saturated with so much water that it cannot drain), *smeery* (wet, sticky surface mud), *stabble* (mud made by footprints), *stodge* (thick, tenacious mud), *stug* (watery mud), *sullage* (filth drained off from a farmyard), *swank* (a bog), *wallow* (the filth in which swine wallow), *warp* (a mixture of fine sand and mud left on a meadow after flooding) and *wichert* (chalky mud).

Most of us go through life ignoring this wealth of choice, relying instead on the patently inadequate 'mud', a bit like only ever using the same two programmes on a fancy washing machine. Yet there are also times when I am running when, notwithstanding all the above, I conclude that the English language simply lacks the resources to do justice to the substances I find underfoot.

Cowgloop, for example. Has no one ever felt the need for a term like that? The question suggests itself on a September day when it is raining so hard that I'm wondering if my clothes might dissolve. It was raining all night, too: the thick hiss of it permeated my dreams. Now the volume has redoubled. I was waterlogged to the skin before I left the first field, and my fingers and toes must be unrecognisably wrinkled from prolonged immersion. As for Nutmeg, her fur is so flattened that she seems to have lost a third of her volume. I don't think this bothers her much, but there is perhaps a bit less exuberance than usual in her body language, as if she were simply doing what had to be done, doggedly.

It's a bit like standing under a high-powered shower. Even my lightweight synthetic leggings are sagging from the weight of it. Yet it feels less unpleasant than it sounds. By the time we reach the sloping, half-flooded path past Grumbler's Holt, I've been soaked and mud-drenched so many times that I blast down the centre of the giant puddles without a second thought. There is a limit to how wet or muddy you can get, and few feelings are so liberating as reaching that limit. The day is fairly mild, with little wind. The rain can do what it likes from now on. I'm happy to be out in it.

The fact that the ground seems to be melting beneath my feet is, if anything, a bonus. I mentioned earlier how rewarding it can be to be totally immersed in a landscape. In weather like this it feels as though the landscape were being immersed in me, or as if we were dissolving into one another; and the feeling of rightness is equally powerful.

There are, however, still practical challenges to be confronted, simply in terms of mud management. For example: there's a field corner that basically has to be waded through; and later on there's a stretch of path so narrow, slithery and uneven that I barely dare go above walking pace for fear of slipping on to the barbed wire alongside it. And then there's the cowgloop.

There is, to be more specific, a big, squarish field next to Plumpton church (the furthest point of this route) that slopes downhill, via a recurring central plash (see above) to a wooded stream and a gateway in the bottom corner that leads to other fields and, ultimately, out into Plumpton Lane. Vast quantities of water drain from all over this field (and, I think, from the one above it) into that small corner, where the comings and goings of people, cattle and farm vehicles have turned the ground near the gate into a brown no-man's-land of slippery sludge, all ruts and holes and puddles and miniature mudslides, as hard to get a purchase on as soap dropped in the bath.

It's a challenge to remain upright on this, let alone to run properly. But it is easy going compared with the wide patch a little to the side of the gateway, which slopes up towards the stile that we need to get to. This area is overshadowed by trees, and regularly frequented by cows, which go there in search of shelter from sun, wind, rain or snow. No doubt they think it's a cool place to hang out, too.

They trample this sodden soil for hours and even days at a time – 'stoaching' is the old word for this – pausing occasionally to defecate where they stand, letting the rain sink in, then stamping and urinating and stirring it all into a squelchy, slippery, foul-smelling slurry – still somehow topped with traces of grass – that is simultaneously unfeasibly liquid and sufficiently firm and glutinous to grab and suck at your footwear like a bogful of hungry river monsters.

Then, as often as not, if a group of them are standing there when I approach, they'll give the whole lot a final frenetic churn, staggering, slipping and lurching as they retreat chaotically to the higher, drier ground. This leaves me with 100 metres or so of impossibly slimy, swanky stug and stodge to lurch and stagger through myself. I suppose you could call it running, but you might not recognise it as such if you hadn't been told. It does, however, provide an intense, thorough, low-impact workout for most of my body. It takes me maybe three times as long as it would take to cover a similar distance on smooth, dry, flat ground; and yet, apart from the lack of an adequate word to describe that kind of ground (hence 'cowgloop'), I'm not unhappy with the experience.

The fact that I'm splashed to at least chest height – and presumably smelling more gloopy than would normally be considered ideal for a sophisticated metrosexual male – is, if anything, part of the fun. On the one hand, it makes me feel as though I've shaken off a few chains of adult respectability, which is always pleasant. On the other, it's all going to wash off anyway, long before I get home. The rain is coming down in such quantities that the sensations remind me of swimming. Water is streaming from the low sky in a dense curtain so heavy that it's hard to look straight ahead with my eyes fully open. My feet are running not so much on the ground as in it and I'm glad I made a special effort to strap on my Fivefingers as tightly as possible. They're a bit more vulnerable to mud suction than conventional shoes.

The last field we cross on the way back to Grumbler's Holt is the wettest of all. A mass of ploughed soil has been washed down to the bottom of the slope, forming the kind of fine, tilthy, liquid paste that you'd expect to get if you mixed 1,000 jars of smooth peanut butter with 1,000 pints of water. I suppose it's a mixture of sleech and warp, with a sadland base, although there's probably a more descriptive term to be found somewhere. Perhaps I should research and publish a proper Dictionary of Mud one day, although I imagine the market for it might be limited.

This particular mixture is, again, not unpleasant for running in, despite being nearly knee-deep in places. I tread carefully, for fear of losing a froggy foot, while Nutmeg manages – more or less – to skim over the top, gathering slab as she does so. (Later on, she can choose between being hosed down or, if she prefers, just lying on her back in the rain for five minutes.)

Further up the slope, there's a bit more grass to give the ground substance, and a bit less water. It's hard work, but at least it resembles proper running. I wonder, in passing, if there is anyone else outdoors at this moment, within a ten-mile radius, who is feeling hot.

By the time we reach the top of the slope the rain has almost rinsed me clean again – but then, for reasons I can't quite fathom, there's another area of quagmire, including a narrow mudslide, with brambles on each side, which I might have struggled to negotiate had Nutmeg not been with me. I let her climb it first and then tug myself up on her lead.

I never imagined when I first started running in the countryside, that I would come to enjoy days like these. But I do. There's something restorative about the kind of rain that seems to wash away the illusory protections of civilisation, leaving just you, a hint of sodden clothing, and nature. The cold, you realise, is manageable: as long as you keep moving, it's not so bad – always assuming you have a waterproof home to go back to in the end.

I suspect, too, that you grow used to the smells of your local fields, including your local mud. Familiarity breeds tolerance. Every now and then, I stay with friends in other parts of the country, go running, encounter their local mud, and feel faintly revolted by it. These are other fields, other woods, with different soil, the traces of different crops and creatures. The mud – the detritus of local life – is alien. It reminds me of the way that, when we're children, the unfamiliar smells, tastes and textures we encounter in someone else's home can make us feel suspicious and homesick. Do rural runners experience something similar? The mud where

I live may be filthy, but at least it's my filth. Other people's mud may be dirty.

That's another mud word for my dictionary, I think, ruminating on these matters as we retrace our steps past the wood: *pooch*, for the kind of dubious, dog-frequented mixture that I've encountered on the outskirts of certain rural towns. (No names, but you know who you are.) And, while I'm at it, *retch*, for the dark, unwholesome brew that tends to gather where rural footpaths pass under major roads. And *snelt*, for the peculiarly sticky, cold kind of mud that is left when a heavy snowfall has just melted. They may not be real words, but if I'm going to the trouble of compiling a specialist volume for mud enthusiasts I might as well ensure that there's something to cover every eventuality. Talking of which, I mustn't forget *sheep-squelch*: an ostensibly milder version of cowgloop that is left when sheep spend a long time in a waterlogged field, leaving the surface grass intact while creating thousands of tiny footprints across the entire field, each involving a deep hole where the foot went in and a volcano-like rim where it came out. Sheep-squelch is harmless enough when it's wet, if a little slippery. When it's dry, however, the mini-volcano rims harden into solid points and edges, so that running on the field feels a bit like running on a coral reef.

The more I think about my dictionary, the more potential I see for it. How could there *not* be a market for a book like that? Then I think: of course there wouldn't be. All those mud words, real and invented, are obscure and forgotten because we no longer have a use for them. Like Yupik city-dwellers who have stopped living with snow, most of us live lives in which mud no longer plays a part.

But the mud is still out there. A few fields from home, I deviate from the path slightly in order to run three sides of a freshly ploughed field. I can remember when I would have thought of even one such side as a dreadful, mountainous challenge. No matter how pluckily you started out, the combination of treacherous, yielding ground with sticky mud that weighed down your feet would reduce you to an exhausted wreck long before you reached the safety of the far side. In my early days in these parts, perhaps haunted by memories of compulsory cross-country runs in my school-days, I would avoid ploughed fields unless there was absolutely no alternative.

Now I seek them out as a treat. They are, for a start, rarer than they were, as farmers leave fields unsown for ever shorter periods. And I have long since mastered the art of running on them. Here I am now, for example, approaching the field's edge with the serious-faced apprehension of a man on his way to battle, taking a metaphorical deep breath and then launching myself into it, with long, slow, measured paces, as if performing a ritual dance. First that furrow, then that; then – oops, a collapsing ridge necessitates a last-second readjustment; keeping the pace slow enough for me to be able to sustain the pattern of never stepping on the same furrow twice; focusing intently on the few yards of mud immediately in front of me, looking for upcoming hazards and opportunities; giving no thought at all to the overall size of the field or how far across it I am; keeping my breathing in step with my leaping, breathing out on take-off and in on landing; keeping just enough muscle power in reserve to deal with the inevitable slips and sinkings; darting to left and right when the lie of the earth requires it, while remaining close to what I remember as my overall line; keeping my steps low, so as to minimise the distance that clinging mud has to be carried; occasionally dislodging large clods with a quick flick; and, throughout, remaining firm in my belief that, eventually, the far side of the field will come back to meet me.

By the time I've done the three sides (the last one uphill) I'm drenched in sweat – or would be if the cooling rain weren't washing it off as fast as it poured out – and am breathing as heavily as I know how. Jogging gently through the final homeward fields, I tell myself that that must have been at least as demanding, and fit-making, as running a mile flat out on a 'normal' surface. But I've used most of the muscles in my body in the process – and subjected my joints to next to no impact.

I've occasionally speculated, as I've become more confident at this kind of running, that someone, somewhere may organise an athletic contest in which the nation's finest ploughed-field-runners test their skills against one another – and that, if so, it might be fun to have a shot at it.

Sadly, the only such contest I've ever heard of is the Robbie Burns Goose Chase, the future of which at the time of writing is in some doubt. It was first organised in 2011 by Ron Gillies, an eccentric maker of fruit wines, on a field on his farm in Errol, Perthshire, to celebrate his combined enthusiasms for ploughed fields, Robert Burns and getting people outside and doing things together in the drab days of January. Runners competing for the Golden Haggis trophy had to make two crossings (there and back) of a relatively flat 400-metre ploughed field. It was described as a 'sprint' but in terms of stamina would probably have more in common with a mid-dle-distance event. Video footage I've seen shows deep, chunky furrows, with mud heavy and sticky enough to cause several competitors to fall over.

The first event was a moderate success, with a few local runners helping to raise a modest sum for the Royal Scottish

Agricultural Benevolent Institution; but the turnout for subsequent runs was so pitiful that, when I spoke to him, Ron was doubtful he'd run it again. 'It's a difficult time of year. Everyone's still reeling from the whole Christmas/New Year thing.' Successive severe winters hadn't helped, either.

But he was glad that he'd tried. 'When I was younger, I used to enjoy running on ploughed fields. I thought it involved a special skill set. I thought, this could be a proper sport.' One particular memory came from his teenage years – roughly the same period as mine – when he was out shooting on the farm. 'I remember winging a goose, and then chasing it over a ploughed field. That was when the idea came to me, and I kind of stowed it away in my mind. Now I wish I'd done it earlier.'

The implication is that he left it too late, but I hope he sticks with it. I'd like to try it one day, just as, one summer, I'd like to try the Maldon Mud Race, a 400-metre low-tide 'sprint' through the deep estuarine silth of the River Blackwater in Essex. Not that I'd expect to do well in either, but such events deserve encouragement.

It's interesting that the Maldon race, too, is a relatively new event, first held in 2010. There are, as an internet search for 'mud race' reminds me, plenty of slightly less rugged modern races on a similarly earthy theme, from Wild Warrior to Tough Mudder.

Does the emergence of such events imply that others share the impulses that underlie my enjoyment of mud-running? OK, so Wild Warrior's mudbaths are man-made, branded and paid for, while mine and Ron's – I would argue – are the real thing. But from most people's point of view there is little difference. If you're a city-dwelling gym-goer, going away for a day of packaged mud, water, exhaustion and falling over can quite reasonably be seen as an escape from the sanitised conventions of 'normal' life, in the same way that my solo immersions in Northamptonshire's waterlogged fields provide me with my escape.

In both cases, the very fact that we're breaking some unspoken taboo feels liberating and refreshing.

Or perhaps it's more than escape. Perhaps it's rebellion: a small but exhilarating act of defiance in a neurotically hygienic age that has forgotten how to value the age-old pastime of mucking about.

19

Birthrights

I woke before dawn and, for some reason, felt utterly refreshed. It seemed mad to get up but madder still to stay in bed. I tried to dress silently, but Nutmeg heard me so I went downstairs to let her out.

It was dark outside; or, rather, it was night. Moonlight was shining on the frost so brightly that I knew at a glance how crisp our neighbours' grey and white lawn must feel. The idea of a run seemed irresistible: now, in the moonlight, while there was all the time in the world, and the world was, to all intents and purposes, all mine.

I decided to head for Sulgrave, over the hills, on one of my longer circuits. We tiptoed out of the village, past the church, along the brambly path – and emerged into a sea of silver and blue-black. Two broad pastures stretched ahead of us, empty and immaculate, every blade of grass dusted with white, every shadow as sharp as the finest calligraphy.

The dark, metallic sky glowed with starlight, each pin-prick as bright as shredded tinfoil in the vast shadow of the night. If the moon wasn't full, it was as near to full as made no difference. It hung directly ahead, pale with age, sliding imperceptibly down to the southern horizon. It was all I could do to avoid getting dazzled by its melancholy face.

The fields were a mysterious blend of whites and greys, detail and confusion. Long, sharp-shadowed grasses blurred randomly to indistinct monochrome, and I misjudged the contours of the ground twice. Yet it all shone with ghostly silver – as though I had travelled back into someone else's life, long ago, in a dream.

Apart from the faintest of distant orange glows to the south-west (Banbury), there was no artificial light of any kind. It is hard to describe how different such a moment feels from the usual state of affairs in our indoor-focused, light-polluted world; or, paradoxically, how normal it feels: how natural and right, like the peace after the passing of a train.

The icy bite of the wet, frost-drenched grass soon shocked me into wakefulness. It would have been knee-high had the night's moisture not weighed it down into heavy clumps. I had to lift my feet vigorously, knees to chest, to avoid tripping. Nutmeg leapt and swooped, but perhaps more hesitantly than usual, as if confused by the darkness.

We were almost out of the field before I realised that there were sheep in it, deep in the frosty grass, watching us silently with their still, black faces. Their wool seemed perfectly white, as if each thread were made of moonlight.

A big stile brought us into a giant, dipping field of grass, the far corner of which has been inhabited by foxes for as long as I can remember. The moonlight was bright enough for me to take the downhill slope at a sprint.

We crossed the long track that splits the field and climbed with difficulty over a tall double stile into a series of hilly pastures that led eventually to a stream and small wood. The grass was shorter here, and I found myself sinking into a more somnolent rhythm, as if I was dreaming after all. One of the fields had cows in, but they showed no interest in us.

Owls were hooting at each other in the trees ahead. I wondered if we might see one – this was, after all, prime time for predators. But their hoots suggested that they had other things on their minds than hunting. A few grey rabbits, chomping the silver turf, showed little concern as we approached.

In the woods it was dark, and I wondered for the first time if I should have brought a torch. But I could just about find my way, moving at little more than walking speed and feeling ahead with my hands for stray branches. A creature crashed through the undergrowth ahead. Probably a badger, I concluded – despite my theory that, if you can hear it, it must be a bird or a squirrel. This sounded far too big for a squirrel, and birds don't crash about at ground level at night.

By now I could see the outline of the footbridge on the far side of the stream, and the grey light beyond. My spirits rose, as human spirits always rise when darkness begins to melt away. This is, of course, one of the attractions of early morning running. Different runners have different preferences about the times of day when they run, many of them deter- mined by commitments beyond their control. I spent many years as an after-work runner and couldn't imagine a better time for it. My body was wide awake by then, and my working day had usually filled me with tensions that it was a pleasure to run off. But when the children were little it became harder to carve out that crucial hour when I wasn't supposed to be doing something else. Getting up early seemed the best solu- tion. It took a while to overcome my lifelong aversion to the practice, but I learnt to appreciate being out in the twilight blur when wildlife is at its most active. And one particular consideration helped to convert me: mornings get better. In terms of light, in terms of warmth, in terms of how alive you feel – all the things that really matter to humans at the deepest level – an early morning always improves as it goes along. However dark it is now, it won't get any worse. In half an hour's time it will be lighter and, almost certainly, warmer. Half an hour after that, it will be better still. That's quite a morale booster, as an underlying law of nature observed every day. For rural running, it's also a practical advantage. Go out into the fields in the evening and, if you misjudge your route or your timing or the state of the moon or clouds, you can find yourself caught out in the middle of nowhere, unable to see your way home as the world becomes progressively colder and darker. Go out in the early morning and, if you can find your way for the first few strides, you know that it won't get worse.

On this occasion, as we crossed the stream on the far side of the woods, the world was still hovering between night and day. A car appeared in the lane, on the far side of the field we were entering, and I closed one eye to avoid its headlights. I hardly needed to: night vision was hardly an issue by now. But my aversion to artificial light when I'm out in the fields is emotional as well as practical. Rural nights unspoilt by light pollution are vanishingly rare in modern Britain. When I'm lucky enough to be out in one, I like to make the most of it.

In the next field, I was struck by how little colour there still was in the landscape. The sheep were monochrome, the grass more grey than green. Yet Nutmeg, who I would have expected to look paler than usual, seemed a rich red gold – the warmest shade in sight. The earth was skull-hard beneath the unkempt grass, and I noticed that I was running in slightly exaggerated zigzags, as if I were leaping from boulder to boulder. It was lucky I wasn't timing myself. This didn't feel like the shortest possible route across the field: just the route the landscape wanted to take me on. The morning must still have been cold but I was already too warm to notice.

Then we were into a ploughed field: wide and alarming as a rough sea, with a skeletal hawthorn tree to mark the place where the right of way should bring us to the far shore. It was frosted solid, which meant that it would be easier than usual but also more hazardous. Running on frozen furrows is a bit like running on wildly irregular, slippery rock. Each step has to be placed with care and precision, on surfaces that are all at different heights and angles, if you don't want to hurt an ankle in a crevasse. It was strange to think that just a few weeks earlier I'd been wading through this stuff, cursing its yielding stickiness.

That's part of the joy of ploughed fields: the same field can pose many challenges. And that in turn embodies one of the great bonuses of all rural running: the challenges vary with the weather and the season. The countryside is, in effect, a giant, miraculously well-equipped gym, providing a beautifully balanced year-round workout. It's hard to predict precisely when the seasons will fall these days, but at different points in the course of twelve months I would normally expect to encounter at least a fortnight's worth of each of the following:

- Hard, frosty ground on which I can run fast.
- Crisp, frozen snow: also quite good for fast running.
- Deep or soft snow, which yields or slips away from under you, creating an effect similar to running on sand-dunes. Bad for running fast. Good for building stamina.
- Mud: many varieties – as previously discussed. Most types involve some degree of yielding or slipping; some also

add weight to your feet. Very good for stamina, although if you never did anything else you would end up with tight hamstrings.

- Smooth turf: ideal for 'normal' running, with a slight trade-off between softness (which varies) and speed.
- Uneven turf. Not ideal, but still has its uses. This kind of ground typically results when mud is churned up by livestock, then dries and hardens, creating a terracotta-hard mini-mountain range of peaks, troughs, holes, ridges and lumps (let's call it 'cattleskid') that is all the more hazardous for (usually) being hidden under grass. This has to be run on with control, especially downhill. In contrast to mud, it is good for the fronts of your legs. And for your ankles, unless you injure them.
- Long, thick grass – normally encountered towards the end of the summer – eventually reaches a height and a density that mean you can't just blast your way through but, instead, have to lift your feet right over it with each step. This knees-to-chest action (mentioned earlier in this chapter) is exhausting and very good for, among other things, the upper leg and the lower abdomen. Very demanding for short-legged hounds.
- Obstacles: these come in many forms, including gates, fences, stiles, ditches, hunt jumps, footbridges, cattle grids and fallen branches and trees. These vary with the seasons, too, as farmers re-arrange them according to their own priorities. (This particular run features, I think, twenty-five such obstacles in a circuit of about seven and a half miles.) All of these obstacles not only have to be negotiated – either with care or with a reckless leap – but also, in many cases, have to have a dog heaved over them. I don't think many Olympic training programmes include

dog-heaving, but it's still good exercise, with particular benefits for core stability. The bigger the dog, the better the work-out.

No doubt I've left out a few but you get the idea. And I haven't even started on the way that even the length and direction of your routes can vary with the seasons, with the same field perhaps being ploughed one week and sown the next, requiring you to run around it instead of across, and then reduced to stubble a couple of months later – and so on. Rural running offers variety for the body as well as the soul.

I'm sure this explains why so many off-road runners (I'm thinking particularly of fell-runners) keep going well into their sixties and seventies. The unpredictability prevents injury as well as boredom. We may be slightly more prone to traumatic injuries, but we're far less susceptible to repetitive strain injuries. It also helps to explain my lack of interest in timing my runs: there are too many variables for comparisons to mean much.

I was reflecting on these issues when we reached the highest point of the run, the top of the broad shoulder of grassland known as Barrow Hill. It was daylight by now: not just half-light but, suddenly, thrillingly bright sunshine, gathering warmth and brilliance with startling speed. We scaled a brambly fence, crossed a deserted lane, scaled a brambly stile, passed the forgotten remains of a Bronze Age barrow (more recently the base of an equally forgotten medieval windmill) and leapt down to a rough, badger-ravaged path that led through to the long, open slope on the far side. I was surprised, as I always am, by the sudden silence that stilled the world as we began the downward run. There must have been a wind before, from somewhere, rumbling in my ears unnoticed. And now, abruptly, all was quiet.

This particular silence – the transition that occurs always at this same spot – has been warming my heart for decades. Something about it makes me feel connected to the land and its past. On a clear day, if I slow down for a minute to look around, I can see a huge circular rim of horizon that cannot be less than a hundred miles in circumference, with swathes of at least three counties within it. You could have visited this hilltop at any point in the past five hundred years and experienced similar things: the cut-off of the wind; the real-isation that mile after mile of sleeping farmland can be seen, spread out in all directions; the illusion that every inch of that vast horizon is thickly covered with dark trees; the slow discovery, as your ears adapt to the relative silence, that the air is pulsating with skylarks' songs; the occasional glimpses of stone church towers protruding from the distant trees; and, a little later on Sunday mornings, the sound of English church bells floating on the breeze.

It was turning into the clearest of days today; in fact, it was hard to believe that it had been night barely forty minutes ago. (Had the world really changed? Or was it just me?) It was also, I realised, a Sunday morning – which made it all the more ridiculous to be out and about so early. I slowed down (as I would never have done in my earlier ages of running) to savour the moment. A little brown skylark popped up from a grassy tussock by my feet. Then the slope began to draw us downwards.

I've always enjoyed this slope. Long, steep and open, it is undeniably hazardous, especially when, as now, a lot of the ground has been churned up in the wet season by horses before drying into the horse equivalent of cattleskid and being con-cealed by grass. But it's also exhilarating, because you can take it at a sprint; and the faster you go the less hazardous it is – up to a point. I opted for medium fast on this occasion. The higher slope was still spattered with frost (a little smear on the northern side of each tuft of grass, strangely arbitrary, like white hairs on an old dog's chin), and I couldn't face the thought of having to limp home with an injury – not at this hour.

I reached the bottom unscathed and got my breath back plodding up the next hill. It's funny, I reflected, how I've never seen anyone else enjoying that sprint (except when I used to race my children and their friends down it). You'd have thought that people would be queuing up for it, given how little green space there is left to go round and how much of it is being eaten up by development and population growth.

That reflection set me off, uncharacteristically, on a train of negative thoughts. At the top of the next hill a dark hare, a rich gravy brown, lumbered out in front of me: so close that I seemed to be able to feel the weight of its footfalls. Instead of smiling, I thought instantly of a news item I had read the previous day, about Britain's brown hare population having fallen by 80 per cent in the past hundred years.

Shortly afterwards my enjoyment of a carpet of dazzling wildflowers on the long, easy slope down to Sulgrave was marred by the related thought that such meadows barely exist any more. Britain has lost more than 97 per cent of its semi-natural grassland since the 1930s (along with up to 50 per cent of its ancient woodland and 60 per cent of its farmland skylarks, and an awful lot more).

Some people would think me incredibly lucky to live in 'real' countryside like this. Others would laugh at the idea that this busy, built-up county, where maybe one person in a hundred earns their living from the land, could be considered properly wild or even rural. Both would be right. Yet in one respect we're all in it together. Whatever kind of countryside we have access to, it's a fair bet that it's vanishing. The 2013 State of Nature report, compiled by twenty-five conservation groups under the umbrella of the RSPB, found that of 3,148 British species surveyed, 60 per cent had declined over the past fifty years and 31 per cent had declined significantly. Since 1962 – two years after I was born – the UK has lost 72 per cent of its butterflies, 93 per cent of its turtle doves and forty-four million pairs of breeding birds. I could fill pages with such statistics, but your eyes would glaze over, as mine always do. We have seen so many of them, each shocking in its own right; and the world continues, and none of us knows what to do about it. The only statistic that matters, where rural England is concerned, is that most of it has gone.

Nor can anyone seriously imagine that such historic losses are the end of it. Our island continues to grow more crowded, more urbanised and more desperate for economic growth at any price. Already, 50 per cent of the land area of England is 'disturbed by the footprint of development' (according to a comprehensive 2007 survey by the Campaign to Protect Rural England). There is plenty more disturbance where that came from. By 2035, nearly five million extra homes are due to be built in England alone. In my county, Northamptonshire, more than 80,000 are likely to have been built by 2020, with planning permission already granted (by 2013) for 35,000. This is all part of the county council's plan to 'kickstart and unleash local dynamism and economic potential'. And, of course, more homes and people means more infrastructure.

We had reached Sulgrave by now, and ran through a village that seemed utterly asleep, sticking to the mown grass verge rather than the pavement so as not to break the silence. A series of 'SAY NO TO HS2' stickers in the windows of parked cars reminded me that in a generation's time (barring major policy U-turns) there will probably also be a giant high-speed railway cutting the countryside in two just beyond Sulgrave, its mile-long freight trains roaring day and night, with only the briefest of intervals between each one. And then, of course, there will be the wind farms – I know of at least two developments that would be visible from Barrow Hill – and the road-widening schemes to service the extra homes, and the extra street lighting, and the extra traffic to take advantage of the wider roads. I can enthuse all I like about mornings like this, but if it all disappears I'm wasting my breath. Perhaps my children's generation are sensible to spurn it – it won't be available in future anyway.

Still, at least no one can steal my early mornings. Except, of course, they can. There's a powerful political movement, led by the 10:10 Lighter Later pressure group, that has been campaigning for years for the UK's clocks to be put forward by an hour throughout the year. The lobbyists insist that the change would, among other benefits, reduce road accidents, lower electricity bills, reduce crime, create 60,000–80,000 new jobs in leisure and tourism, encourage active lifestyles, reduce obesity, 'make the nation happier' and 'improve quality of life for older people'. Rebecca Harris, the Conservative MP who tabled a private member's bill on the subject in 2011, has claimed that it would 'boost the economy by up to £3.5 billion a year'. Perhaps she and they are right. Some of the claims seem implausible to me, but presumably they wouldn't just pluck them out of thin air (would they?). In any case, the lobby seems unwilling to take no for an answer.

Yet for me, listening to the yellowhammers in the hawthorn hedge as Nutmeg and I make our quiet way back up Barrow Hill from the far side of the village, the thought of such a change is heartbreaking. This golden hour that starts each day, when the land comes alive again, and each living thing rejoices at the ebb of darkness – this daily interlude of sanity and groundedness, when my running habit brings me closer to the natural world around me than at any other moment in my life...Could a bunch of metropolitan politicians simply cancel a chunk of my life at the stroke of a pen?

The thought was so depressing that I almost stopped running. What if that actually happened? What if people like me – runners who use the window of daylight before work for a daily dose of reinvigorating exertion and joy – are simply too small a minority for our views or needs to matter? What if all this became impossible?

The hill grew steeper, and the extra effort required began to distract me from the accumulation of gloominess; in fact, I upped the pace deliberately, pumping away with impotent anger as I used to do in London thirty years earlier. Eventually the gloom dispersed, but it took a while. The problem with most of these issues is that they aren't easily resolved. Most of us can appreciate that there might be a need for wind farms and freight trains, or homes for a growing population, and that even skylarks can't necessarily be a national priority in difficult times. But we also know how much our countryside has to offer, to us and to those who haven't yet learnt to value it. We can see, without sentimentality, that it is in no one's interests to let our rural heritage slip away, irretrievably. We don't know what the answer is, so we sink into apathetic despondency.

But running and despondency aren't natural bedfellows; in fact, they abhor one another. By the top of the hill I had shaken off most of my pessimism. The sun was shining brightly now, the skylarks in the immediate vicinity seemed to be in good voice and a warm breeze blew unexpectedly in my face. Those last traces of frost seemed to have vanished in an instant.

I ran the final miles in, or possibly on, a cloud of optimism. OK, so there were shadows on the metaphorical horizon. There were none on the real one. I had no idea, really, what the future would bring. Meanwhile, today's world was gleaming more brightly every minute.

I lengthened my stride along the long, up-and-down track that brought us back to the fields where our run had begun. I could sense the sun drying the sweat on my face, and it felt as though I could see its warmth, too, glowing back at me from the stones of the church among the familiar trees.

In the final field, the monochrome sheep we had seen earlier were still there, still staring, their feet rooted in the same spots in the long grass. But their perfect moon-white fleeces were now warm with colour, the finest threads of gold and silver glinting within their rich cream wool.

Lifting my knees, I accelerated through the drying grass as if I were sprinting up a mountain. As I did so, I took advantage of yet another rather neat aspect of 'natural' running: if you don't run with headphones, you always have the option of streaming music direct from your brain.

Arms, feet, knees and lungs pounded in perfect rhythm, and the birdsong was drowned out by the voice of Janis Joplin, pumping through my veins: 'Get it, want it, need it, hold it, get it while you can! Yeah, honey, get it while you can!'

20

Manhunting

A few years ago I drove past a road race in Oxfordshire and noticed that large Day-Glo signs had been affixed to various lamp-posts and railings along the course, warning runners of such hazards as 'DIP' or 'BEND'. I'm pretty sure this isn't common practice: I've seen nothing like it since. None the less, it has stuck in my mind as a vivid symbol of the fact that, however much running and adventure may once have been associated with each other, today they are almost opposites.

I still can't quite put my finger on the 'when' or the 'why', but at some point in the twentieth century running ceased to be synonymous with thrills and spills and became associated instead with health, weight loss, sobriety and self-improvement – or, for the elite, with fame, fortune, medals, records and the science of marginal gains. Runners expect their running experience to be as smooth as the surfaces they run on, and those who sell such experiences make every possible effort to exclude irregularities. It's not just risk and discomfort that are considered inappropriate to the sport. Even unpredictability, the essence of adventure, is shunned.

A few people still run for kicks: at Cooper's Hill, for example. But they are running against the tide of the times. Even the famously fearless sport of fell-running is increasingly constrained by the twin forces of consumer culture and health and safety.

Yet there is one place where, unknown to almost anyone apart from those who do it, a form of running is practised that has nothing to do with weight loss, prudence, records or racing. Instead, it's to do with the raw thrill of running as nature intended: in the wild, with a purpose. There are seasoned stuntmen in Hollywood who might think twice before trying it.

Its headquarters, in so far as it has one, is an old stone guesthouse in the heart of Cumbria, where blurred black and white photographs of whiskery, respectable men hang by the wide wooden staircase. I shouldn't think many guests give a second glance to the names and dates that identify them – or, if they do, give a second thought to the exact nature of the 'hunt' of which each man was at some point Master.

That's probably just as well – because the hunt in question is a manhunt.

I won't say where or when it takes place. The sport thrives largely because (unlike the Cooper's Hill cheese-rolling) it has kept itself anonymous. Only a few dozen people are involved, although hundreds have taken part in the 116 years since it began. It isn't strictly a secret, but it shuns publicity. For most of us, in any case, the location and date are irrelevant: it's a private affair, enjoyed by a small group of families and friends for their own private reasons. However, I do think it's worth describing, because of the light it casts on my own musings about the relationship between running and landscape.

The Trevelyan Manhunt – to give it its proper name – was

first held in 1898. The rules have barely changed since. A group of around thirty-five people assemble once a year at a preordained place in the heart of the Lake District and spend three days hunting one another. They are divided into Hares – usually four per day – and Hounds – everyone else. The Hares get a half-hour head start, which they use to make themselves scarce in the mountains. The Hounds then set off to catch, or 'kill', them. A kill is made by touching. And that's it.

It doesn't sound dangerous, until you think about it. Think, for example, about the word 'mountains', and all that that implies: rocks, gullies, cliffs, scree, mud, heather, bog, bracken, boulders, crevasses, steep slopes, sheer drops, extreme weather and, of course, disorienting cloud. Think, too, about the word 'touching'. Then think of the intensity of a playground game of 'tag' – the headlong sprints, the desperate lunges, the evasive twists and turns. And then mix the two together...

The Hunt takes place over a ten-square-mile area of the Lake District National Park. The Hounds tend to hunt in a loosely cooperative fashion, often in small groups, but are not formally coordinated in the way that a real pack is. Each Hare acts independently. No one is allowed to stray beyond the agreed boundaries, and the hunting day lasts from 8.30 a.m. to 5 p.m. I think those are the only formal rules. The informal rule is that Hares, who wear bright red sashes, are expected to 'give good sport' – which means that, rather than simply hiding away beneath a distant boulder, good Hares with no one on their scent will draw attention to themselves from time to time until they are actually chased. They carry hunting horns for this purpose.

The challenge of the game lies in the fact that ten moun- tainous square miles is an enormous area for a game involving fewer than forty people. The joy is that success depends partly on fitness, partly on fearlessness, partly on guile; but also, largely, on mastery of the landscape. The best hunters – Hounds and Hares – know the Hunt's terrain intimately, and understand the threats and opportunities offered by each square foot of ground.

Any amount of cunning is permitted, by all concerned. Tales from hunts gone by include incidents of Hares climbing trees, hiding in farmyards (with refuges including a hayloft and a waterbutt), melting into parties of tourists, burrowing under a boulder beneath the feet of the pursuing Hounds, swimming out to the middle of a tarn and, in several cases, escaping so far up or down precarious rockfaces that hostilities had to be temporarily suspended while more pressing questions of survival were addressed. There was even one incident, too obscure to explain, involving what was in effect a car chase. It is hard to imagine a more adventurous extreme sport.

I stumbled upon it by accident quite recently and, after delicate negotiation, was allowed to join in part of the 2013 Hunt. It was a day of glorious sunshine – unusual for those parts – and, as a result, I was able to see at least some of what was going on. But the process is, for a novice, baffling. A Hare appears on a distant skyline, sounding a horn. You set off in pursuit, but by the time you get there – maybe half an hour later – the Hare is, of course, long gone and far, far away.

That's where the subtleties come in. The thoughtful Hound – or, better, group of Hounds – will think before chasing. What are the Hare's options, leading from that spot? Are there impassable crags to the north of him? A tempting descent to the west? Where might he (or she) hide? Which slope might he have in mind for a speedy getaway? Which direction or directions should we approach from, to cut off his likely route or to shield us from his sight? Which other Hounds are near? Is there scope for luring him into a trap?

My first day's hunting involved an hour or so of cheerful ascent from the valley, chatting to fellow Hounds, followed by perhaps another hour of wandering alone (having been sent in fruitless pursuit of a Hare who had shown herself twice but then vanished); after which I bumped into two other Hounds, who appeared simultaneously from different directions.

'Is Mary somewhere round here?' asked one.

'I just killed her,' said the other, coolly. 'Just on the other side of that ridge.'

We both congratulated him and listened to his account of Mary's final moments: the last breathless pursuit through the heather; the desperate dodging and weaving on a patch of half-dry bog; the lethal lunge and touch. Then, after brief discussion, we headed off as a pack towards some different fells, picking up another Hound on the way. (Convention dictates that dead Hares are left to their own devices for a while, enabling them to re-enter the game a little later at a moment and place of their own choosing.)

After a while, we reached a high ridge from which we could see several square miles of the hunting area. In the brilliant clarity of the mountain sunshine, you could sense the texture of the far side of the valley: the dry bristling turf, the warm boulders crusted with sun-baked lichen. Oddly, in the shadows of one high gulley, there was still a patch of snow. This would, we agreed, offer excellent scope for a high-speed downward slide, should a Hare's descent need to be cut off in that area.

There was, as yet, no sign of a Hare, but it seemed inconceivable that none was around. We spread out, sweeping slowly down one slope with eyes straining to spot signs of our prey on the slopes on the far side of the valley. Every now and then, someone would spot movement. Was that a Hare? A Hound? An ordinary tourist? Or perhaps even an ordinary four-legged hare?

For most of this time we were walking rather than running, eating up the miles without noticing. We were near enough to chat, just about, and spoke mainly of the hunt. Who had seen what clues? What would we do, if we were Hares, on a day like this? Then someone spotted a figure running down from the skyline, about a mile away. 'That Hound looks like his blood is up,' said the Hound nearest me; which sounded ridiculous, except that it was true.

If you've ever seen an animal or group of animals – canine, feline, vulpine, whatever – closing in on its prey, you would recognise the body language. The Hounds around me began to move in a different way: heads forward, bodies coiled and alert, striding purposefully, swiftly, stealthily. I realised that I was doing the same. Then someone said 'There he is', and our gaze miraculously followed the speaker's just in time to see a sashed figure, further down the far hillside than his pursuer, scurrying towards the cleft where that slope disappeared behind ours. We spread out and ran, fast and silently, down and across the fell, instinctively following lines that would maximise our chances of cutting off the Hare before he rounded the promontory.

Soon many of us were heading down slopes at least as steep as Cooper's Hill, but longer and less even, with boulders and random holes and gulleys adding to the hazards. It helped that there were no Double Gloucesters or drunken bodies bouncing around us. None the less, there was an obvious tension between the need to keep track of the Hare's movements and the need to focus intently on the ground beneath. We dealt with it simply by concentrating – hard. I felt a sense of hyper-alertness: that feeling you get in a car crash of everything being in slow motion. But it was not fear that was pumping adrenaline through my veins: it was a kind of bloodlust. I suspect I may even have been sniffing the air, hungry for my prey, seeking information of any kind to maximise the chances of a kill.

Then, somehow, the Hare vanished. There didn't seem to be any cover for him to hide in, but there were so many indentations and obstacles in the valley that it was easy for our line of sight to be interrupted. We tried to sweep around carefully, in such a way as to be sure that he was in front of us. I think we succeeded, but we couldn't be certain that he hadn't found an emergency hiding place among the boulders. Down the valley we prowled, more slowly now, until a shout of 'Tally ho!' echoed down from a third ridge, to the north and to our right. Another Hound, too distant to identify, had spotted our Hare creeping up the heathery slope towards him.

We sped off in pursuit, cursing. How had he managed to put so much distance between himself and us? How could we cut him off? And, more pressingly, how could we get from our slope to his without losing half a mountain's worth of height and then having to get it back again?

Our mini-pack split in two, approaching in a curved pincer movement. Another Hound appeared far below; we called for him to join us. Some time later – and it could easily have been fifteen or twenty minutes, because the distances and heights we had to cover were quite substantial – a group of five or six of us converged on the heatheriest, steepest, most bouldery bulge in the hillside, convinced that, somewhere within our circle, the Hare was hiding. We began to tiptoe, signalling to one another with gestures rather than shouts, hoping to sneak up on him, pitting our guile against his. Surely we had him now . . .

Some time later, a horn blew from the fellside we had originally started from and a red-sashed figure was seen jogging smugly up towards the northern skyline, waving his hunting horn and giving occasional provocative toots.

Once again, we set off in pursuit: not angrily, but with the kind of grim determination that you imagine a cheetah must feel, knowing that if it doesn't get this gazelle, it will starve. At some point it dawned on me that I was the nearest one to the Hare. If I didn't get him, we would all starve.

I forced myself into a near-sprint, thankful that the uphill gradient of the chase made it relatively easy to pick my steps on the rough ground. After five minutes, I was cursing the gradient. The effort was killing me. No matter how much I strained to close the gap between us – initially no more than thirty or forty metres – I couldn't get him within touching distance, or anything like it. Sometimes I seemed to be closing on him. Then he'd vanish behind some mini-ridge, and the next thing I knew he'd have changed direction, negating any advantage that my painful surges had gained me.

Eventually I lost sight of him for a minute or more, and the next time I spotted him he was half a mile away. (He was, in fairness to me, one of Britain's top fell-runners.) Utterly spent, I gave up – but vowed revenge.

Our day's hunting lasted eight and a half hours, over nine mountains and five valleys and I hate to think how many thousands of feet of ascent and descent, or miles of running. I failed to make a kill of my own, and have been mulling over the 'might have beens' ever since: that uphill chase when maybe I should have just put everything into one early sprint;

or that episode near the end when, had I only spotted the Hare creeping above me on the rocks a bit earlier, I could surely have run him down in a desperate death-or-glory chase... It's as futile and addictive as visualising the goals you didn't score playing football.

I was, however, vaguely involved in two catches. For one, a couple of us tracked down and crept up on the Hare who had eluded me earlier, then lay in wait behind a boulder to ambush him. He was heading towards our trap – but then another Hound, who we hadn't realised was there, leapt out from behind another boulder and made the kill. The Hare didn't even get a chance to make a dash for it.

For the other, two of us managed to harry another Hare along the side of a valley, one from below and one from above, until eventually, vaulting a drystone wall to avoid me, he fell into the hands of my fellow Hound.

But my inexperience meant that a lot of the action passed me by. Other Hounds had more of a knack of being in the right place at the right time. They also knew better than I did when it was worth going for the kill and when it was better to be patient. (Subsequently, observing Thelma and Louise hunting mice and rabbits, I've concluded that the cat that catches the most – Louise – is the one that waits longest before making her final leap.)

I was struck, too, by how much better my fellow Hounds understood the landscape than I did. I had thought that I knew these particular mountains well, but it turned out that I knew only the tops and the ridges connecting them. Most of the landscape – the hollows and buttresses, the streamlets flowing into the larger streams, the bubbles, dents and folds in the lower slopes, the patches of valley vegetation – had simply passed me by in a blur over the years, as if seen through a car window. No wonder the Hares outwitted me so easily.

Yet already I was getting a sense of how addictive this game can be, testing not just athleticism but guile, mountaincraft and spirit. This complexity allows it to accommodate a wide range of abilities and ages. The youngest Hound I spoke to was fourteen. The oldest was sixty-five. In between, there were two or three who could reasonably be described as elite fell-runners; perhaps a dozen who were definitely in their prime; and at least a dozen more (including me) who definitely weren't. I heard several mutterings to the effect that 'I'm slower than I used to be' or 'I tend to rely on cunning these days'. Six of the thirty-six participants were women. I'm pretty certain that no one felt left out.

Subsequent debriefings confirmed that there had been eighteen kills that day: an unusually high total that probably owed much to the unusually good visibility. (But no one Hound would have seen more than about half a dozen of these.) There had been other casualties, too. As we slumped afterwards in the garden of the guesthouse, drinking tea and orange juice and exchanging tales of daring and farce, I totted up: two sprained ankles (one severe); one knee that had had a giant ice pack applied to it; two bright red shins (on the same person), torn raw by a sprint through a patch of gorse; and at least one blistered foot (whose owner's shoe had disintegrated in a bog).

No one seemed particularly bothered by this; and, indeed, reading through the Hunt's handwritten records – lovingly bound in Hunt Books going all the way back to 1898 – you can see that this has never been a sport for the faint-hearted. The earliest accounts offer little more than lists of hunters and tallies of catches. As the years go by, however, they become more detailed, with the daredevil incidents described in delighted detail. The one that pleased me most involved a young Hound who leapt down on his quarry from a high crag and broke his ankle: 'The first thing he said to the Hounds at his side (not entirely realistically) was: "Whatever you do, don't tell my dad."' A few descriptions are embellished with diagrams or drawings: showing a Hare hiding up a tree, for example, or an incident in 1997 when a Hare was surprised while hiding on a ledge and leapt 'forward and outward' without thinking about where he was, somersaulting over the pursuing Hound and landing on his back fifteen feet below ('a dangerous manoeuvre'). In another entry, a decade earlier, a Hare gets similarly carried away when pursued up a tree and simply 'leaps out, arms spread' and hopes for the best. The fact that both men lived to tell the tale does not negate the folly of such practices.

Yet most people involved in the Trevelyan Manhunt are no fools. On the contrary, they tend to be staggeringly intelligent. The hunt was founded by three Cambridge undergraduates – George Macaulay Trevelyan (later a celebrated historian, Fellow of the Royal Society and Master of Trinity College, Cambridge), Geoffrey Winthrop Young (later a noted author, mountaineer and educator) and Sidney McDougall (a brilliant engineer who was killed at Gallipoli in 1915) – and a strong Oxbridge link has remained. Of perhaps seven hundred people who have taken part in the Hunt in its 116-year history, I estimate that at least a third (and possibly many more) must have been Oxbridge-educated; there is also a separate Trinity Lake Hunt, an offshoot of the original Hunt for members of Trinity College, Cambridge, which operates along similar lines at a different time of year. Many Trevelyan hunters have been (or have gone on to become) distinguished academics – for example, the aforementioned C.E.M. Joad. Others have ended up as senior civil servants or politicians (including one Chancellor of the Exchequer, one Home Secretary, two Secretaries of State for India and a Governor of Hong Kong).

My sense is that it's a bit less rarefied now. As years became decades, those Oxbridge men married, had families; children began to come along, to wait in the valley or to go on their own adventures; and then, as they grew older and tougher, the keenest were admitted to the Hunt themselves. The names of around twenty families (some rich, some not) crop up again and again in the Hunt's history, and for most current members it is family or friendship, not education, that have drawn them into the sport. The existence of a separate Trinity Lake Hunt has weakened the original hunt's Oxbridge link further. In any case, the general decline of outdoor hardiness and mountain know-how has greatly reduced the likelihood that any given academic high-flier will have what it takes to participate in a mountain manhunt. In recent years, people have been brought in by the current Master, Jethro Lennox, a top-class fell-runner, for their excellence in his sport.

None the less, the manhunt is clearly as rooted in privilege as the cheese-rolling of Cooper's Hill isn't. Yet I think there is more to it than that. There is, for some reason, a strong link between the Hunt and social idealism. G. M. Trevelyan was not just a historian but a social reformer, who taught at the Working Men's College in London – as did other early hunters such as Hilton Young and Francis Cornford. Charles Trevelyan (G. M.'s elder brother) was one of the few politicians with the courage to oppose Britain's entry into the First World War, resigning from government in order to do so. G.W. Young, a pacifist, led an independent ambulance unit on the Western Front; when the unit moved to the Italian front, G. M. Trevelyan joined him. Both men were decorated for their bravery in rescuing wounded men under fire. Young ultimately lost a leg in Italy (but subsequently learnt to climb with an artificial one).

G. M. Trevelyan was an early advocate of the creation of a Lake District National Park. A subsequent Hunter (and Trevelyan descendant), John Dower, did more than anyone else to make National Parks a reality; and Kenneth Spence, founder of the Friends of the Lake District, is another figure who deserves the gratitude of anyone who enjoys the beauties of the Cumbrian mountains today. Other enthusiastic members of the Hunt included Edwin Montagu, who helped move India towards self-government in the 1920s, and William (later Lord) Beveridge, who in the 1940s almost single-handedly created the welfare state. More recently, Hunt members such as George Lowthian Trevelyan (Charles's son) and Roger Orgill have devoted enormous efforts to promoting the education of the underprivileged young, through a mixture of New Age spiritual dialogue and outdoor activity. They may have been an unusually privileged bunch, but it is hard to disagree with the proposition that, if you took away the contributions that Hunt members have made to British life in the past century or so, the lives of the less fortunate majority would be less fortunate still.

Is there something the rest of us can learn from this? I suspect that depends on the political preconceptions you bring to the question. But there is a school of thought within the Hunt that holds that the sport is – to quote one former Master – 'ennobling'. And my own preconceptions, about landscape and running and outdoor adventure, predispose me to give that idea a sympathetic hearing.

I spent part of the Hunt on a long traverse from one ridge to another, chatting with a Hound from Herefordshire about mountains and adventure and the motivations of the men who explored and hunted on them in generations gone by. We both happened to have been reading books about George Mallory, the pioneering mountaineer who died on Everest in 1924, and had been struck by the relationship between Mallory's experiences on the Western Front in the First World War and his determination to explore the extreme limits of his talents thereafter. He could so easily have settled down in comfortable post-war security with his adored wife, but insisted instead on testing himself one more time against Everest (and then one more time after that; and, fatally, another after that).

It wasn't just him. As one of the books (*Into the Silence: The Great War, Mallory and the Conquest of Everest*, by Wade Davis) makes clear, a whole generation of mountain adventurers, including most of Mallory's companions on his Everest expeditions, had been similarly shaped by their wartime traumas; and it seemed to us, discussing it now with mighty grey crags towering all around us, that in certain crucial periods of its history something comparable must have happened to the Trevelyan Manhunt. You have only to study the Hunt Books – peppered as the volumes are in wartime years with entries commemorating those who have 'died since the last hunt' – to see that it, too, must for much of the twentieth century have been largely driven by survivors of world wars who were determined to squeeze every last drop of joy out of whatever moments remained to them. 'They'd been through such horrors in the trenches, they weren't really afraid of things any more,' said my fellow Hound. 'Not the way we are.' Or, in Wade Davis's words: 'They were not cavalier about death – they all wanted desperately to live – but they had seen so much that it had no hold on them. What mattered was how one lived.'

It is hard to imagine an outlook more alien to the spirit of twenty-first-century Britain, which has a very different view about the relative importance of, on the one hand, living life to the full and, on the other, the avoidance of risk. It is also hard not to feel a twinge of regret at this reversal of priorities. We are, after all, still going to die, health and safety or no health and safety. Aren't moments of magic and delight worth at least as much as an illusory sense of living in a risk-free world?

'Get it while you can', the phrase I quoted earlier, can have different meanings in different contexts. For the flower children of the 1960s, it meant sex and drugs and rock'n'roll. For the archetypal twenty-first-century fat-cat director, it means lining your pockets with company money while you can get away with it. For several previous generations, including hundreds of early Trevelyan Manhunters, it may well have meant something more like: 'Get it while you can. Life is short at the best of times, and these are not the best of times. Make the most of every moment given to you, before you are snuffed out.'

Perhaps I am getting carried away. From a different perspective, the indifference to risk that underpins the Trevelyan Manhunt is, clearly, childish – irresponsible, even – rather than noble. Maybe the Hunt's founders simply didn't consider the possible downside of their activities. Geoffrey Winthrop Young, as an undergraduate at Trinity College, Cambridge, was a keen nocturnal roof climber, who might well have been sent down from the university had he been exposed as the anonymous author of a pamphlet – still in print – called *The Roof Climber's Guide to Trinity*. (Luckily for him, the college appointed a young Fellow called G. M. Trevelyan to head the panel that was set up to track down the pamphlet's author.)

But perhaps the two explanations don't have to be mutually exclusive. We can be immature in our behaviour for all sorts of reasons; and sometimes there is a nobility in our immature moments — just as there can be an ignobility in the habitual caution of maturity. Did the Manhunters who rescued the wounded from the carnage of the Great War act with exhaustively considered courage, or because, childishly, they hadn't really thought about what might go wrong? The answer is: it scarcely matters.

Yet it is striking that so many intelligent people, rather than telling Trevelyan, Young and McDougall to grow up and get a grip, have embraced their reckless game with such warmth and enthusiasm. And it is striking how liberated so many of them seem to have felt by the experience of playing it. A pamphlet produced in 1998 to mark the Hunt's centenary quotes from thank you letters sent by satisfied hunters over the years. 'I have rarely found myself subject to such extremes of physical and mental alertness as I experienced on the third day when I found myself being hunted from three directions,' enthuses one. Another says: 'As I settled into the seat of the 747 last night, I looked at my fellow passengers around me and a glow of well-being seemed to come over me from nowhere. None of them could ever appreciate the satisfaction of chasing a hare in driving rain from the slopes of [one mountain] across the top of [another], round [a third] and down the screes...'

Of course, we cannot be made fundamentally better people by behaving recklessly in the mountains, no matter how much we enjoy it. I doubt, however, that we are often made worse people by our moments of childish fearlessness. And it seems highly unlikely that one can spend three days straining every fibre of body and mind in adventurous pursuits and not return somehow enhanced: if not a better person, then perhaps at least more of a person: more alive, more awake to the world. As Robin Dower, a Northumberland architect (and Trevelyan descendant) who was Master from 1987 to 1998, put it a few years ago: 'It is very natural that the spirit should exult as it meets the timeless challenge to mind and strength that underlies our relationship with the mountains.'

Perhaps that's why the Hunt seems so unbothered by the fears of litigation that plague other 'extreme' sports. Those who take part see it as a privilege to do so, and the freedom to take risks is part of what they value. In fact, it's not even clear that the Hunt actually has a 'provider' (a key concept in health and safety legislation), although I'm sure an ambulance chasing lawyer could argue the case, if hired by an injured participant. (There is a limited company associated with the hunt, set up half a century ago to buy and manage the boarding house, otherwise open to the public, where most Hunt members stay on the Hunt weekend.) At any rate, no one seems unduly bothered by the prospect of someone seeking damages over a Hunt-related injury. As one older Hound put it: 'Yes, it could happen. But it doesn't.'

Perhaps that's as good a way to deal with the issue as any other. Indeed, perhaps this private, informal approach is the key to enjoying many kinds of adventure in the modern world. We live in such a public age that it is sometimes hard to believe that we have the option of just doing things privately. Not paying a 'provider' to organise the activity; not participating in a recognised event whose brand, commercial or otherwise, legitimises our achievement. Just doing it.

The Trevelyan Manhunt, despite the sense of public duty historically associated with it, remains deeply private: an eccentric game, passed down through several generations of families and friends, with no more public significance than the games of hide-and-seek you might play with your children. You don't do it in order to brag about it. You do it in order to do it. (As another high-powered Hound put it: 'It's very existential.') Anyone reading this who wants to take part in a Manhunt will just have to hope that, one day, someone invites them. You can't apply.

Alternatively, you could always organise your own landscape-based game. You won't get a T-shirt to show for it, or a medal.

But you may, for a few short, shining hours, feel alive.

21

Fun and gamification

Once a year, on a November weekend in Surrey, the British branch of Big Running has its annual equivalent of a party conference. Representatives of more than a hundred brands converge on Sandown Park racecourse to swap ideas, innovations, contact details and marketing initiatives. New models of running shoe are unveiled (exhibitors in 2013 included Mizuno, On, Newton, Brooks, Asics and Puma); some generate scarcely less excitement than a new iPhone launch. But that's just the tip of the iceberg. There are also new lines of apparel, accessories, nutrition, training and – the industry's gift that keeps on giving – injury management.

Even for a cynic like me, it's hard not to get caught up in the carnival atmosphere. The crisp, dew-rinsed racecourse outside sparkles in golden autumn sunlight; visitors pour through the big glass doors as eagerly as shoppers at sales time; and, once we're inside, there's an intoxicating sense (as there generally is at big running events) of a shared relish for life.

The list of exhibitors tells its own story: 1,000 Mile Socks, Aftershokz Sport Headphones, Apres Recovery,

Beyond the Ultimate, CherryActive, CompresSport, CurrexSole, Fit Brands, Garmin, Halo Headband, Hilly Clothing Company, Hyperperformance Nutrition, Ithlete, Kinetic Podiatry, LessBounce, Nip Guards, Precision Hydration, RealXGear Cooling Products, Shock Absorber, Sub-4 Health, Sure Clinic, TomTom, UK Race Equipment Hire, Workplay Bags, Xtenex Laces, Yurbuds, to name just a few. All running life is here, from adventure race organisers to sock specialists, medal-makers to headphone-makers – and, not least, runners.

It's hard to be certain where the enthusiasts and bargain-hunters stop and the product-pushing professionals begin. Many are here in more than one capacity, and most project much the same air of fit, relaxed, well-informed enthusiasm as ideas are exchanged and explained. But the distinction barely matters. The sense of being at the sharp end of an energetic, endlessly innovative industry is overwhelming.

The exhibitors aren't all the absolute giants of Big Running. (They'll be at the equivalent US event a couple of weeks later, in Austin, Texas.) But even the smaller names are the sort of innovators who, if all goes well, might hope to do a lucrative deal with a big global operator a few years down the line. If you want to get a sense of what runners en masse will be spending their money on next, this is the place to start.

The difficulty is knowing where to stop. There's hardly a stand that isn't buzzing with activity, and, at each one, a must-have product or service is being marketed. I'm successively persuaded of my pressing need to stock up with: clothes made of fabrics that warm up when they come into contact with sweat (causing it to evaporate); cooling bandages that become ice cold when you add water; innumerable items of compression apparel (shorts, tops, socks) that will either help my injuries to heal or prevent me from getting them in the first place; a windproof reflective running top with a flashing light built into its back; a range of inserts that will chemically cleanse my running shoes of smells; special running head-phones that will allow me to hear 'situational noise' as well as my music (and, in one case, my digitally uploaded workout instructions); a revolutionary silicone-based powder that pre-vents blisters by waterproofing the feet; a special spray to take the stink out of sports bags; any number of specialist nutrition products, including special £10 Marathon Packs; a 'revolu-tionary training app' that analyses the variations in your heart rate to determine how hard you should be training on any given day; and a range of coloured KT tape (£20 per self-ad-hesive roll) that allegedly helps injuries to heal.

A couple of stands offer sweat-testing services – to help me to determine what kind of 'bespoke drink formulation' I need to purchase; several offer free biomechanical or gait analysis; and a host of therapists and podiatrists offer physio, massage, sports injury advice and (in the case of the podiatrists) recommendations for 'bespoke sports orthotics'.

At the firefly™ recovery stand, a woman called Kate is demonstrating a strap-on product (£45 for a starter pack) that uses electrical impulses to increase blood flow to the lower leg, which allegedly speeds up post-race recovery. She has one on each knee, and her bare calves are twitching as a result. By Sunday evening, they will have been twitching in the call of duty for 15 hours. The small print on the flyer she gives me concedes that the device 'is not cleared by the US FDA and is not available for sale in the USA'; but the principle of stimulating blood flow seems reasonable enough. The encounter reminds me that, in my fell-running days, I used to apply a natural version of the same therapy to my own injuries, deliberately stinging the affected joint with nettles. Any pain was offset by the thought that each throb was a sign of the blood doing its healing work.

But it's the Xempo stand that impresses me most: not for its technological inventiveness but for sheer chutzpah. The company is promoting a range of running apparel that comes in nine colours, from red to gold, according to your standard. 'They're colour-coded to reflect your personal best,' explained one of the cheerful young men at the stand. 'So as your times improve, you can buy new colours.' The harder you push yourself, in other words, the more money you are allowed to spend. It's arguably the perfect running product.

But the Running Show isn't just about products. It is a celebration of the running industry, designed to send visitors away fizzing with enthusiasm. So there's also a pacing masterclass and a physio clinic; and workshops in, among other things, running technique (from The Running School) and nutrition; and cut-price analytical tests of lung power and skinfold body composition by, among others, the Surrey Human Performance Institute (one of the show's sponsors). On the second day, there are races for various ability levels on the hard tracks adjoining the grass racecourse. And there's a series of well-attended seminars: I notice discussions on 'Knowing When to Train'; 'Nutrition in Running'; 'Choosing the Right Kit'; 'Understanding the Motion Patterns that Create Injury'; and 'Hydration for Running'. The latter is overseen by a 'Lucozade Sport Scientist'.

By the end of the weekend, up to 6,000 people will have passed through the show, most of them young, active and passionate about their sport. And they are only the beginning: the core of professionals and super-enthusiasts from whom new ideas and innovations will filter down over the coming months to several million ordinary runner-consumers.

According to David Townsend, the Show Director: 'The show is designed to help all runners – whether preparing for their first five-kilometre or gearing up for their tenth ultra-marathon – get the most out of their sport.' A more cynical interpretation would be that it helps the running industry to get the most out of ordinary runners, helping it to hone its products and get them talked about. It seems unlikely, at any rate, that exhibitors would pay £525 + VAT each for a stand (including carpet, name sign and lighting) if they had no outcome in mind beyond increasing the satisfaction of the running public.

'Are you interested in learning how science can improve your performance?' asks a bright young woman from Surrey Human Performance Institute, as I wander towards the exit with a bulging goodie bag in my hand.

I think about this proposition for a moment and then, trying not to sound rude, say honestly: 'No, not really.'

Events like The Running Show remind me that there are at least two irreconcilable philosophies of running. One is my minimalist one. Its opposite is captured in the blurb of 2XU, the compression-wear specialists exhibiting on stand K24: '2XU engineers products with the single-minded goal of equipping the athlete to feel more prepared, race ready and capable than the competition. As they put on their technologically advanced garments, athletes also put on a desire to perform beyond expectation and be greater than ever before. Armed with 2XU technology, another piece of the finely balanced athletic equation is in place to multiply your human performance...' You could use this spiel, with the odd adjustment, as a rationale for almost any running product you care to name.

There was a time when I was a sucker for this kind of stuff. I'm not now. But is 'sucker' the right word? That's another question to which the answer is likely to be determined largely by prejudice. When I see an industry making money hand over fist (bookies; payday lenders; energy suppliers), I instinctively conclude that the consumers concerned are being taken for a ride. Others look at industries that are making money hand over fist (search engines, supermarkets) and conclude that they are simply providing consumers with a much-needed service.

Maybe both are right. It does, I admit, seem unlikely that running could have become the hugely profitable industry that it is if most of its products didn't deliver, most of the time, at least some of the benefits they promise. Yet I still find it slightly galling that, instead of selling us the cheap and cheerful kit that most of us actually need, the giants of Big Running put all their energies into peddling absurdly overdesigned copies of the specialist kit that top professionals use. I suppose it's a bit like football's replica shirt industry. In each case, ordinary enthusiasts are persuaded to part with startlingly large sums of money in return for kit that feeds the illusion that they have lots in common with their elite heroes. There's nothing wrong with that, if you are such an enthusiast and it works for you. But don't let anyone kid you into thinking that you're the one doing well out of the transaction.

One can hardly blame the running industry for seeking higher profits and stronger balance sheets. But look at a publication such as *Running Insight*, a leading US magazine aimed at running retailers, and you'll be struck by the subtly different language that advertisers use in their product descriptions when addressing industry insiders: 'builds incremental sales'; 'presents attractive margins and repeat sales'; 'translates to repeat purchase and increased profitability'; 'perfect impulse item for consumers'; and so on. Can you detect a theme?

You'll also be struck, if you read such publications, by the industry's relentless ingenuity in finding new ways to squeeze money from the market. Not a year goes by without a crop of new must-have products appearing from nowhere – iliotibial band compression wraps, plantar fasciitis-relieving socks, Stay Cool fabric to lower your skin temperature by 6 degrees F – as inevitably as new style imperatives are conjured up by the fashion industry. In other cases – running shoes, for example – a slight tailing-off in demand has been offset by a substantial increase in prices. In every case, it's not that running has somehow become more expensive to do: it's just that ordinary runners have been persuaded to pay more to do it.

The industry's most brilliant innovation of recent years has been the digital wristband or 'mobile health device' – unknown and unimaginable to virtually every runner in history but now considered so indispensable that hundreds of thousands of runners have paid up to £129 for a Nike+ FuelBand or one of its many rivals (the Fitbit Flex, the Jawbone Up, the Under Armour E39, the Striiv Play, the Misfit Wearables...in the US there's even a FitBark, for between $59 and $109, for dogs). As you'll probably be aware, such devices allow users to monitor fitness-related data – steps taken, calories burnt, miles covered (and, in many cases, much, much more); and, crucially, to upload the information to an online site where you can compare it with your targets or, if you prefer, with other people's data.

There are obvious attractions to such devices as motivational tools – especially if you don't much like running in the first place. None the less, it's one more thing for the hard-pressed recreational runner to shell out for (or to feel inadequate without). And it's worth remembering that Nike alone saw an 18 per cent increase in the profits of its equipment division in 2012, its first year of selling the Nike+ FuelBand.

Such devices embody what some analysts predict will be the biggest business trend of the coming decade: 'gamification' – that is, the use of the concepts of computer games to incentivise real life. If your coffee shop gives you a reward card, with a free drink each time you get ten stamps on it, that's gamification. If your supermarket gives you reward points, or an airline gives you frequent flier points, that's gamification. Increasingly, however, gamification is based online, and the incentives are not material ones but, instead, virtual rewards such as badges, points and admission to new levels. Health and fitness lend themselves particularly well to the process, but it's also good for education (try it for language learning), transport management, workplace productivity and more. A 2011 report by the analysts Gartner predicted that, by 2014, more than 70 per cent of the world's leading companies would have at least one gamified application, while 'a gamified service for consumer goods marketing and customer retention will become as important as Facebook, eBay or Amazon'. It is, among other things, a great way of getting your customers to do your marketing for you.

What interests me particularly about this trend is the way that gamification takes a real activity and subordinates it to a virtual one. Instead of focusing on the thing itself, you focus on the game that has been superimposed upon it. That's fine if the thing itself doesn't interest you: for example, if you hate exercise but know that you need to get fit for health reasons. But what if the activity – running, for example – is already an enthusiasm? Aren't you then simply paying to replace real joy with an artificial version – as you increasingly derive your pleasure from the 'rewards' you are accumulating rather than the process of running itself?

The purest example of this exchange is that short-lived Trailblaze concept I mentioned at the beginning of this book: never mind that beautiful National Trail you are running on, just think of what all these miles will mean for your online profile. But the same process is at work with every gamified running device, from Garmins to FuelBands. And, as Xempo's range of colour-coded kit shows, the scope for further expansion is vast. In each case, it's less about just doing it than about just saying you've done it.

It all comes back to the relatively lo-tech question: what do you actually need to be a runner? The answer is that, if you are an actual or potential champion, you may well need every possible refinement that science can invent and money can buy. The rest of us, to varying degrees, don't. What matters, for most of us, is having a functioning pair of legs and a sustainable relationship between running and the rest of our lives that allows us to enjoy both.

No amount of paid-for gamification will achieve that for you. In fact, I'd go so far as to suggest that, if the idea of a run that isn't overlaid with gamified incentives doesn't excite you, you might want to consider another sport; or, alternatively, to look again at the kind of running you do, and ask yourself if there might not be a more exciting way of doing it. In that context, developing a rural running habit could do more for your quality of life and your quality of running than any number of fancy wrist devices, satellite trackers, sweat tests, compression shorts and bespoke orthotics. And you won't have to pay through the nose for it.

The economics of the running industry defy logic. No

matter what happens to the rest of the Western economy, the sector just keeps on growing. Yet the facts remain the same. Most of us have at least a decade of declining wealth ahead of us, maybe more. Is it really so inappropriate to consider adopting a more minimalist, back-to-basics approach to a hobby that for most of human history has been a low-cost activity?

Perhaps that's what bothers me most about Big Running: the fact that it has more or less convinced the world that its kind of running is the only kind there is. Rival views of the sport are withering in its shadow. It's a bit like the argument about out-of-town superstores. The likes of Tesco and Sainsbury's do little harm in themselves: on the contrary, they grow because they give consumers what they want. Yet their success leaves consumers, in the long run, with less choice. Little, idiosyncratic, out-of-date local shops go out of business; the high street dies; and eventually there is only one way of shopping left.

Is it too far-fetched to suggest that something similar is happening with running?

These arguments won't convince everyone. Big Running has all the weight of received opinion behind it, as well as some of the world's biggest corporations; and shiny new kit is, let's face it, pretty irresistible.

But Running Free, by contrast, is at least free.

22

Everyone suddenly
started running

One of my most vivid recollections of rural running is a strange one: not because what happened was out of the ordinary but because it has, strangely, emerged from the recesses of my brain during the writing of this book. It seemed trivial at the time but has recently begun to replay itself in High-Definition Memory, as if it were somehow important.

It was a race – call it 400 metres – and, unusually, I won it. But that wasn't really the point.

We were on a beach, on the Gower Peninsula in South Wales. There were, I think, nine or ten contestants, or possibly more. It was low tide, and the flat course curved eastwards, parallel with the smooth sea. Jagged, grass-fringed cliffs, dark and knotty, towered over us from the left, like a dragon's spine. The finish was a pool of water beneath an arch of rock on the corner of the bay. Sky and sea were complementary shades of deep, heart-warming blue, and a gentle breeze from the sea eased what might otherwise have been stifling midday heat.

It wasn't an elite contest, but the line-up was still intimidating. There was...But why am I telling you this?

The question has been nagging me for a while now. Why am I telling you any of this? Why do I imagine that anyone, except perhaps my immediate family, would take the slightest interest in my running memories and musings? I hardly know. But perhaps – now that I've raised the question – it's because I imagine that some of you might be a little bit like me: not in the detail, but somewhere inside.

Each runner's life is different. Yet for all but the tiniest handful of us the same three self-evident truths apply that apply to me:

- We are not, and never will be, world champions. (A few of us may find this hard to accept.)
- We are growing older and, if we are much over thirty, will tend to become slower, not faster, with the passage of time. (Again, some find this tough to face.)
- Notwithstanding the above, we wish to run, and feel that running has a sufficiently important role to play in our lives for it to be worth our while to go to all the trouble of doing it. (Think how much simpler it would be not to bother.) Running is, to borrow Samuel Johnson's definition of the purpose of literature, something we do because it enables us better to enjoy life, or better to endure it.

If this book has a purpose, it is to point out that there is more than one way in which running can enrich an ordinary life; and to suggest that, at different points in life, some approaches to running have more to offer than others.

Each life is a journey; and in each runner's life there is a journey within a journey, during which our relationship with the sport shifts and develops. Such journeys can lead us in various directions, and bring various degrees of reward and frustration. Mine has taken me in a vast circle.

It began, as described much earlier, as an escape from youthful fecklessness; became a healing habit, then a passion, then an obsession; and then, more recently, became another escape – this time from the grey routines of middle age. Yet that same journey could, I realise, be described in other, more negative terms. In that post-teenage daydream, I was living permanently in the present, unfocused and unable to think ahead. Running taught me to postpone current indulgence in order to achieve long-term satisfaction – which social scientists claim is the key to 'success' in life. But this, insidiously, sucked me into the habit of not living in the present. Long-term outcomes assumed disproportionate importance. Before I knew it, I was wishing my life away.

Many runners must do the same: it's part of the sport. If I can just squeeze in one more training run this week, we think, I'll be that much faster at the weekend. If I can just ignore the pain for the next couple of miles, the race will be over and I'll have achieved my objective. If I can just get through the next six months of painful training without getting injured or losing willpower, I'll be able to knock five minutes off my marathon time. And – who knows? – if I could just fast-forward through four years of super-intense training, without distraction or interruption, I could challenge for an Olympic medal...

If you're not careful, you can fast-forward through half your life. And when I say you, I mean I.

Eventually, thanks largely to therapy from the countryside around me, I began to escape from that excessively outcome-focused mindset, and relearnt the value of living in the present. And so, in a sense, I am back where I was when I started, before I became a runner.

Do I regret that circular journey? Of course not. Each stage in it – road-runner, time obsessive, marathon runner, adventure racer, kit junkie – brought me pleasure and satisfaction and helped me to develop as a person. Yet I am glad to have moved on from each stage when the time came. The point is not that any one approach is wrong: it is that each approach is more appropriate to some sets of circumstances than to others.

Two anecdotes from my old sport of fell-running come into my head as I write this. One concerns Mark Hartell, a Warwickshire-born IT consultant who in 1997 set a (still unbroken) record for the greatest number of Lake District peaks scaled in twenty-four hours. While he was doing so, Mark was surprised to bump into an old friend from college on a remote mountain path. They hadn't met for nearly a decade. The friend said hello. 'Sorry, can't stop,' said Mark – and continued on his incomprehensibly difficult and intense seventy-seven-peak race against the clock without even slowing down.

About ten years later, a friend of Alistair Brownlee, future Olympic triathlon champion but then still a fell-runner, was walking in the Yorkshire Dales – and, on a windswept hilltop, was surprised to see Alistair running towards him. He, too, said hello. Alistair stopped to chat. After a few minutes, some other runners appeared over the brow of the same hill. Alistair glanced up. 'Ah,' he said. 'I'll have to go. I'm in a race.'

One sport, two diametrically opposite attitudes. Yet neither attitude was wrong: each was appropriate to the circumstances. In different situations, I can easily imagine each athlete taking the opposite approach. (I don't think Alistair would have stopped for a chat on his way to Olympic gold at London 2012.)

So it is, I believe, with the rest of us. We recreational runners have more approaches available to us than we are encouraged to believe. We all know about (and most of us have tried) the 'peak performance' approach: spend, train, feed, calculate and obsess your way to becoming 'greater than ever before'. That's the approach that Big Running sells us, day in and day out. It's not the wrong approach. Nor is it the only one. For many of us, in many circumstances, it's not always the right one.

I've often forgotten this too easily, and not just in my road-running days. For example: I remember running in the Borrowdale fell race several years ago. It was a hot day for any kind of running, let alone a seventeen-mile Lake District circuit involving four large mountains and 2,000 metres of ascent and descent. Halfway through, I was struggling. There were more people behind me than in front, but only just, and all I could think of was how much it was hurting: how bruised my joints felt, how thirsty I was, how limp my legs were, how the glare of the sun was making my dehydrated head ache. I don't think I was actually cursing my misfortune out loud, but I was certainly grimacing. This was torture, and only my inner reserves of courage and pig-headedness were keeping me going.

On the long slog up Great Gable, I slowly caught up with a skeletal, grey-haired runner. Drawing level, I realised that it was Joss Naylor: the most celebrated of all long-distance fell-runners, decades past his prime – he must have been nearly seventy by then – but still moving with the quiet determination that had allowed him to push back the frontiers of human endurance, and become a sporting legend, in the 1970s and 1980s.

'Hello, Richard, how're you doing?' he said, as full of the warmth of friendship as he always is.

I gasped something non-committal.

'Isn't it a glorious day?' he continued, gesturing around us. 'Unbelievable.'

I looked around and had to admit that, now he mentioned it, the unbroken views of half the Lake District National Park – ancient, shimmering, perfectly delineated – were somewhat breathtaking. I wondered why I hadn't noticed before.

'Makes you grateful to be alive,' he continued. 'To come out here and have all this. Glorious.' Then he paused to chat with a spectator who was shouting encouragement from a nearby rock.

I plodded on, flushed with shame. For the past couple of hours or so I had been dragging myself grimly through one of Britain's most beautiful and friendly races with a wildly inappropriate attitude. If I hadn't been lucky enough to bump into one of Britain's most inspiring athletes in mid-race I would have missed the whole point of the experience.

It wasn't the dogged determination that was inappropriate. No one gets round a long fell-race without a certain amount of that; and, in any case, seeing how close to your limits you can push yourself is, for most of us, one of the pleasures of running. What marked me out as a fool was the way I had allowed that result-focused approach to leave no room in my head for appreciating all the other aspects of the race that mattered: the environment, the atmosphere, the romance, the adventure – and our sheer good fortune in being able to go out running in a place like that, with people like that, on a day like that.

Such blinkered vision might have been justified, perhaps, had I stood the remotest chance of winning, or setting a record. But I didn't. Like 90 per cent of those running, I could hope for no more than to finish the race in a position

I felt reasonably proud of, preferably in one piece and ideally a bit faster than last time; and then to enjoy the post-race camaraderie with my friends.

That is all that most of us can aspire to, in most races. It is not an aspiration to be scorned. To achieve the time and position part of it usually requires focus, determination, guts and passion; sometimes it involves finding strength from the core of your being. Yet the goal itself doesn't amount, ultimately, to a hill of beans. Surely it's worth leaving a little space in your brain for living as well?

And if that sounds like a plea for a non-competitive approach to running, it isn't. I've nothing against going for a gentle jog when that's what circumstances demand, but no one will ever convince me that running isn't largely about running as fast as you can. The speed, over long distances or short, is at least half the joy of it. But speed can be achieved in many ways, and sometimes it's more effective, as well as more rewarding, to run with a different focus. I can't swear to this, because it's never seemed important enough to check methodically, but I'm pretty sure that, since I became a convert to what I've called Slow Running, my ability to run fast in races has improved. Any loss of scientific intensity in my training has been more than made up for by increased enthusiasm.

All of which somehow brings me back to that beach in Wales: to a moment that must rank among my finest athletic achievements.

It was, as I mentioned, an intimidating field, despite a wide range of age and ability. This was because it had been organised, on the spur of the moment, as an old-fashioned handicap, with different starting lines for different runners. The youngest runner – Sammy, aged five – was assumed to be the slowest. I was not quite the oldest – of five or six adults in (then) their mid-forties – but was judged to be the fastest. So I started right at the back, with Sammy starting getting on for 350 metres in front and the others distributed at various points in between according to their estimated speed. I'm not sure that all the children took part, or even all the adults (we were on a three-family camping holiday), but there were certainly four or five under-twelves, of whom I judged the main threats to be my son, Edward, then aged eight and starting off what seemed to me an absurdly generous handicap; Isobel, my ten-year-old daughter, who didn't usually put her mind to running fast but could be startlingly quick when she felt like it; and David, Sammy's seven-year-old brother, who had already shown keenly competitive sporting instincts in the beach cricket and who also seemed kindly handicapped.

The adult to beat was probably Ada, who a couple of decades earlier had been an almost-elite 400-metre-runner – a far better athlete than I had ever been – but who had used a few recent years of relative inactivity and a few pounds of extra weight to justify a fifty-metre head start. And then there were the unknown quantities: Clare, for example, who can't have run for years but is none the less quite hardy in outdoor matters and tends to be quite gung-ho when she throws herself into a challenge; Alice, who's always kept quietly fit as an adult through activities like yoga and dance; Nick, a prolific hiker who seemed to have wangled himself an absurdly generous handicap; and George, Ada and Alice's ten-year-old son, whose long legs were already starting to resemble his father's.

The race began. Almost immediately, the heavier among us realised that it was going to be harder than we had thought.

The firm looking sand, still not quite dry from the retreat of the sea, yielded beneath our pounding feet. The bigger the runner, or the greater the attempted acceleration, the greater the yielding. My shoes – one in each hand – felt worryingly heavy. None the less, I felt sure that, if I paced myself, I could gradually run them all down.

The handicapping had been done in the most haphazard way but turned out to be astonishingly accurate. All the gaps were closing simultaneously. By the time I had run 100 metres it was still almost anybody's race. Except mine. Nearly everyone else was far closer to the finish than they were to me. The only way I stood a chance would be if I ran the race of my life.

I decided to do so. There was something about the moment that made anything seem possible: the gleaming sea, the stately cliffs, the spontaneous burst of rediscovered youth among my middle-aged friends. If they could decide to cast off physical caution for a moment, so could I. So I focused my mind on running-related thoughts: relax the jaw, relax the shoulders, drive with the arms; breathe with your rhythm, deep into the lower back; relax the hands (but don't drop the shoes). Don't try to close the gap all at once, I told myself. Just wind up the pace gradually and they'll come back to you.

Instead, it got harder. The nearer we got to the finish, and thus to the sea, the wetter and more yielding the beach became. The others, ahead, had already noticed this, and squeals of mock horror were emanating from, among others, Clare and Alice, as gobbets of wet sand splashed all over them. By the time I had completed roughly half the distance, most of the others were all in a bunch, and everyone was splashing everyone else. The thought that I was too far behind to be affected was not encouraging. In fact, it occurred to me that I might well come last – and that maybe, to avoid losing face, I should give up now, pretending that I wasn't trying.

But I was, and I didn't. Instead, I kept plugging away, feeding my morale with thoughts of the shining sea; and the simple, natural interaction of bare feet with wet sand; and the limitless supply of clean ocean air that was there for me to gulp in as fuel.

Finally, they began to fade. I can't remember who eased off first – I think it was an adult – but gradually exhaustion (combined, in some cases, with giggles) picked them off. Clare, Alice, Nick, Flossie, Isobel: one by one they slowed, in some cases to a walk, as they realised that the sand was, in effect, doubling the distance they had to run.

Meanwhile, unlike them, I had years of racing experience to draw on: I was warmed up, focused and running rhythmically. All I had to do was blot out the pain and...well, it then occurred to me that even that might not be enough. George was still going, but could probably be picked off before too long; likewise Edward and David, who weren't going to give up but would be defeated by sheer lack of stride length as long as I kept going. But that still left Ada, who was running with a strength and purpose that I hadn't seen in him for years; and, most worryingly, Sammy, who was still staggering away, waving his arms and turning occasionally with a big grin on his face – and had almost reached the finishing pool already.

There was nothing for it but to accelerate, even though I felt nauseous from oxygen debt. Pump the arms. Pump the knees. Breathe in that sweet sea air. Relax everything. Remember that, if I'm suffering, they're suffering too. Turn the screw and blast them out of the water.

Before long I was almost level. Was there a voice in my

head that said: 'You sad bastard. You're not seriously going to half kill yourself in order to deprive a five-year-old boy of the pleasure of winning a beach race, are you?' – or words to that effect? Er, I don't know. I was too busy focusing on Ada to give the matter much thought. Luckily, Ada overtook Sammy first (or that's my story), so the responsibility ceased to be mine.

Now only one question remained: whether or not I could complete what might be the toughest 400 metres I had ever run, and use timing, tactics and mental strength to turn my speed into triumph.

I turned up the intensity one final notch, summoning every motivational image from my memory bank (Sebastian Coe coming off the bend in Los Angeles in 1984; Steve Cram holding off Steve Ovett for a whole lap at Crystal Palace in 1983; Hicham el-Guerrouj battling with Bernard Lagat in the Athens home straight in 2004). No one ever won anything worthwhile without pain, I reminded myself; what was to prevent me, too, from conquering it? 'Faster, it's only pain,' Percy Cerutty used to yell at Herb Elliott on the sand-dunes of Portsea; or, as Franz Stampfl used to put it when training Roger Bannister for his four-minute mile: 'It's only pain, Roger. Just ignore it.' I found a still place in my mind where the rising tide of discomfort couldn't reach me, let my bare toes find their own instinctive compromise with the water-logged sand, and thought only positive thoughts: keep breathing, keep relaxing, keep driving, keep focusing on the ground ahead.

With less than twenty metres to go, I was matching Ada stride for stride, but had at least a metre still to catch up. Surely I didn't have to dig deeper? But I did; and, amazingly, I succeeded. With a couple of strides to spare I drew level, edged ahead, thrust out my chest like a sprinter and flopped into the shallow pool.

There was no timekeeper, no spectators, no official result. In fact, I've no real way of confirming that any of this happened at all. Discussing it now with some of those involved, I find that no one else remembers it except in the vaguest terms. Yet I still recall the race with absurd delight.

That's partly for reasons unrelated to running. It's a precious memory from a family adventure, shared with some of my oldest and dearest friends. Of course I cherish it.

It's also because, absurd as it may seem, that race was among my finest running moments. It wasn't an achievement to boast about – obviously – but I suspect that, objectively speaking, I can rarely have run better. Never mind the lack of serious context: I honestly believe that, for those few sand-spattered minutes, I was the best runner I could possibly have been, blending fitness, technique, talent and mental strength to produce a near-perfect performance for an athlete with my genes. Does the fact that no one measured it, or that I don't have a medal or a T-shirt to show for it, make the moment count for less? Probably; but I don't really see why it should.

But there's another thing, too. I think this may be the important thing. The part of this memory that really brings a smile to my face is the thought of all those sensible, middle-aged adults spontaneously behaving as though they were decades younger. It's not the first or last time I've seen that particular group doing so; and, of course, parents often throw off some of the restraints of adulthood in order to share their children's in-the-moment excitement.

But this race seemed to be about more than that. It was about adults being excited on their own behalves, too, as they

278

liberated themselves from the habitual restraint of adulthood: friends I have known since they were teenagers rediscovering their teenage selves through the utterly natural activity of running as fast as they could – and being surprised by how much they liked it.

It made me think of Siegfried Sassoon's great First World War poem, 'Everyone Sang':

> Everyone suddenly burst out singing;
> And I was filled with such delight
> As prisoned birds must find in freedom...'

One moment we were normal, responsible grown-ups. The next we were throwing off our shoes, throwing off our dignity, throwing off our suspicion of sudden, violent movements, stretching our legs and opening our lungs and winging wildly across the wet sands, allowing our whole beings to express themselves via the age-old human instinct to run and race. No special equipment or special preparation was required: just a certain capacity to rejoice in what comes naturally.

Strictly speaking, of course, there is nothing remarkable about that, either. But you don't see it very often.

I find that sad. And the saddest thing of all is that you don't even see it very often among the two million or so British adults who describe themselves as runners. Never mind how young they are at heart: convention demands that they pursue their passion in the approved way, dressing appropriately, preparing appropriately, attaching their timing chips correctly, warming up, warming down, behaving appropriately at all times.

There's something horribly constraining, in a purely physical sense, about being grown up. You're expected to remain upright (at least when sober), to keep your clothes unmuddy and untorn, to avoid doing anything that might cause you to drop your car keys or your credit cards – and certainly to avoid activities that might leave you with unsightly bruises or grazes. Most people over thirty seem to accept these constraints meekly. I wonder how many really want to?

That's one of the reasons why I value regular rural running. Regularly coming home from training runs in a soaked and filthy state, with occasional scratches or bruises you barely noticed yourself getting, is a more acceptable antidote to adult respectability than, say, regularly returning in a similar state from nights on the town. (Trust me: I've tried both.)

But only very recently – only since I started thinking again about that race in Wales – have I come to realise how many levels of liberation natural running can bring you. It's partly about the countryside itself: the raw materials of mud, puddle, grass, trees and so on. Of course you are going to feel liberated to some degree if you run in it. But different people bring different attitudes to the experience. At one extreme, you can run in a respectable way, clinging to the conventions of 'normal' running and trying to keep your kit clean and your dignity intact. At the other, you can break out of that straitjacket of physical caution and throw yourself into the rural environment with more joy than sense. You can, in other words, run like an adult – or run like a child.

The attractions of the latter are obvious, and the fact that the drawbacks are obvious, too, should not be taken as an overwhelming argument against exploring what the concept has to offer. In fact, I'm increasingly inclined to embrace it, not just as an occasional indulgence but as a distinct and delightful Sixth Age of Running. We all have an inner child. Can it really be healthy not to let it out to play occasionally?

I'm sure obstacle racers find a similar liberation in the indignities of Tough Mudder and its rivals. Yes, such events are partly about proving that you're tough enough to rise to the challenge, but they're also about the buzz of taking childish risks: of falling flat on your face, immersing yourself in repellent substances and generally making a fool of yourself. Rural running brings much the same benefits, but more simply and cheaply. It's hard to get back from each day's run with bits of the countryside spattered all over you and still think of yourself as a fully respectable member of the adult species. And so, by default, your mindset remains young. Well into my fifties, I still instinctively think of myself as the least mature member of any group I'm in: the junior sibling; the person whose future is still before him; a child who just happens to have ended up, by an amusing accident, in an adult role. I'm not proud of that. But I am glad of it.

Whether or not this strand of immaturity is enough to justify my hunch that this might be a Sixth Age of Running is open to debate. It's certainly both possible and enjoyable to allow yourself to enter the athletic equivalent of a second childhood, running not for outcomes or results or health or self-improvement or even relaxation, but for wonder and joy – running as we used to run down corridors and crowded pavements, while adults shrieked their disapproval – in short, running because it's fun.

Yet it's hard to argue that this phase follows logically from the previous ones. It could just as easily come anywhere else in the sequence; and, indeed, in my journey I seem to have stumbled on it while I was still embarking on my Fifth Age of Running – the 'slow running' phase – even though it's taken me the best part of a decade to become fully aware of it.

But perhaps that's the real lesson we should take from the

idea of the Seven Ages of Running: that it's a range, not a progression. There is no rule to say that the phases should happen one at a time, in a particular order, with each representing a kind of progress. The secret is to open yourself up to new approaches, not to close yourself off to old ones.

One of the things that delights me most about that memory from a Welsh beach is that the running was joyful at three or four levels. There was the joy of running in a beautiful place, on a beautiful day, with the sun on my face and nothing between my bare feet and the sea-washed sand. There was the joy of sharing a happy moment with family and friends; and the joy of full-blooded, lung-bursting, win-if-it-kills-me racing. And, simultaneously, there was the joy of running like a child: casting off restraint, caution and decorum and charging madly towards the beckoning water. Pull those four joys together, as I sometimes do now when I relive those moments in my head, and you have a template for a kind of natural running that sounds pretty close to my idea of athletic heaven on earth.

So, let's call it the Sixth Age of Running. And the great thing is that, if I'm right about there being seven such ages, that still leaves me with a whole new phase that I've yet to discover.

Perhaps I am becoming fanciful. But are these speculations and reflections really any more far-fetched or absurd than the idea that we should all carry on running in the same repetitive, results-focused way for the rest of our lives, just because that's the only language Big Running knows how to talk to us in? Consider again these hard facts: most adult runners get into the sport in their twenties or early thirties; most give it up in their late thirties and early forties; the main causes are, overwhelmingly, injury and boredom. Natural running, in the various forms described in this book, avoids most of the pitfalls that tend to cause this mass dropping out: hard roads, repetitive movements, hi-tech running shoes, overemphasis on results and 'performance', and a narrow, consumerist idea of what running is for. Natural running with a 'running-like-a-child' mentality adds a further benefit: if you're doing it purely for liberation and joy, you are unlikely to tire of it. Run freely and naturally, for fun, in environments that make you happy, with the exuberance and unthinking wonder you ran with in childhood, and you are far more likely than the average 'consumer runner' to carry on running, happily and healthily, well into an active old age.

Call it natural running, or rural running, or in-the-moment running, or slow running, or running like a child, or what you will: they're all variations of the same idea. For brevity's sake, let's call it Running Free.

23

The Cloud

We step outside into silence. It is neither wet nor dry, light nor dark: just grey, cold and dank. Freezing fog clings to everything. It drips thickly from the hanging branches of the bedraggled trees, oozes over the dirty lane, seeps into the spiky hedgerows and glistens on the wool of the sheep as they sulk, slumped in the watery grass.

The grass is actually doubly wet, with fog moisture clinging to an underlayer of frost. In the big field beyond the copse, there is a third degree of wetness. The turf is waterlogged from weeks of rain, and its hard, frosted crust breaks beneath nearly every footfall. My almost-bare feet feel hard slivers of ice as I sink into the frozen water, my toes burn – and I wonder, as I occasionally do, if perhaps I might have got all this wrong.

Perhaps people avoid experiences like this with good reason. Perhaps they prefer gyms, with heated floors and fluffy towels, because they are sensible. Here I am, flirting with hypothermia, wet and filthy already, aching in every joint, wiggling my gloved fingers to stop them burning, too, breathing in a miserable damp miasma of evaporated mud, and seeing – give or take a few square metres of sodden turf – nothing. What could this kind of running possibly have to recommend it?

I know the mood will pass, but it's proving harder than usual to keep my spirits up. The air is so damp it might as well be raining; so cold that the moisture seems to be freezing to my face. It wouldn't surprise me if my hair and eyebrows were frosted white. As for the wonders of nature, it's hardly worth keeping my eyes open: I don't spot the gate out of the big field until we're within ten metres of it.

In the fourth field, just before the woods, a big dog fox lopes across our path. I barely bother to watch his dark shape recede into the murk: he's just patrolling his territory, like me, probably with no more coherent sense of his reason for passing this way than I currently have of mine. Nutmeg seems similarly unmoved. She must have noticed his scent. Perhaps, like me, she's not in the mood to be excited.

There's less chill in the air on the path through the woods, and some rotting leaves crunch beneath my feet as though parts of them could almost be dry. But you always find dryness in woods: it doesn't make the damp beyond seep any less insidiously into the bones.

In the field on the far side there are more icy puddles; more patches of lank grass flattened into frozen mud patches. I notice that a bitter wind is slicing through me, even though the fog is motionless.

Then a damp, low-flying buzzard distracts me, dragging itself westward with slow, heavy flaps. A bird wouldn't really allow itself to get waterlogged, would it? Not properly soaked so that it could barely fly? The fog swallows it before I can study its feathers properly.

I turn to find the way ahead barred by a flash-mob of sheep: a whole field's worth, crammed for some reason into one dank corner, glowering. They make no effort to shift as we apologetically weave and jostle our way through them. Puffs of mist rise from the saturated grass beneath them, blue-grey like cigarette smoke.

Not for the first time, I feel a pang of affinity for these dumb beasts, quietly enduring the discomforts of the fields just as I do, not because they are especially tough but because the discomforts are there and so are they. It's odd that our ideas of endurance running don't usually encompass this kind of endurance. It's an underrated quality.

Splashing on through the next, empty, field, I notice that my numb feet feel as heavy as a wet buzzard's wings. I glance down and see that, in places, the lower parts of my leggings are frozen solid. The weight of the ice drags like mud from a ploughed field. Oh well, I tell myself: at least the extra work will warm me up. But my joints still yearn for a hot bath, and my fingertips still burn with what feels like (but isn't) frostbite.

A casual observer might conclude from this and previous descriptions that I am a running masochist: that there must, despite all that I have written about joy, be an element of self-flagellation to my training regime. It's a reasonable inference, but that's not how I see it at all. Once, it's true, in my first Ages of Running, I welcomed pain: both because learning to deal with it would make me a better runner and because it felt as if it was somehow expiating my youthful decadence. If it hurt, it served me right.

But my rural running in more recent years has, by contrast, been almost entirely motivated by the pursuit of happiness. I am no longer a tortured runner. I run because it makes me feel good, not bad. And I do so in wild fields partly because it is easier than banging out fast miles on the road. The latter requires huge self-discipline; the former is just a question of not whingeing about cold toes.

Yet the fact remains that, sometimes, rural running does expose me (and will expose you, if you try it) to forms of physical distress that are rarely encountered in cities or gyms. And – I admit it – the fact that I don't actively seek out such distress doesn't mean that I don't, in a curious way, welcome it when it comes.

It's not about self-conquest. It's about coping – a word which, perhaps more than any other, defines the daily challenge of most ordinary, middle-of-the-pack adult lives. Never mind the details of our different circumstances: if we want to be self-respecting grown-ups, we all have to cope with what life throws at us. For men, this seems to mean achieving a perfect, elusive balance of sensitivity and indestructibility. You must be hardy, resilient, self-sufficient; support your family, keep a roof over their heads, hold down a job, know how to mend and maintain every household object, be a solid rock in times of adversity; have neither too much nor too little assertiveness; and remain in touch with your feelings without being unduly vulnerable or afraid. In short, you must be rather more of a man than I sometimes feel. Women, of course, have their own burden of impossible expectations to bear. I won't presume to define them. But coping, again, seems as good a one-word summary as any.

It's not an impossible demand; perhaps not even an unreasonable one. But it doesn't get any easier. And I, for one, find it helpful to warm up for the task each morning with a bit of outdoor coping, dealing with whatever discomforts and inconveniences nature happens to have cooked up for me. Ideally, no major distress is involved – although if it is, so be it. But anything that awakens a response of quiet stoicism is to be welcomed, as a perfect preparation for the day ahead.

The trick, for humans if not for sheep, is either to think about something else or, where possible, to focus on the alleged unpleasantness and look for things to enjoy about it. Today, for example: the way the boundaries between sky and land, earth and water, man and mud, have dissolved – isn't that something to relish rather than resent? And even the fog has its uses. Some big brown bullocks in the next field we come to don't notice us until it is too late for them to molest us. A few rear away as we appear from the shadows. Who knows what kind of creature they think we are? By the time they turn to look back at us, we've gone.

In the field above Plumpton church, the fog seems to lift slightly – or perhaps it is just that the sloping field falls away from under it. About halfway down, there's that giant plash that sometimes forms in the dip. There is a silvery gleam to it this time, despite the lack of sunlight. As we approach, it shatters into countless ripples, like dropped mercury, as forty or fifty ducks take off from it all at once. They form almost instantly into a perfect 'V' and ascend into the gloom. It would never have occurred to me that there could be so many ducks together in a place like that; nor that they would fly away in formation. But the frenzy of quacking that accompanies the display leaves no room for doubt.

We regain height in the next field, where the fog is thicker than ever: still pressing down on everything like yellow-brown mould; still damp and mud-flavoured and so dense that I want to claw my way through it with my hands. But is it perhaps a little warmer than it was?

We climb the corrugated hill patiently, ridge by ridge. In the absence of sun, moon or stars, my sense of direction has evaporated. I have to infer our route from the shape of the slope and my memories of previous runs here. All I can hear is my own breathing, and a barely perceptible whiffle of dog behind me. I see moisture dripping from a couple of shrivelled thistle clusters, but the drips are silent. I wonder if the fog is stifling all other sounds or if the world has actually become noiseless.

About halfway up, I am startled by a hawthorn tree. Its black, bedraggled mass seems to leap from the shadows, startlingly close – like a ghost ship bursting from the sea mist on a desolate, distant ocean. I take an instinctive evasive side step before I make sense of its dark, dripping shape. As I do so, the idea of being lost irretrievably at sea takes a temporary grip on my mind – and I feel a shiver of physical fear tingle up my neck.

Our part of south Northamptonshire has always had fog issues. We're on high ground, much of which is wet much of the time. Sometimes cold air brings the fog down; sometimes warmth draws it up from the earth. Either way, once it's there, it settles, sometimes for days: as thick as cotton wool and as clingy as cobwebs. When we first moved here, the fogs frightened me. I remember asking myself, after three unbroken days of the stuff: what if, one day, it never cleared – ever? What if our children grew up in a world so ecologically sick that this was all that remained?

Now I think: perhaps all human hopes come down to this – the hope that this fog, this darkness, real or metaphorical, will not last for ever; that a time is coming when the gloom will pass and we will see clearly again.

Then I think: maybe that's what keeps drawing me out here, day after day, into this dank mess of mud, damp and cloud. It's not self-flagellation; it isn't even self-discipline – despite my earlier thoughts about coping. But it is, perhaps, another kind of self-improvement: the kind that results from *going outside*.

Our instinct – mine as much as anyone else's – is to crave

clarity and certainty. We yearn to know everything about everything, past, present and future; ideally, we would like to preserve that knowledge, physically or digitally. We struggle to believe that anything can sink untraceably into oblivion, just as we struggle to believe that anything can happen randomly, without someone, somewhere, being responsible.

But we're wrong. The reality of life is a cloud of unknowing. Nothing is fixed. Most things vanish. We can't see where we're going. There is no guarantee that tomorrow will resemble today. All we can do is choose: between despair and hope; or, if we must, self-deception.

And part of the appeal (or scariness) of running in wilder contexts – outside the illusory reassurances of civilisation – is that it forces us to face up to uncertainty. In the branded, regimented, packaged world of Big Running, the delusions of certainty are deafening: pay for this product and you *will* improve your performance by three per cent; enter this race and you *will* be fed, watered, timed, told where to run, photographed, rewarded with a medal and reunited with your kitbag. In the ungoverned outdoors, the harshness of reality is less escapable: anything might happen.

I make a point of shrugging off whatever unexpected challenges the countryside inflicts on me before I start each day, not because I want to be tough but because I might as well start as I intend to go on. Countless urban runners must do much the same, when they go out to cope with the semi-tamed, weather-exacerbated challenges of their local parks, paths and patches of wasteland. It's about reminding ourselves, day after day, that the way ahead is neither clear nor likely to be easy. Shrugging off discomfort and dealing with uncertainty are what we must do to survive. Embracing uncertainty is what we must do to thrive.

I suppose you could think of a run like this as a Tough

Fogger: challenging and uncomfortable, and sometimes dis-concerting; but no more demanding athletically than any other kind of run – and tame compared with the challenges that real adventurers face. Knowing that there's nothing to be afraid of doesn't entirely dispel the instinctive response of unease. Fear of fog is part of the human condition, and the best response to it is hope. Practising that response does us no harm whatsoever. It's not self-discipline: it's self-awakening.

So it is that, this morning, I find myself not just becoming resigned to the fog but, increasingly, welcoming it. I have only the broadest sense of where I am, but I am starting to enjoy the sense of dislocation. Have I really not noticed that spinney here before? Or am I in fact not 'here' at all but somewhere else? And, if so, how liberating is that? It's a bit like swimming in the sea and letting the waves take you where they will.

Eventually, we reach the far side of the field, at an unex-pected point, and we run the next couple of miles with a field boundary of some kind always in sight: over the brook, up the hill, along the side of the wood. As we do so, I notice how the dimness of the half-light has softened the hedgerows' autumn hues. Instead of a kaleidoscope of reds, browns, yellows and fading greens, I see stiff, grey twigs smudged with pale hints of barely noticeable colour, delicate as lichen. The beauty, now I finally see it, is mesmerising.

And I think, too, of all the other times I have been lost in fog – in mountains, in strange lands, even in towns – and marvel that I could ever have felt disheartened by the expe-rience. Now that I have surrendered to the fog, and to the mud and the moisture, I feel renewed by them. As for my earlier doubt and self-pity, their last traces have long since vanished.

And then, less than a mile from home, the fog itself clears. I've been vaguely aware for several minutes of something changing, without quite noticing what. Then, just as the thought is forming that it is growing lighter, and that there is a hint of warmth in the air that reminds me of sunlight, the gloom simply parts and vanishes.

The abruptness is breathtaking – like a curtain being snatched aside.

The western sky resolves itself as I watch into a clean, watery blue; and then, in a minute or less, into the rich, deep azure of a warm autumn morning. The bedraggled landscape starts to sparkle beneath it as it dries. It is as if a pencil sketch had been transformed into a watercolour, and then into a lustrous oil painting – all in the time it takes to run 200 metres.

A warm, physical glow of hope surges through my body. I notice, too, that the frayed hedgerow on my left is splattered with sloes and hawthorn berries: little bright paintballs of brilliant blue and red among the shiny wet leaves. How could I have failed to see them on our outward journey?

Nutmeg glances up at me, and we both launch ourselves into a joyful semi-sprint along the edge of the water-logged stubble.

She is soon ahead – she doesn't sink into the mud as I do – and I notice something from behind the breathtaking per-fection of her camouflage. The unkempt stubble's pale straw colour grows dramatically darker near ground level, where it has presumably been splashed by mud – and exactly the same applies to the unkempt, low-slung hound. It seems unlikely that she evolved for the precise purpose of this carefree race, let alone that I did. But right now, for a few joyful moments, it feels as though it might be true.

As we work our way along the field, I find myself splashing

through ever more waterlogged ground: slippery, marshy, splashy, with patches of calf-deep standing water. I feel gloriously indifferent to the consequences: I'm waterlogged already. But I notice that the bigger the splash, the better it feels.

Then I think: I am doing it again; I am running like a child.

That is: I am running with an adult's strength, an adult's stamina, an adult's understanding of pace, distance and the irrelevance of short-term pain; but I am also running with a child's instinctive sense that certain circumstances and environments demand certain responses – and that, in some cases, only a flat-out charge will do. I doubt one child in a hundred could look at this archipelago of puddles, and at the sodden hound splashing joyously on the stubble beside them, and not feel a primal urge to run, fast, into the middle of it all.

I can't. I'm throwing myself forward with no trace of a care for anything, zigzagging slightly so as not to miss any aquatic action, at one with the world, immersed in the texture of everything. My arms feel as loose as rubber, and I think I may be dribbling with exertion. I can see the colours of the morning refract as inverted waterfalls shoot up between them and me. Somewhere in a little corner of my mind are vague memories of childhood sensations of running wild: in playgrounds, corridors, beaches, shopping centres, parks and pavements.

I've just enough vestigial sense of adult values to realise how childish this is, but not enough to care. But the adult in me is also thinking: is that what this is? My Sixth Age of Running? Is this the secret of running happily in middle age? And, if so, does it come from the countryside? Or is it just a state of mind?

The questions slip from my mind unanswered, like so many others before them, as the run itself intervenes. Nutmeg waits for me at the gate to the big penultimate field. I brush the mud from my eyelashes with a muddy hand (bad idea) and open it for her, and we start the final stage of our race on almost level terms, although she doesn't wait as I close it. On the skyline to our right, a couple of miles away, the 750-year-old tower of Canons Ashby church looks back at us imperturbably from the trees, solid and calm. The sun glows on the pale front of the old manor house beyond it, and the whole valley seems to shimmer with reassuring warmth as it dries. Even the distant radio mast, glinting like a glass minaret on the furthest horizon, seems to sprout organically from its hilltop, as if the whole landscape were at one with itself.

In front of us, our mile-long shadows stretch out ahead, right across the huge penultimate field. Each wet blade of grass is shining now, like a tiny sliver of sharp metal; the last leaves glitter over the scrappy copse beyond, in a thousand nameless shades of red, gold and brown, while sunbeams bounce from bright little acorns on the big oak tree beside it.

Inflamed with unexpected joy, we race for the far corner with demented intensity. Nutmeg has no intention of giving up her head start, and we wind up the pace with a relentless ferocity that would enthral an athletics stadium.

Surge for surge we match one another; stride for stride (actually four of hers for two of mine). Then, just as I'm drawing level, her shaggy coat begins to gleam like living gold, transformed by a crescendo of sunlight from a grubby straw colour to rich textured shades of flame. My short, dumpy, nondescript hound seems suddenly bathed in nobility and grace, like a great lion, racing her heart out for the glory of the animal kingdom while even the sun struggles to keep up.

And for a moment I, too, have ceased to be a dumpy, nondescript jogger and am simply a human being, running free, barefoot, fearless and full of life.

Acknowledgements

Without many people's kindness, patience, insight and forbearance it would have been hard not just to write this book but even to have had many of the experiences it describes. I am grateful to each of them.

The names of some appear in the text and do not need repeating. Of the rest, perhaps the largest group comprises the farmers and landowners, large and small, local and far-flung, on whose property I have spent so many happy hours running. I thank them all, along with all those unsung visionaries who have campaigned, legislated, litigated and made a nuisance of themselves over the generations to ensure that so much of our lovely land is accessible to ordinary people – through National Parks, National Trails, protected areas of natural beauty, municipal green spaces and, not least, ordinary rights of way. Little glamour attaches to the small battles that keep the countryside open by these means, but much joy often results from them. I don't suppose many people have as much cause to be grateful as I do.

I should also say thank you to (in chronological order): Lisa Markwell, editor of the *Independent on Sunday*, who asked me to write the short article, published in 2010, that was the kernel from which this book grew; her colleagues Mike Higgins and Rebecca Armstrong, who helped me fulfil that commission; Brie Burkeman, my agent, who urged me to do more with the story; Matt Phillips, editorial director of Yellow Jersey, who commissioned the book; and, also at Yellow Jersey, Frances Jessop, who edited it with a patience, tact and incisiveness that makes me look back in disbelief at the unwieldiness of my initial draft.

I am grateful, too, to the following, for their helpful comments on some or all of my text: Graham Harbor, Jethro Lennox, Nicholas Rudd-Jones, Dr Mick Wilkinson; and, not least, to my sister, Anne Askwith, an incomparable copy editor who has once again given me the benefit of her expertise, encouragement and wisdom.

My thanks also to Renaud Vaschalde at NPD Inc., Matt Powell of SportsOneSource and William Boston of the *Wall Street Journal* for their specialist advice; and, especially, to Robin Dower, Jethro Lennox and Peter Trevelyan, for welcoming me so generously to their manhunt.

In terms of published sources, my many debts will mostly be self-evident. I should, however, make a special mention of Scott Keneally, whose superb exposé of the obstacle racing industry in *Outside* magazine in 2012 made the work of writing Chapter 8 considerably easier. I am also grateful to Claire Maxted, editor of *Trail Running* magazine, for first making me aware of the scale of the obstacle racing boom. Some of the material in Chapter 8 originally appeared in *Trail Running*, or in *The Independent*.

I am also indebted to the work of Professor Roger Robinson, Emeritus Professor of English at Victoria University of Wellington, New Zealand (and former elite runner): both for his classic, hard-to-obtain *Running in Literature* (Breakaway Books, 2003) and for his erudite articles in *Running Times* (especially one about early paper-chasing, 'On the Scent of History', published in December 1998). I should also acknowledge Edmund Gray's *100 Hunts: A Chronicle of the Trevelyan Manhunt 1898–2007*, a specialist, even-harder-to-obtain work that is none the less authoritative or fascinating for that. Other niche publications that deserve a mention include *Cheese Rolling in Gloucestershire*, by Jean Jefferies (Tempus Publishing, 2007) and *Follow the Saltire: The Annals of the Thames Hare and Hounds* (by John Bryant et al., 2012).

The quotation in Chapter 2 from 'Big Yellow Taxi', by Joni Mitchell (© 2007 Crazy Crow Music), is used by kind permission of Alfred Music; as is the quotation in Chapter 19 from 'Get It While You Can', by Jerry Ragovoy and Mort Shuman (© 1971 (Renewed) Unichappell Music Inc. and Mort Shuman Songs). The quotation in Chapter 5 from *The Matchmaker*, by Thornton Wilder (© 1955, 1957; earlier version under the title *The Merchant of Yonkers*, copyright © 1939 by The Wilder Family LLC reprinted by arrangement with The Wilder Family LLC and The Barbara Hogenson Agency, Inc.; all rights reserved. The quotation in Chapter 22 from 'Everyone Sang' by Siegfried Sassoon (© Siegfried Sassoon) is reproduced by kind permission of the estate of George Sassoon.

I am more grateful than I can say to the countless running companions, human or otherwise, who have shared and, in many cases, made possible the years of running happiness that I have been lucky enough to enjoy. In particular, since I never got round to doing so before, I would like to say a special 'thank you' to two of my oldest friends, Adrian

Fowkes and Gawain Barnard, who between them were largely responsible, many decades ago, for coaxing me into becoming a runner. Without that unsolicited gift, my life would have been unimaginably different.

Above all, and finally, I thank Clare, Isobel and Edward: for their patience, their support, their love – and for everything else.